SOME BOOKS BY YVONNE YOUNG TARR

The Complete Outdoor Cookbook
The Farmhouse Cookbook
The Great East Coast Seafood Book
The Great Food Processor Cookbook
The New York Times Bread and Soup Cookbook
The New York Times National Foods Dieting Book
The Squash Book
The 10-Minute Gourmet Cookbook
The 10-Minute Gourmet Diet Cookbook
The Tomato Book
The Up-With-Wholesome Cookbook
That's Entertaining

SIMON AND SCHUSTER

NEW YORK   LONDON   TORONTO   SYDNEY   TOKYO   SINGAPORE

Yvonne Young Tarr's
Low-
Cholesterol
Gourmet

Illustrations by
LAUREN JARRETT

Simon and Schuster
Simon & Schuster Building
Rockefeller Center
1230 Avenue of the Americas
New York, New York   10020

SIMON AND SCHUSTER and colophon are registered trademarks
of Simon & Schuster Inc.

Designed by Nina D'Amario/Levavi & Levavi
Manufactured in the United States of America

1   3   5   7   9   10   8   6   4   2

Library of Congress Cataloging in Publication Data

Tarr, Yvonne Young.
[Low-cholesterol gourmet]
Yvonne Young Tarr's low-cholesterol gourmet / Yvonne Young Tarr;
illustrations by Lauren Jarrett.
p.   cm.
Includes index.
1. Low-cholesterol diet—Recipes.   I. Title.   II. Title: Low-
cholesterol gourmet.
RM237.75.T37   1990
641.5′6311—dc20   90-35892
                                                                              CIP

ISBN 0-671-52321-X

I affectionately dedicate this book to two very dear friends, Hilva Landsman and Ernestine Lassaw, with many thanks for their help, concern, and bushels of friendly advice. Without them life would be a lot less lively.

Acknowledgments

A very special thank you to doctors Harold Rifkin and Rodney Ryan for stealing time from frantic schedules to evaluate, and comment on, this book. Their wisdom, scientific insights, and guidance were of inestimable value.

The making of this book came about with the support, encouragement, and hard work of four very talented women: my former Simon and Schuster editor, Carole Lalli; my present Simon and Schuster editor, Kerri Conan; my agent, Christine Tomasino; and my long-time friend and editor, Ruth Grossman. I wish to thank them from the heart for their good sense, patience, and humor under stress.

Foreword

Yvonne Young Tarr's newest book entitled *Low-Cholesterol Gourmet* is a superb contribution to the literature on nutrition. It is a cookbook written for individuals who wish to improve their present approach to eating, and also for patients who have been advised by their physicians to follow a low-cholesterol and high-fiber diet.

Significantly, this book translates the essential information and guidelines of various medical and other professional associations into a gourmet approach to this healthful way of eating, simultaneously serving as a practical guide to a low-fat and low-cholesterol intake. It makes preparing food relatively simple, permitting increasing freedom and flexibility.

Deluxe, sophisticated lunches, picnics, and dinners are described carefully, taking into account various ethnic considerations. Ms. Tarr's writing style is as clear as the menus delineated in the book. The basic information relating to the science of nutrition is accurate and understandable. The recipes are written by a professional who is a charming and charismatic hostess, who herself loves to prepare food, set a delightful table, and eat well.

Harold Rifkin, M.D.
Professor of Clinical Medicine,
New York University School of Medicine, New York
Clinical Professor of Medicine
Albert Einstein College of Medicine,
New York

Yvonne Tarr's newest masterpiece exults in the advocacy of low-cholesterol, high-fiber diets. She tempts the palate and promotes good health and long life with creative menus for every season and a delightful tour of the world's greatest cuisines.

There are simplified menu versions and more elaborate preparations, but all achieve the balance so important for a more healthful life. In a highly informative and readable style, Yvonne Tarr elaborates on the background of all the low-cholesterol foods she uses in her menus. Information is included on availability, quality, storage, and preparation that will help the cook prepare fresh, vitamin-rich, and zestful dishes that will be both satisfying and enriching.

Recent advances in human nutrition have helped us understand how our dietary habits could be improved to be more in tune with a modern life-style and prolonged good health. From a medical point of view, Yvonne Tarr's emphasis on high-fiber diets holds additional appeal.

High-fiber diets have gradually been recognized to be beneficial in the prevention of many disease processes, including cardiovascular and bowel diseases. The high-fiber intake also reduces the absorption of calories while satisfying the appetite, helping reduce the risk of obesity. The lower calorie intake along with the reduced cholesterol is an excellent way to reduce cholesterol and triglyceride levels.

Salt intake in the modern diet is also excessive. When preparing these delicious international menus, Ms. Tarr suggests keeping the salt intake to a minimum to allow the delicate natural flavors of the fresh vegetables to stir your gustatory senses.

Finally, Yvonne Tarr does show that a low-cholesterol diet can be varied and can add the right spice to your diet life with nutritional good sense.

Rodney Ryan, M.D.
Gastrointerologist
Southampton Hospital, N.Y.

Contents

Introduction

This book is about enjoying really delicious food while monitoring dangerous blood cholesterol levels that, if left unchecked, could lead to heart diseases. Once, practically any ingredient that enhanced the taste, texture, or toothsome qualities of a dish was wisked in without regret. But now, good sense has come in the kitchen window. High-cholesterol ingredients are reduced or simply avoided like poison. To bring forth a serving of eggs benedict dripping with hollandaise is to be regarded suspiciously. Any dish that doesn't mind its peas, beans, oats, and unsaturated fats is unceremoniously dismissed, out of hand and off the plate.

When friends inquired about my new book, instead of yawning at the prospect of a low-cholesterol vegetable book as I feared they might, they responded enthusiastically. "Low-fat gourmet? Exactly! We're all bored to distraction with humdrum, low-cholesterol, high-fiber diets. Besides, what on earth do we serve when friends come to visit?" The more enthusiasm I encountered, the more I realized this was a book that many seemed to need as much as I did.

Cardiovascular disease causes one out of three deaths in America, killing one citizen every minute. In 1987, the National Heart, Lung and Blood Institute (NHLBI) and the National Cholesterol Education Program assembled a panel that was a cooperative effort sponsored by the institute and twenty-three major medical associations and health organizations, including the American Medical Association, the American College of Cardiology, and the American Heart Association. They subsequently issued a historic report emphasizing that dietary treatment should be the foundation of all therapy to reduce blood cholesterol levels, and drugs prescribed only for those with genetic forms of high cholesterol.

In fact, respected independent medical groups, the American Heart Association, and the American Medical Association have joined voices with federal agencies, the Food and Drug Administration, and the Surgeon General's office advising us to reduce our consumption of cholesterol, fat, and calories. Also reporting findings on nutrition and health, the prestigious National Research Council, the research arm on the National Academy of Sciences, has recommended in its most recent comprehensive review that Americans eat less fat, cholesterol, and salt to avoid a wide range of diseases.

The challenge is clear. How can we drastically reduce—or virtually eliminate—our consumption of many of our most delicious foods like cream, butter, eggs, cheese, fried foods, most red meats and still enjoy the pleasures of the table?

It can be done! With a little sleight of spoon and some judicious substitutions, it is possible to create dishes that are delicious, nutritious, and pose no hazard to your health. The recipes that emerged from my test kitchen to form the backbone of this book are rich, creamy, attractive, and flavorful, while giving little indication that they are low in fat and, for the most part, based on vegetables.

To begin eating more healthfully this minute without reading the dozens of books on this subject or worrying about which ingredients you may use and in what quantities, you can start with this book. I've eliminated the no-no's and made more healthful substitutions. If you are bogged down by a typical American high fat/cholesterol/salt diet, you'll soon be on the road to recovery when you begin using these low-cholesterol gourmet menus.

These are *real* foods—lasagne, jambalaya, chili, and even sukiyaki. Although I have deliberately kept the quantity of meat, fish, or poultry to about one ounce per serving, mainly for flavor, your palate will never be the wiser. Even avid red-meat eaters will not feel deprived.

Don't hesitate to mix and match the menus to suit yourself. If you are interested in further lowering calories, simply reduce the amounts of oil and substitute sweeteners for sugar. Although this is meant first to be a food book, I have included some basic nutritional data for your information. If you haven't already explored the low-cholesterol story for yourself, you'll want to check out pages 16 to 18. For in-depth reading see titles on page 225.

Remember, this food is to enjoy. You owe it to yourself—and your food-loving family and friends—to make the most important substitution of all—low-cholesterol gourmet for perilous high-fat cooking.

Here's to you and to a long, healthy life.

Low Fat, Low Cholesterol Made Easy

The subject of low cholesterol and the way it affects your health can be a bit confusing. From now on, for clarity, when I use the term *cholesterol* I am referring to the total amount of naturally produced and dietary cholesterol found in the bloodstream. Chemically speaking, all fats, including vegetable oils, are a mixture of three types of fatty acids. Canola oil, for instance, is 7 percent saturated, 55 percent monounsaturated, and 33 percent polyunsaturated. At the other end of the scale, coconut oil is 86 percent saturated, 6 percent monounsaturated, and only 2 percent polyunsaturated.

Depending on the amounts, these fatty acids may influence blood cholesterol. It is important to remember that in order to reduce blood cholesterol levels, it is essential to reduce total calorie intake from dietary cholesterol and fat, especially saturated fat. Here are some basics you should know for the sake of your heart.

Understanding Fats

Cholesterol: A naturally occurring waxy substance in the blood and in many of the foods we eat. One of a number of fats (also known as lipids) found in the blood. Also a general term for all these fats. Cholesterol is essential to our bodies; it performs several major biological functions without which we could not function. However, an excess of it can build up in the arteries, which can cause heart diseases.

LDLs (low-density lipoproteins): Substances that carry cholesterol through the bloodstream to blood vessel walls, where it can accumulate and lead to the formation of artery-clogging plaques that cause most heart attacks.

HDLs (high-density lipoproteins): Substances that carry cholesterol away from blood vessels and are thought to help protect against heart disease.

Triglycerides: Fatty substances manufactured by the body that are part of the blood lipid picture but different from cholesterol. Their levels fluctuate more than cholesterol and depend in greater measure on fat in the diet. When present in the blood at high levels, they can be a cause of heart disease.

Saturated fats: The liver uses saturated fats to manufacture cholesterol in the body. When too much builds up in the bloodstream, the coronary arteries may become clogged, choking off the blood supply to the heart. The culprits are fatty meats (pork, beef, veal, lamb, etc.), dairy products (whole milk, cream, cheese, egg yolks, ice cream), coconut, palm and palm kernel oils, and hydrogenated vegetable fats.

Polyunsaturated oils: Sources are all vegetable oils that are *not* hydrogenated or partially hydrogenated—safflower oil, sunflower oil, corn oil, sesame oil, and soybean oil.

Monounsaturated oils: Some sources are canola oil, olives, olive oil, peanuts and peanut oil, and avocados. These will not add to the amount of cholesterol in the bloodstream and may even decrease it.

The American Heart Association's Three-Phase Program to Help You Avoid Heart Disease

Phase 1: A daily maximum intake of 300 milligrams of cholesterol total fat intake not to exceed 30 percent of total number of calories consumed (10 percent saturated, 10 percent polyunsaturated, and 10 percent monounsaturated fats and oils). If this first diet is unsuccessful, a nutritionist should be consulted and Phase 2 embarked upon.

Phase 2: Same as Phase 1 but cholesterol intake not to exceed 250 milligrams per day. If unsuccessful, embark on Phase 3.

Phase 3: Fat intake should not exceed 20–25 percent of the calories consumed and less than 10 percent should come from animal sources. Total cholesterol intake should not exceed 100 milligrams per day.

Hints and Tips for Lowering Cholesterol

A general rule of thumb. Avoid or partake sparingly of foods from animal sources—red meats, sausage and cold cuts, organ meats; dark meat and skin of poultry; egg yolks; butter; hard cheeses. Most very creamy cheeses are high in cholesterol and some are extraordinarily high. The yolk of a single egg is 250 grams. A cup of chicken livers has 800 grams. Just 3 ½ ounces of brains total 2,100 grams!

Become a label reader. Avoid any product that contains hydrogenated shortening or palm or coconut oils. Seek out foods that are labeled no cholesterol, or are low fat, polyunsaturated or monounsaturated.

Choose low-fat meats. Skinless white meat chicken or turkey (young birds have less fat); lean cuts (those with little or no visible fat or marbling) of beef (round, chuck, or loin); trimmed cuts of veal (except commercially ground); leg or shoulder of pork; leg, arm, or loin of lamb.

Skim off fats. Whenever possible, prepare soups, stews, etc., in advance. Chill and skim off the fat that rises to the top.

Prepare foods wisely. Use non-stick cookware when sautéing or pan-frying.

These Are the Foods I Look For

If these aren't on your "must have" list, they should be.

Milk: 1 percent low fat or buttermilk made from skimmed milk
Cottage cheese: 1 percent or 2 percent low fat

Other cheeses: Part-skim mozzarella, Dorman's Lo-Chol, a tablespoon or two of grated Parmesan and other hard cheeses you love, but avoid double and triple cremes completely.

Margarine: Soft (tub) or liquid rather than sticks (which are hydrogenated). One tablespoon butter for very special occasions.

Egg substitutes or only egg whites: Avoid yolks.

Frozen yogurt and ice milk: Instead of ice cream.

Vegetable oils: Safflower, canola, sunflower, corn, peanut, soybean (see pages 18 to 19), but never palm, palm kernel, or coconut.

Olive oils: Extra-virgin, virgin, "pure" blends (page 23).

Grains: Especially oats and barley, whole grain breads and cereals.

Dried peas and beans: See pages 199 to 201.

Bean curd: One of the world's most perfect foods (pages 25 to 26).

Fish: Especially fatty cold water/ocean varieties—tuna, salmon, bluefish, mackerel, trout, herring, sablefish, shad, and butterfish.

Seafood: Clams, mussels, oysters, and scallops are low in cholesterol. Lobster, shrimp, and crabmeat have a somewhat higher cholesterol content but are still low in fats and high in Omega-3.

Poultry: White meat of broiler or fryer with no skin (large birds have more fat). Turkey breast in cutlets or ground to order.

All fruits and vegetables: Especially apples, carrots, leafy green vegetables, garlic. If a high percentage of your calorie intake comes from carbohydrates found in vegetables, it will help you keep your weight down. Food fat easily converts into body fat; the body is much more reluctant to convert carbohydrates.

Nuts: Straight from the shell, not fried or roasted in oil. Avoid coconut, palm, or palm kernel oil like the plague.

About Oat Bran, Oatmeal, Vegetables, Legumes, Fruits, and Other High-Fiber Foods

Yes, it's true. Today, high-fiber, low-fat foods are recommended to help reduce the risk of a number of ailments including heart disease, colon cancer, and obesity in addition to helping to control diabetes and hypoglycemia. Oats, oat bran, whole grain breads and cereals, vegetables, legumes, and fruits provide these essential fibers.

Fiber has been broadly classified into two types: water-soluble and water-insoluble. Both have different functions in the body and are found in varied amounts in foods. While some foods contain both, most foods are better sources of one form of fiber than the other. Insoluble fiber is made up of those plant parts—seeds, skin, cell walls, husks, stems, and the like—that cannot be broken down by our digestive enzymes and therefore pass through our systems intact to serve as natural laxatives, adding bulk and absorbing water, speeding elimination, and diluting the effects of cancer-producing carcinogens.

Water-soluble fibers—vegetable gums, pectins, and the like—combine with water in the intestines to produce a glutenous mass that aids digestion. They help to lower cholesterol and control blood pressure, and enhance the absorption of sugar, which in turn assists in controlling diabetes and hypoglycemia.

How much of a drop in cholesterol levels can you expect when you increase water-soluble fiber consumption on a regular basis? According to two studies done at Northwestern University Medical School, it is possible to lower a cholesterol count by about 3 percent by eating 35 grams of bran daily. (It's possible to get even better results—up to a 10, or even 20, percent drop—if you don't mind consuming 100 grams of the stuff daily, or one bowl of pure bran cereal in the morning and five no-cholesterol bran muffins during the day!) Probably the most efficient way to get daily fiber is with a single ⅔-cup serving of hot oat-bran cereal or quick-cooking oatmeal. Equally efficient, eat a ½-cup portion each day of pinto, black, kidney or navy beans, chick-peas, split peas, or lentils.

Sodium, Potassium, and Hypertension

Many people who are interested in lowering their cholesterol to prevent heart attacks are also concerned with the roles sodium and potassium play in reducing the risk of hypertension and strokes. Norman Kaplan, head of the Hypertensive Section at the University of Texas Southwestern Medical School and author of *Clinical Hypertension, Prevent Your Heart Attack,* and *Hypertension,* recently discussed this in an interview in *Nutrition Action Healthletter,* issued in May 1989 by Center for Science in the Public Interest. He stated that about 50 percent of the people who cut their sodium intake by half will have a significant fall in blood pressure. Patients with mild hypertension can bring their blood pressure down to normal simply by reducing dietary salt, and thus avoid the potential risks of drugs.

Although there is not as much evidence that eating potassium-rich foods can lower blood pressure as much as a low-sodium diet will, there have been a number of studies showing that doubling an average 2,000 to 3,000 milligrams daily intake of potassium can lower blood pressure by 3 to 5 mm. Hg.

POTASSIUM-RICH FOODS FOR YOUR HEALTH

To increase the potassium in your daily diet, include more of these low-cholesterol, high-fiber fruits, vegetables, beans, and legumes.

	Potassium (mg.)
Fruits and Fruit Juices	
Avocado (½ medium)	602
Watermelon (¹⁄₁₆)	560
Banana (1 medium)	451
Cantaloupe (¼ melon)	412
Orange juice, frozen (6 ounces)	284
Raisins (¼ cup)	308
Grapefruit juice (6 ounces)	284
Orange (1 medium)	237
Apple juice (6 ounces)	222
Pear (1)	208
Beans and Legumes (cooked, 1 cup)	
Soybeans	886
Lentils	731
Red kidney beans	713
Split peas	710
White navy beans	669
Black-eyed peas	476
Vegetables (cooked)	
Potato (1 large)	844
Squash, acorn (½ cup)	446
Spinach (½ cup)	419
Sweet potato (1)	397
Rutabaga (½ cup)	344
Squash, butternut (½ cup)	290
Brussels sprouts (½ cup)	247
Carrot, raw (1)	233
Zucchini (½ cup)	228
Peas (½ cup)	217
Cauliflower (½ cup)	200

About Oils

VEGETABLE OILS

Polyunsaturated vegetable oils—canola, safflower, corn, sunflower, sesame, soybean—or monounsaturated peanut oil lend themselves gracefully to a wide variety of heart-safe recipes. Extra virgin olive oil, also monounsaturated, adds distinctive flavor and aroma to more vibrant ethnic dishes.

Basically, the difference between one vegetable oil and another is the amount of saturated fat each contains. These levels vary, with canola having the least, and the tropical oils—coconut, palm kernel, and palm—containing the most. (Avoid these last ones completely.)

Fat Profile of Vegetable Oils*

Type of oil	Percent Saturated	Percent Monounsaturated	Percent Polyunsaturated
Canola	7	55	33
Safflower	10	12	75
Corn	13	24	59
Soybean	14	23	58
Olive	14	72	9
Peanut	19	46	30
Tropical oils			
Palm	49	37	9
Palm kernel	81	11	2
Coconut	86	6	2

*The total percentage of all three types of fat will not add up to 100 percent because oils contain small amounts of other ingredients.

Source: U.S. Department of Agriculture

CHOOSING OILS: A GUIDE

Almond oil: Distinctly non-nutty, with a mildly sweet taste. Use for salad dressings or as a substitute for butter when greasing a cookie sheet.

Avocado oil: Sharp and slightly nutty flavor. Blend into salad dressings. Although avocados are good sources of important nutrients, California avocados get 86 percent of their calories from fat, while those from Florida get 76 percent. One half of one fruit will yield about ⅕ the total amount of fat the average adult should consume in one day, even though very little of the fat is saturated.

Canola oil: Pressed from the seed of rape, a mustard-family plant, this oil is lower in saturated fat than any other vegetable oil. It contains only 7 percent saturated fat, 55 percent monounsaturated fat, and 10 percent alpha-linolenic acid, an Omega-3 fatty acid believed to reduce cholesterol. Procter & Gamble's Puritan Oil (made from canola oil) won the American Health Foundation's 1987 Product of the Year Award.

Coconut oil: The high amount of saturated fat in this tropical oil prohibits its use in any low-cholesterol diet.

Corn oil: A light flavor and high smoke point make this polyunsaturated oil one of the most popular in the kitchen. An all-around oil whose flavor can be heightened by judiciously combining with more fragrant oils.

Cottonseed oil: Higher in saturated fats than any other of the polyunsaturated oils. Use it sparingly or not at all.

Grape seed oil: This exotic and costly oil gets most of its flavor from the dried herbs that are often blended into it. You can duplicate its flavor by adding your own combination of dried thyme, basil, rosemary, and fennel to a light-flavored oil. Useful in marinades.

Hazelnut oil: Redolent of toasted nuts, this lovely but expensive golden-brown oil is generally kept for tossing into salads.

Olive oil: The best quality olive oil is extra-virgin, and the finest of the extra-virgins are those that are cold-pressed from the first pressing of the olives. Look for labels that say "unfiltered, cold-pressed, extra-virgin olive oil." Reserve the top-quality, fruity olive oils for salads, or add a tablespoon or two "alla Italina" to steamed chard, spinach, or broccoli.

Virgin olive oil is from the second pressing and may be used similarly to extra-virgin. "Pure" olive oil is from subsequent pressings and is lighter and milder than the first-press variety. Use this for dishes with ingredients that are outstanding on their own. Blended olive oils may be used for sautéing.

Peanut oil: A monounsaturated oil which has a smoking point only a little lower than that of corn oil. Its light flavor makes it tops for stir-frying or sautéing. French peanut oils have the nuttiest flavor and should be reserved for use in salads.

Safflower oil: Next to lowest in saturated fats and high in polyunsaturates (with only 10 percent saturated fat), safflower oil is the ideal cooking oil for cholesterol watchers. Unfortunately, it has little flavor and when used as a salad dressing, tends to make greens overly greasy. Blending it with a tablespoon or two of olive oil helps, as does the addition of fresh or dried herbs.

Sesame oil: Darker varieties of this oil are favored for use in Oriental dipping sauces or stir-fried veggies. Try the paler variety to add accent to your salad dressings.

Soybean oil: Often a component of the partly hydrogenated vegetable oil blends that line supermarket shelves. The most flavorful soy oils can be found in Oriental groceries.

Sunflower oil: A highly polyunsaturated oil with a strong oil flavor that intensifies with cooking. Popular in Europe, in the Soviet Union, and in the Near East and Mexico. Also useful for complementing raw fresh vegetables.

Walnut oil: A subtly flavored oil best used in cold dishes where the lovely walnut essence may be appreciated without being destroyed by heat. The French import is far superior to the health food–store product.

PROCESSING OILS

The way in which an oil is processed, as well as the seed, fruit, or nut used for its making, affects its culinary properties. Processing can provide the robust flavor found in fruity extra-virgin olive oil or a smoky sesame oil, or yield a less assertive light oil suitable for home cooking.

All oils—whether olive, peanut, sunflower, corn, avocado, soybean, or any other—are extracted through one of two processes. The pre-press chemical solvent method yields a stable oil that is not likely to burn, smoke, or foam at fairly high temperatures, nor turn rancid easily. True cold pressing results in a fragrant, flavor-rich oil that has been pressed by physical or mechanical means only, without additional heat or any chemical solvent.

An oil's true character is revealed through appearance, aroma, and taste. When buying oils for any purpose other than to cook with—to dress fresh greens, for instance, or to use in a vinaigrette or marinade—look for an oil with a rich color, emphatic bouquet, and tantalizing flavor strongly reminiscent of its vegetable or fruit origin. These are all signs that very little processing has been involved in its preparation. Be aware, however, that cold-pressed oils, because of the minimal processing they undergo, do have a shorter shelf life than their blander counterparts, because they turn rancid a bit more quickly and will burn at lower temperatures. Buy these flavorful oils in small quantities and keep them refrigerated. The cloudiness and thickening that may result will not affect their quality and should dissipate when the oil returns to room temperature.

When choosing an oil for cooking, keep in mind that heat intensifies the flavor.

ABOUT ENHANCED OLIVE OILS

The glorious inflow of precious and semiprecious olive oils to this country is cause for celebration. No longer are we restricted to one or two dreary brands (bottled who knows when) that once stood gracelessly on our grocery store shelves. Now this liquid gold gleams through ornate bottles like so many vials of pricey perfume—with price tags to match. Outrageously rich? Perhaps. But it seems to me that one tablespoon of this gorgeous, pale-green extra-virgin essence can do more to elevate a commonplace dish than can any other single ingredient. I for one would far rather indulge myself in a few drops of this treasure than in a quart of cologne. So much for priorities. That said, I contend that even perfection can be embellished. Witness these aromatic, herb-scented gems.

Experiment with a variety of oils until you find those that please you most. (My favorites are Badia A Colto Buono, Sicilian Madre Sicilia, and, for use in quantity, Colavita. Then give them even more flavor with sprigs of fresh thyme, rosemary, oregano, marjoram, or tarragon. Hot red pepper, garlic, and cracked peppercorns, or any one of these in combination with herb twigs, also start wonderful dressings.

ABOUT FISH OILS

The debate over fish oils and their place in a healthy-heart diet contributes to the confusion about which foods to eat for the sake of your well-being. In the past, nutrition experts urged us to avoid fatty fish and shellfish—salmon, shrimp, and the like—but new evidence indicates that the Omega-3 fatty acids found in the oils from these fish actually diminish the risk of heart attack and strokes.

Interest in the potential of fish oil to prevent coronary heart disease began back in the 1970s, when Danish researchers became aware that Greenland Eskimos, whose diet typically consists of large quantities of whale blubber, seal meat, and/or fish, rarely suffer heart attacks.

Because few people are likely to eat as much fish—not to mention blubber—as do Eskimos, it was inevitable that fish-oil capsules were soon being touted as an alternative. The problem is that to get an effective amount of Omega-3 it is necessary to take 15–20 capsules of oil daily. Even then no one knows for sure what fish oil taken in this form can and cannot do.

What is known is that, taken in sufficient quantities, Omega-3s in their natural form do have the potential to lower the amount of harmful fats and cholesterol in the blood. Researchers now theorize that these fats also help when cholesterol deposits begin to form in an artery due to some kind of microscopic injury to the blood vessel wall. Fish oil, it appears, may inhibit these events by reducing the numbers and adhesion of clot-forming blood platelets, thereby helping keep artery walls free from buildup.

Most people will derive the greatest benefit from the action of Omega-3s by substituting cold-water fish for those foods—red meat and dairy products—that promote formation of fatty plaques in artery walls.

About Bean Curd (Japanese tofu, Chinese dow foo, bean custard, soybean cake)

If ever there was a miracle food, one that was rich in nutrition, low in cholesterol and calories, versatile, inexpensive, and easy to prepare, bean curd would have to be that super food. The Chinese call it "meat without bones" and for good reason. Made from pureed soybeans, it is a rich source of protein and lecithin containing amino acids.

White, ranging in texture from custardy to firm, bean curd comes packed in water in plastic containers, refrigerated, and sold in most supermarkets and health food stores. Some brands are labeled "soft," "medium," or "hard," and one Chinese variety, called yakidoufu, is quite firm. Although it is best used immediately, if you change the water in the package every day you can refrigerate it for up to seven days (it does not freeze well).

Not only is bean curd a perfect food when it comes to nutrition, it's versatile as well. Steam it, stir-fry it, grill it, add it to vegetable dishes, stews, or soups. Mix it with egg whites for a creamy texture in a variety of cooked recipes, or chill it and serve it with chopped scallions, dried seaweed, and grated fresh ginger.

If you don't care for the soft variety you may firm its consistency by wrapping it in cheesecloth or paper towels and weighting it down with a heavy plate for an hour or so.

I've included bean curd in many recipes in this book, mostly the conventional soft, medium, or firm varieties. However, here are other bean curd treasures you might experiment with if they become available to you.

BEAN CURD STICKS

This version (made by both the Chinese and the Japanese and available in Chinese groceries or other specialty food shops) is dried bean curd, folded into sheets or sticks. These keep unrefrigerated, up to 2–3 months, but no longer since they will, like other products, eventually become rancid.

To use, soak in water for up to an hour, slice, and use like conventional bean curd.

FERMENTED BEAN CURD

This product is available packed in brine in cans or jars, red or white, in various sizes. White is usually salty and cheeselike in flavor. Red (some brands mild, some spicy) is fermented with wine and colored with red rice.

Store in a tightly lidded jar in the refrigerator for up to 3 months.

Use sparingly as a condiment or seasoning in sauces, with poultry, meat, or in salads. The white curd may be eaten raw with rice.

Low-Cholesterol, Fat, and Salt: Other Sides of the Story

As was perhaps inevitable with so widely acclaimed a doctrine, over a period of time a few dissenting opinions have been heard. Some nutrition experts have been sending mixed messages concerning the trio of dietary no-no's—cholesterol, fat, and salt. It is only fair to bring these to your attention. Consider the following, but let moderation be your guide. The questions raised pertain to the validity of testing healthy individuals on a regular basis, were the reductions in blood-cholesterol levels less dramatic than once was thought, and so on.

While acknowledging that high levels of blood cholesterol are statistically associated with high rates of heart disease, several experts have suggested that reducing dietary cholesterol may not act to lower blood cholesterol as much as previously thought. Other prominent scientists have challenged the dominant consensus among medical authorities and government agencies that a lower sodium intake is a necessity, even for people who don't suffer from hypertension.

Thomas J. Moore is among those who doubt that reducing cholesterol intake has other than modest effect on blood cholesterol levels. In his book, *Heart Failure* (Random House, 1989), part of which was excerpted in a widely publicized article in the September 1989 *Atlantic Monthly* entitled "The Cholesterol Myth," Moore marshals his evidence against diet as a means for reducing high blood-cholesterol levels by reexamining several well-known federal studies.

Along with the authors of *Balanced Nutrition,* Drs. Frederick J. Stare, Robert E. Olson, and Elizabeth M. Whelan (Bob Adams, Inc., 1989), Moore argues that these studies are inconclusive because all the participants were middle-aged men. Although some of the studies did establish a connection between blood cholesterol and diet, he continues, the average reduction in blood-cholesterol levels was less than dramatic and brought no significant decline in mortality.

These authors also question the wisdom of the government's National Cholesterol Education Program, which advocates (1) that everyone over the age of two have his or her blood tested for cholesterol, and (2) that the 60 million Americans whose counts exceed 240 mg./dl. reduce their cholesterol intake by whatever means necessary, whether through diet or drugs.

To add to the confusion, the researchers have found that there is actually one saturated fat, called stearic acid, that does not raise blood cholesterol. Because beef and chocolate contain fairly large amounts of stearic acid, this finding has prompted the beef and chocolate industries to herald that the saturated fat in these products may not be so bad for us after all.

In the case of stearic acid, the fuss focuses on the fatty acids that make such a difference in fat's impact on health. As we know, some fatty acids are saturated, others monounsaturated, and still others are polyunsaturated. Researchers aren't certain why saturated fatty acids raise blood-cholesterol levels, nor are they sure exactly why unsaturated fatty acids tend to lower them. All they know is that is what happens.

Scott Grundy, a researcher at the University of Texas, conducted the major experiments that showed stearic acid to be one of the few saturated fats that does not raise cholesterol. Grundy, who also happens to be the man who first alerted the nutrition world to the cholesterol-lowering properties of the monounsaturate olive oil, used pure stearic acid in his experiments. And therein, it seems, lies the problem. Half of the saturated fat in beef and chocolate may be stearic acid, but the other half consists of palmitic acid, which actually raises blood cholesterol levels.

The challenge to the conventional view that everyone should reduce sodium intake to prevent the development of high blood pressure in the future also hinges on whether it makes sense to extend such a restriction to normal healthy people.

None of the experts involved argue that reducing salt in the diet is not absolutely vital to control the blood pressure of the millions of Americans already diagnosed as hypertensive. Instead, they contend that the current emphasis on sodium as the key dietary component in hypertension is misplaced. They maintain that other factors—age, body weight, race, genetic profile, kidney infection, and dietary components other than salt—may be just as important.

While considering the above, it is important to realize that despite the conflicting evidence about risk factors involved, there is no longer any question that excessive intake of foods high in cholesterol, fat, and salt is hazardous to your health.

Food—"New American" Style

What makes the dishes in the menus that follow nontraditional is that they contain very little meat. In fact, they are based primarily on vegetables and rise from the premise that a variety of fresh, superior raw materials, chosen at their peak and used in imaginative and provocative ways, will result in delicious, sophisticated, and refreshingly unusual fare.

Splendid vegetables and fruits, harvested at their peak, are critical to the success of developing a cuisine that is less dependent on meat. In "Star Vegetables" (pages 197 to 224), I explain how to choose and use them. For the extraordinary abundance of once-exotic or nearly impossible-to-find food produce that currently overflow roadside vegetable stands and even appear in supermarket produce sections, we thank the practitioners of the "New American" cuisine.

This new, inventive style of cooking, dedicated to taste and texture, color and freshness, relies exclusively on the use of distinctive natural ingredients. The young chefs and other visionaries who lead this movement satisfied their passion for preparing vegetables that would have the "just-pulled-from-the-soil" immediacy they sought by acquiring the best produce local farms had to offer. As they got to know their suppliers, they began to enlist the help of these farmers and cottage-kitchen operators, urging them to grow specific items, unusual specimens, perfect in form. The rest is culinary history.

The number and choice of vegetables and fruits being grown has increased dramatically. Old varieties have come back into favor. Exotic new hybrids are being swiftly introduced. Sugarsnap peas and snowpeas, a fanciful array of exotic mushrooms, sprouts of all kinds, dazzling assortments of beans and peppers, and even bean curd in several textures have become the rule rather than the exception. Coast to coast, consumers are responding to natural foods, the spread of the "New American" heart-safe way of cooking and their own newfound knowledge of—and healthy respect for—exquisitely fresh produce.

Spring

A Spring Dinner with Oriental Overtones

MENU

Summer Squash and Squash
Blossom Soup

Chicken Velvet with Stir-Fried
Spring Vegetables

Brown Rice (page 183)

Cherries in the Snow

SUGGESTIONS

The summer squash soup may be prepared using canned consommé or broth. Scallion tassels and cherry tomato slices can be substituted for the squash blossoms.

If you're in a hurry, choose vegetables for stir-frying that do not require blanching or pre-cooking such as mushrooms, sweet pepper, scallions, and snow peas, or chinese cabbage. Become familiar with this tasty, simple-to-prepare Oriental staple. You'll be amazed at its versatility.

If your time is limited and creating and clarifying your own stock is out of the question, never mind; simmered-down canned uncondensed broth may be substituted.

Summer Squash and Squash Blossom Soup

When your mood, or the occasion, calls for a subtle, delicate soup, this combination is lovely both to see and to taste. The soup stock is best simmered down to its essence and clarified so that the color and flavor are at their richest. If no flowers are available, cut the summer squash creatively and add a few scallion tassels (page 193) and seeded cherry tomato slices.

NOTE

Think of flowers not as a mere curiosity but rather as another colorful ingredient. Lately, squash blossoms are more readily found at produce stands and specialty shops. Some places even stock nasturtium blossoms and flowering herbs. If a number of these are available, go ahead and present your guests a riotous bouquet in a bowl. If not, substitute violets, lilacs, or rose petals that have never been sprayed or exposed to the pollution of passing cars. (Don't use the *leaves* of any flowers unless you are certain they are edible and avoid specimens from your florist—these might be sprayed.)

Serves 6

2 quarts Chicken Consommé, Homemade Chicken Broth (pages 187 and 186), or canned broth

2 large onions, peeled and finely chopped

1 tablespoon minced fresh ginger

½ teaspoon minced lemon zest (the yellow outer skin of the lemon with none of the bitter white underskin)

Generous pinch each of saffron threads and turmeric

2–3 of the smallest available, finger-length if possible, summer squash, squash blossoms, nasturtium blossoms, violets, herb blossoms, rose petals, and/or seeded cherry tomato slices or a combination of these

Simmer the consommé or broth, onions, ginger, lemon zest, saffron, and turmeric, partially covered, for 15 minutes. Strain the soup and return the fortified broth to a clean pan. Just prior to serving, run the tines of a fork lengthwise down the squash to form long stripes, then thinly slice them. Heat the squash slices in the hot soup for 3 to 4 minutes.

Cut the squash blossoms in ¼-inch horizontal slices, leaving the stem end with the stamens attached, which will resemble little flowers. Serve the soup hot, garnished with the squash slices, squash flower petals, or any of the other flowers or garnishes mentioned.

Chicken Velvet with Stir-Fried Spring Vegetables and Brown Rice

There is a unique cloudlike delicacy to this classic Chinese omelet prepared with egg whites (no cholesterol) and pureed white meat chicken. Partner this with an assortment of the most glorious fresh stir-fried spring vegetables available, and serve with highly flavored brown rice for an unusually satisfying meal. The ham, which adds richness at less than 1 tablespoon per person, is one of those ingredients that seem to be worth more than their weight in flavor, but it can be eliminated to keep the cholesterol to a minimum.

Serves 6

2 small chicken breasts (or 1 large one, approximately 8 ounces), skinned, boned, and with all bits of tendon or gristle removed

2 tablespoons sherry

1 teaspoon plus 1 tablespoon cornstarch
Salt to taste (optional)

5 egg whites

½ cup cold water

5 tablespoons peanut oil

1¼ cups Chicken Consommé (page 187) or one 10½ ounce can chicken broth, undiluted

¼ cup light soy sauce

¼ cup finely sliced trimmed scallions (include some of green top)

1 tablespoon sesame oil

2 teaspoons minced, peeled fresh ginger

3 tablespoons finely chopped smoked ham (optional)

6 cups Stir-Fried Spring Vegetables (recipe follows)

1 recipe Basic Brown Rice (page 183)

This is really a snap to prepare in either a blender or a food processor, with the steel blade. Cut the chicken breasts into 1-inch cubes and puree, adding 1 tablespoon of the sherry, one drop at a time. Then, with the motor running, whirl in the following ingredients: 1 teaspoon cornstarch, salt, if desired, and 1 egg white. Gradually beat in ¼ cup of the water, a few drops at a time (don't add the water too quickly, or the mixture will separate).

In the bowl of an electric mixer (or a medium-size mixing bowl), beat the remaining egg whites until they form soft peaks; do not let them become stiff and dry. Fold in the chicken mixture. The omelet is now ready to cook.

Heat 3 tablespoons of the peanut oil in a heavy 10-inch skillet or omelet pan. Add the chicken mixture and cook, without stirring, over low heat for 1 minute, then remove the pan from the heat and stir rapidly to incorporate the oil into the chicken mixture. Return the pan to low heat and cook 1 minute more. Heat the remaining 2 tablespoons oil in another 10-inch skillet, turn the omelet over into this pan, and cook 2 minutes more. Turn off the heat but let the pan remain on the burner.

If you are using an electric stove, allow the pan to remain on the burner only 2 minutes or until the omelet is moist but not runny inside.

Meanwhile, heat the consommé or broth, the remaining tablespoon sherry, the soy sauce, and scallions in a small saucepan. Mix the remaining 1 tablespoon cornstarch into ¼ cup cold water until the mixture is smooth. Stir this into the consommé mixture, and bring to a boil, stirring continuously until the sauce is thick and clear. Add the sesame oil, ginger, ham, if desired, and salt if required.

Serve Chicken Velvet with the hot sauce poured over, surrounded by a ring of Brown Rice and the Stir-Fried Spring Vegetables.

STIR-FRIED SPRING VEGETABLES

Stir-frying is a cooking technique that renders vegetables half tender, half crunchy, and at the height of their flavor and color. The secret to achieving this harmonic synthesis of fresh taste and glowing good looks lies in proper preparation and cooking.

Stir-frying is quick cooking. The idea behind it is to seal in the juices by tossing the vegetables quickly in hot oil, then to finish them in their own or some other liquid.

Proper preparation calls for cutting or slicing each vegetable into pieces of equal size and thickness, just before you're ready to cook them. A general rule of thumb is to cut soft vegetables vertically; slightly harder ones such as broccoli, carrots, cauliflower, and green beans, and slower-cooking ones such as carrots, cauliflower, and winter squash, on the diagonal. To shorten the time needed to stir-fry these diagonally cut vegetables, parboiling or blanching them in advance is recommended.

NOTE

To blanch, use a strainer and plunge the vegetables first into boiling water, drain then immediately submerge in cold water to stop the cooking action, and drain again. To parboil, cook the vegetables in the boiling water until slightly less than half done, then transfer to the cold water. Drain well. Parboil green vegetables just long enough for them to turn bright green; cook nongreen vegetables until they are crisp-tender. Be sure all vegetables are perfectly dry before adding them to the hot oil.

Use 6 cups of any of the vegetables listed below for your stir-frying, preparing them as directed. For interesting contrasts in color and texture, try them in a variety of combinations.

PREPARING VEGETABLES FOR STIR-FRYING

Asparagus: Break off woody stems, scrape the stalks, and cut on the diagonal into ½-inch pieces; leave tender tips intact. Blanch stalks only.

Bok choy: Cut the bright green leaves of this Chinese celery into thin shreds; cut stalks into ½-inch pieces on the diagonal.

Broccoli: Cut florets apart and thinner stalks in half. Thinly slice larger stalks on the diagonal. Peel them with a vegetable peeler first if they seem tough. Blanch.

Carrots: Scrape or peel and cut into thin slices on the diagonal. Parboil.

Cauliflower: Separate into small florets; slice stalks thinly on the diagonal. Parboil.

Celery: Remove all strings; trim leaves and ends. Cut diagonally into thick slices. Blanch.

Chinese cabbage: Also known as Napa cabbage. Cut this subtle and delicate cabbage variety into thin shreds.

Chinese eggplant: A small white variety of the vegetable, with a pulpy, delicate flesh. Peel and dice.

Cucumber: Peel. Thinly slice small cucumbers. Cut larger ones in half, scoop out seeds, and cut into ¼-inch slices.

Green beans: Trim ends and cut into 1-inch slices on the diagonal, or leave whole. Blanch.

Leeks: Use only the white or palest part of the vegetable. Wash well and shred thinly.

Mushrooms: Trim stem ends and wipe caps with a damp cloth. Slice large specimens vertically; leave small ones whole.

Onions: Peel and slice very thinly.

Peas: Shell and blanch.

Scallions: Use only the whitest or palest green parts; trim and cut on the diagonal.

Snow peas: Available fresh or frozen. Break off tips and remove strings from fresh specimens.

Spinach: Remove tough stems and wash leaves thoroughly; shake and pat dry before using whole or shredded.

Summer squash or zucchini: Peel and slice thinly on the diagonal.

Sweet peppers: Seed and slice into strips, or cut in squares. Blanch just long enough to brighten their color.

Tomatoes: Peel and seed. If small, cut into quarters; cut larger ones into cubes.

Winter squash: Peel and cut into thin slices or julienne. Parboil.

Cherries in the Snow

When early spring fruits and late winter snows coincide, scoop up a pristine bowl of the latter and decorate with the former for dramatic effect. The cherries may be presented on cracked ice if Mother Nature fails to cooperate.

Serves 6

4 quarts clean snow, or cracked or shaved ice
1½ pounds black cherries (with stems if possible)

Mound the snow or ice in a large glass bowl and arrange the cherries attractively over the top. Place the bowl on a tray and serve immediately.

A Deluxe Vegetable-Pizza Dinner

MENU

Fresh Peas with Seasoned "Salt"

Fresh Vegetable Pizza

*Salad of Fresh Young Sorrel
Leaves, Cherry Tomatoes, and
Daikon Radish*

Red Fruits in Dubonnet Rouge

SUGGESTIONS

The pizza dough may be prepared the evening before or you may purchase it from your local pizza parlor. It isn't difficult to stretch and roll it out to fit a baking sheet.

If sorrel and daikon are not available in your area, prepare the salad instead with fresh spinach and white or red radishes.

Fresh Peas with Seasoned "Salt"

When fresh-picked peas are at hand, this makes an original, refreshing nibble to serve with drinks. Guests pop open the shells, sprinkle with seasoned salt, and eat the raw peas.

Sugarsnap peas make a nice substitute. Rub one end of each lightly with egg white, then dip in seasoned salt, and allow to dry.

Serves 6

1 pound fresh-picked young peas
¼ cup seasoned salt substitute
¼ cup minced fresh herbs (or 1 tablespoon dried) (optional)

Rinse the peas in their pods, roll them loosely in paper towels, and refrigerate for several hours. Mix the salt substitute and the herbs. Just prior to serving, arrange peas in an attractive silver or glass dish with a smaller glass dish to hold the seasoned salt.

Fresh Vegetable Pizza

Besides being an original first course for dinner, this also makes for a good main course at a company lunch, or a knockout one-dish dinner.

Serves 6

1 recipe Pizza Dough (recipe follows)
7 large ripe tomatoes, peeled, seeded, and coarsely chopped
1 large clove garlic, peeled and minced
1 teaspoon granulated sugar
¼ teaspoon salt (optional)
6 tablespoons good-quality olive oil
Oregano, fresh or dried
1 each small zucchini and yellow summer squash, very thinly sliced
2 tablespoons plus 2 teaspoons vegetable oil
1 each medium-size green, red, and orange peppers, seeded and sliced in rings
1 cup shredded snow peas (page 214)
6 slices low-fat mozzarella cheese

Prepare the pizza dough as directed. While the dough is rising, prepare the topping. Place the tomatoes, garlic, sugar, salt, if desired, and 3 tablespoons olive oil in a saucepan and cook over low heat, stirring from time to time, about 30 minutes, or until most of the liquid evaporates.

Preheat the oven to 425° F.

Roll out the dough to fit a large rectangular cookie sheet, approximately 10½ inches by 16 inches, with sides. Oil the pan and press the edges of the dough up against, and a little higher than, the sides. Spread the tomato sauce over the dough. Sprinkle with 3 tablespoons olive oil and oregano to taste. Bake for 20 minutes.

Meanwhile, sprinkle the squash slices lightly with salt, arrange them between paper towels, and weight them down with plates for 10 minutes so they shed their moisture. Pat dry.

In a non-stick skillet, sauté the squash slices until lightly browned on both sides, turning once. Set the slices aside and drain on paper towels. Add one teaspoon vegetable oil to the same pan, sauté the pepper rings until barely tender, and set them aside. Add another teaspoon vegetable oil to the pan and toss the snow pea shreds over medium heat for one minute.

To serve, arrange the pepper rings on either end of the pizza, the squash slices down the middle, and the cheese in between. Sprinkle the snow pea shreds over all. Return the pizza to the oven and bake 5–10 minutes longer, or until the cheese bubbles and turns light brown. Cut into 3-inch squares and let guests choose their favorite toppings.

Pizza Dough

Makes enough dough for 1 large or 6 individual pizzas

   4 cups all-purpose flour
1½ teaspoons granulated sugar
   ½ teaspoon salt
   ½ package (1½ teaspoons) dry active yeast
   ¼ cup lukewarm water
   ⅔ cup skim milk, at room temperature
   3 tablespoons vegetable oil

Place the flour, sugar, and salt in the bowl of a food processor fitted with the metal blade, and process just long enough to mix. Dissolve the yeast in the lukewarm water and add to the bowl along with the milk. Process by turning the motor on and off quickly 8 times. Add the oil and process again for 15 or 20 seconds, or just until the dough forms a ball. If the dough fails to form a ball, add a bit more milk; if it seems sticky, add a bit more flour.

Turn the dough out of the bowl, and divide it into 8 pieces. Return the pieces to the bowl, press them down against the blade; replace the lid and process just long enough for the dough to form one ball again. Repeat this process 4 or 5 times.

Shape the dough into a large ball and set in a warm, draft-free place for 2 hours, or until double in bulk (page 195).

Salad of Fresh Young Sorrel Leaves, Cherry Tomatoes, and Daikon Radish

When fresh young sorrel leaves are available in peak condition, it's time to try this sprightly salad. Since the sorrel itself is slightly lemony, the pungent olive oil alone may be dressing enough. Have a taste to determine.

You may have to buy more than 2 pounds of sorrel to get enough small leaves for this salad. The extra amount may be cooked the following day (as you would cook spinach), or dressed with garlic oil. If daikon can't be found, substitute an equivalent amount of any white or red radish.

Serves 6

2–4 pounds sorrel, well—but not roughly—washed
   ½ pint small sweet cherry tomatoes
   1 8-inch piece daikon radish, peeled, rinsed, and thinly sliced (if you substitute red radishes, do not peel)
   1 teaspoon salt (optional)
   1 lemon
   2 teaspoons Toasted Sesame Seeds (page 192; optional)
3–4 tablespoons Garlic-Enhanced Olive Oil, or 1 clove peeled and crushed garlic mixed with plain or herb-flavored olive oil (pages 24 and 190)

Select about 2 pounds of the smallest leaves from the bunches of sorrel; wash and dry well. Cut the cherry tomatoes in half. If you wish, drop the radish slices into a pint of water to which the salt has been added. To make the lemon slices more attractive, use a vegetable parer or small sharp knife to cut from the lemon four narrow strips of peel, including the bitter white underskin. Thinly slice the lemon.

Arrange a small mound of greens on each of 6 salad plates. Next to this, arrange a row of cherry tomato halves. On the edge of the plate, fan out 6 slices of daikon. Garnish with sliced lemon and sesame seeds, if used. Guests may squeeze the lemon slices over the salad if it is not tart enough. Pass plain and garlic oils in cruets.

Red Fruits in Dubonnet Rouge

Present these sweet red fruits in champagne glasses. Be sure to add the fragile raspberries just prior to serving.

Serves 6

1 cup Dubonnet Rouge
2 2-inch strips lemon peel
2 pints strawberries, cut lengthwise
   into quarters
1 cup red raspberries

Place the Dubonnet in a 4-cup bowl that has been rubbed with the skin-side of the strips of lemon peel. Twist the strips over the Dubonnet, then drop them into it. Marinate for 15 minutes, then discard the peel.

Place the strawberries in the bowl and toss with the Dubonnet. Refrigerate for 1 hour. Spoon the mixture into champagne glasses, top with the raspberries, and serve at once.

An East-West Dinner

MENU

Gado-Gado Endive

Teriyaki Sea Scallop "Coins"

Sushi Rice

Salsify Pancakes

*Fava Beans and Zucchini in
Garlic Oil with Coriander*

Raspberry-Yogurt Pie

SUGGESTIONS

If coriander is not available, substitute Italian parsley in the Gado-Gado; also red radishes for the daikon.

Cook the rice a day in advance, mix it with the vinegar-syrup, form into ovals, cover tightly, and chill overnight. Grate and refrigerate radish and cucumber several hours early.

To simplify the meal, omit the salad or the salsify cakes, and instead of the pie, just serve the berries topped with a squeeze of lime juice mixed with a bit of warmed raspberry jelly.

Gado-Gado Endive

This version of Gado-Gado is a pleasant addition to any array of cocktail nibbles.

It is not unusual in Africa and in Indonesia for a condiment made from ground peanuts, in combination with hot chili oil, paste, or powder (Gado-Gado), to be used to enrich and enliven sauces, rice, and vegetable dishes. Since very nearly every commercial peanut butter contains all or partly hydrogenated oil (not to mention salt and sugar), it's best to buy the freshly ground, additive-free variety now available in many gourmet markets and health food shops. Or use your blender or food processor to grind your own from fresh roasted nuts.

Slightly bitter endive leaves partner beautifully with the sweet-hot flavor of the dip and also look attractive standing upright in the sauce. Guests can scoop up the creamy mixture in the leaves. Although readily available ingredients have been substituted for some of the hard-to-find authentic ones, and yogurt replaces milk to diminish the richness, the finished product is extremely satisfying.

This version of Gado-Gado is a pleasant addition to any array of cocktail nibbles.

Makes 2 cups

1 cup crunchy peanut butter
½ cup coarsely chopped sweet onion
1 tablespoon sesame oil
1 tablespoon soy sauce
2 large cloves garlic, peeled and crushed
1 teaspoon minced fresh lemongrass (optional)
1 teaspoon hot oil or ulek sambal (Indonesian chili paste) or chili powder
½ teaspoon each ground dried coriander and cumin
2 tablespoons peanut oil
½ cup plain yogurt
1 tablespoon finely chopped fresh coriander (if available)
3 Belgium endive

Whirl first nine ingredients in a food processor or blender until well mixed. With the machine whirling, add first the oil in a thin stream and then ¼ cup of the yogurt.

Spoon the mixture into an 8-inch, flat-bottomed bowl (a soufflé dish works well) and refrigerate for at least an hour or overnight. Remove the dip from the refrigerator about 30 minutes prior to serving, and let it stand at room temperature for 20 minutes. Fold in the additional cold yogurt thoroughly but gently. Sprinkle with fresh coriander. Separate the endives into leaves and stand them up close together in neat concentric circles, starting just inside the rim of the bowl. Serve immediately.

NOTE

It's interesting to serve hot, room temperature, and chilled foods at the same time as is called for in this recipe.

Teriyaki Sea Scallop "Coins"

Ask your fishmonger for large, perfect sea scallops; the smaller specimens or fragments won't do here. The scallops must be cooked at very high heat so that they caramelize almost instantly while remaining underdone at the centers. Have the Sushi Rice and grated garnishes already artfully arranged on the serving plates, then, working quickly, prepare the sea scallops.

Serves 6

12 large, perfect sea scallops
 2 tablespoons vegetable oil
 ¼ cup sake or 3 tablespoons sherry
 3 tablespoons light brown sugar
 ⅓ cup soy sauce
 1 teaspoon vinegar
 1 recipe Sushi Rice (recipe follows)
 2 tablespoons grated fresh ginger
 ⅔ cup grated fresh daikon radish or unpeeled red radishes
 ½ cup peeled, seeded, and grated cucumber

Cut the scallops crosswise across the center to form each into 2 perfect thin slices. Blot dry on a towel. Heat the oil to sizzling in a large non-stick pan. Fry the scallops for a second only, turning once. This is just to seal in the juices. Remove immediately from the pan and drain on paper towels.

Bring the sake, soy sauce, and vinegar to a rapid boil in the same pan until it is syrupy and just covers the bottom, taking care not to burn it. Arrange the scallops in 1 layer in the pan and cook over very high heat for a second or two on each side; they should caramelize almost immediately. Serve hot with small ovals of Sushi Rice and garnish with ginger, daikon, and cucumber.

Sushi Rice

Makes about 20 ovals of rice

1½ cups Japanese short-grain rice or long-grain white rice
1½ cups water for short grain; 1¾ for long-grain (or follow package directions)
 ⅓ cup Japanese sweet rice vinegar (or mild vinegar with a teaspoon of sugar added)
 ¼ cup sugar
 2 tablespoons mirin, sake, or sherry
     Wasabi, powdered (Japanese green horseradish powder) (optional)

This flavorful rice can also be rolled into small balls and topped with bits of raw or parboiled vegetables or small bits of fresh fish. Serve with Sweet and Salty Dipping Sauce (page 178) or Sashimi Dipping Sauce (page 178).

If you are using short-grain rice, wash it in a strainer until the water is no longer milky. Stir the rice into the boiling water, and when the water returns to the boil, cover, lower the heat, and simmer for 15 minutes or until the water has been absorbed. Cover and let stand 15 minutes more. In the meanwhile, boil the vinegar and sugar together until syrupy. Mix the hot syrup into the rice fanning it vigorously to hasten evaporation. Spread on a flat dish, and refrigerate until well chilled. Roll between your palms to form ovals about 2 inches by 1 inch. Chill until ready to use. Mix Wasabi with water to a smooth paste; cover and let stand for 10 minutes. Brush rice ovals with Wasabi if desired.

Salsify Pancakes

These small golden pancakes are just savory enough to complement medallions of chicken, duck, turkey, salmon, tuna, or, in this case, scallops.

Serves 6

1 recipe Salsify Puree (page 182)
1 egg or ¼ cup (2 ounces) egg substitute equivalent to 1 egg
   All-purpose flour
   Vegetable oil, for frying

Beat the Salsify Puree into the egg or egg substitute with just enough flour to make the mixture a little thicker than heavy cream. Drop the batter by tablespoons into ¼-inch hot oil in a non-stick skillet. Fry to golden on both sides, turning once. Serve hot.

Fava Beans and Zucchini in Garlic Oil with Coriander

Serve this at room temperature to heighten the mellow flavors.

Serves 6

1½ cups shelled fresh fava beans
   (about 2½ pounds)
¼ cup Garlic-Enhanced Olive Oil
   (page 190)
1½ tablespoons lemon juice
   Salt and freshly ground black
   pepper to taste
2 tablespoons minced fresh coriander
4 finger-length zucchini, thinly
   sliced then pressed between
   paper towels for 10 minutes
3 tablespoons chopped walnuts

Steam the fava beans until tender (about 15 minutes) and place them in a salad bowl. Toss with the garlic oil, lemon juice, salt and pepper, if desired, 1 tablespoon of the coriander and the zucchini. Let stand from 15 minutes to 1 hour. To serve, sprinkle with walnuts and the remaining coriander.

VARIATION

Slightly undercooked fresh or frozen baby lima beans can pinch-hit for the fava beans, but be sure the beans are still warm when you mix them with the other ingredients and put them aside to marinate.

NOTE

While this dish is at its peak when served as above, leftovers are also tasty when served cold. If the zucchini has caused the dressing to become watery, drain and toss with a little additional garlic oil.

Raspberry-Yogurt Pie

This exceptional pie can be varied by using one type of berry in the filling, another on top. Try blueberries in the pie, for example, raspberries on top. Or, if raspberries are hard to find, or are too pricey, buy frozen ones, puree, and strain them to add to the yogurt cheese, and top the pie with blueberries. Whatever way you prepare it, you're sure to enjoy this beautiful dessert.

1 9-inch Three-Grain Pie Crust (recipe follows)
2 cups raspberries
½ cup honey
1 teaspoon vanilla
1½ cups Yogurt Cheese (page 47) or low-fat farmer cheese
1 cup soft bean curd, well drained
¾ cup warmed and strained raspberry jelly

Prepare the pie crust, let it cool in the pan, then chill.

Puree and strain ¾ cup of raspberries, reserving the best-looking ones for the top. Mix the puree with the honey and vanilla; blend thoroughly with the Yogurt Cheese and bean curd, using a food processor. Spread the mixture into the crust and top attractively with the remaining raspberries.

Melt the jelly, cool slightly, then drizzle over the top of the pie. Chill at least 2 hours, but not more than 4 or 5. Remove from the pan and serve chilled.

Three-Grain Pie Crust

One try will convince you that this crust tastes terrific. It's actually good for you, but you shouldn't hold that against it.

Makes 1 9-inch crust

1 cup finely crushed graham crackers
3 tablespoons toasted honey-wheat germ
3 tablespoons oat bran
1 tablespoon liquid margarine
2 tablespoons plain yogurt
2 tablespoons honey
¼ teaspoon ground cinnamon
Generous pinch nutmeg

Preheat oven to 325° F.

Mix together the graham cracker crumbs, wheat germ, and oat bran. Use your fingers to rub the margarine into the mixture as evenly as possible. Mix in the yogurt, honey, and spices. Generously oil the bottom and sides of a 9-inch springform pan, turn the crust mixture into it, and press firmly over the bottom and part way up the sides. Bake 10–15 minutes or until lightly browned; don't let the crust get too dark. Cool to room temperature, then chill. Fill as directed.

A Late Spring Picnic

MENU

Eggplant Appetizer

Peasant-style Baked Vegetable
Cake with Black Olive Sauce and
Sweet Red Pepper Mayonnaise

Garlic Bread

Seasonal Fruit with Yogurt
Cheese

SUGGESTIONS

Eggplant appetizer keeps for weeks, so prepare it when you have spare time. I often double the recipe and serve it with a number of meals as it complements a wide range of entrées.

When preparing the vegetable cake, cook the Swiss chard and the pumpkin in advance and chill these overnight in separate bowls. If Swiss chard is not available, omit it and double the amount of spinach. Frozen winter squash puree may be substituted for your own cooked pumpkin, but since it is very moist and fine-textured it must be baked or boiled down to a thick paste.

Use canned kidney beans, available at your supermarket, rather than home-cooked ones, and frozen spinach rather than fresh. You'll need several packages. Drain well.

Black Olive Sauce may be prepared with canned and drained pitted black olives rather than pitted oil-cured ones.

Substitute commercial roasted red pepper or pimiento for the home-broiled ones, if necessary.

Eggplant Appetizer

Serves 6

1 large eggplant, peeled and cut into ½-inch cubes
  Salt
1 large sweet onion, peeled and coarsely chopped
3 ribs celery, coarsely chopped
6 medium-size mushrooms, wiped clean and coarsely chopped
1 tablespoon vegetable oil
3 tablespoons each honey and catsup
2 teaspoons lemon juice
¼ teaspoon cinnamon
⅛ teaspoon each ground cloves, thyme, and marjoram

Delicious on crackers or sliced daikon.

Sprinkle the eggplant cubes very lightly with salt and let stand for 10 minutes. Drain well, and press lightly between paper towels to remove excess moisture (and most of the salt).

In a large non-stick skillet sauté the eggplant, onion, celery, and mushrooms in the oil until lightly browned. Add the honey, catsup, lemon juice, and spices and boil, stirring continuously, until thick. Serve well chilled or at room temperature.

Peasant-style Baked Vegetable Cake with Black Olive Sauce and Sweet Red Pepper Mayonnaise

Makes 1 10-inch vegetable cake

2 pounds spinach, well washed, with coarse stems discarded
1 pound small young red Swiss chard, well washed with leaves stripped from the stalks
1 lemon, cut in quarters
4 tablespoons fruity olive oil
1 pound mushrooms, coarsely chopped
1 medium-size onion, peeled and finely chopped
¼ cup (2 ounces) egg substitute equivalent to 1 egg
⅓ cup grated Parmesan
  Dash of ground nutmeg
  Freshly ground black pepper to taste
1 cup cooked white kidney beans, well rinsed and drained
¼ cup fresh basil, chopped
3 cups cooked, coarsely mashed rutabaga or new, unpeeled red potatoes
3 large cloves garlic, peeled and minced
1 recipe Black Olive Sauce (recipe follows)
1 recipe Sweet Red Pepper Mayonnaise (recipe follows)

There's something so home-style, so downright gratifying about a simple rustic country dish like this one. I guarantee you won't even think about meat or the lack of it with this on your plate. Slather with Black Olive Sauce and include a bottle of lusty red wine for a picnic you'll long remember.

Cook the spinach in the water that clings to the leaves for about 5 minutes, cool, then press out excess liquid (page 217). Set aside. Cook the Swiss chard leaves in boiling water for 10 minutes or until tender. Cool and press out excess liquid, and squeeze the juice from one lemon quarter over it (page 220). Set aside.

Heat 1 tablespoon oil in a medium-size non-stick skillet, add the mushrooms and the juice of another lemon quarter, and sauté until the excess moisture has cooked away. Set aside. Heat 1 tablespoon oil and sauté the chopped onion until the pieces are soft and translucent, but not browned.

Preheat the oven to 350° F.

To assemble the vegetable cake, add half the egg substitute to the spinach and half to the Swiss chard; add 1 tablespoon Parmesan to each, and season with nutmeg and pepper. Press the spinach mixture into the bottom of a heavy, shallow 10-inch round earthenware dish or ovenproof porcelain dish. Layer with the mushrooms, then the beans, the basil, the rutabaga or potatoes, and, finally, the Swiss chard. Mix the crushed garlic with 1 tablespoon of Parmesan and 2 tablespoons of oil. Spread this over the top of the cake, sprinkle with the remaining cheese, and dribble the remaining olive oil over all.

Bake for 1 hour. The top should be a light golden brown. If it isn't, raise the heat to 400° F. and bake a few moments more. Let cool and serve at room temperature. Pass the two sauces.

VARIATION

Bake an autumn vegetable cake substituting cooked kale for Swiss chard and pumpkin or winter squash for the rutabaga or potatoes.

Sweet Red Pepper Mayonnaise

This fine sauce is enhanced by the addition of charbroiled sweet red pepper. Even if the flavor weren't sublime (and it is), the color might be reason enough to add the mayonnaise to a selection of very special recipes. In fact, this mayonnaise is so versatile even this rather large quantity will disappear before you know it. Try it with fish!

I whirl mine up in seconds in my mini-food processor, but if you prefer to use your standard-size processor, you will have no trouble; the quantity is ample to fill the bowl right up to blade level.

Makes almost 2 cups

1 tablespoon Dijon mustard
¼ cup (2 ounces) egg substitute equivalent to 1 egg
1 garlic clove, peeled and quartered
  Salt (optional)
½ cup Lite Mayonnaise (read ingredient lists carefully—not all of these are low in saturated fats)
1 teaspoon lemon juice or balsamic vinegar, heated
½ cup light olive oil
1 large sweet red pepper, charbroiled (page 214)
  Cayenne pepper

Whirl the mustard, egg substitute, garlic, and salt until well mixed. While the motor is running, add the mayonnaise a teaspoonful at a time, waiting until each has been assimilated before adding the next. Through the spout, add ½ teaspoon hot lemon juice or vinegar, then add ¼ cup of the oil, a drop or two at a time. At this point, add the remaining oil in a thin, steady stream, stopping when the mayonnaise is unable to absorb any more oil. Whirl in another ½ teaspoon hot lemon juice or vinegar.

Blot the red pepper between paper towels, then cut it into ½-inch-wide strips about 2 inches long, discarding seeds and pith. With the blade whirling, add the pepper strips, one at a time, to the mayonnaise mixture, waiting until one strip is incorporated before adding the next. Whirl in cayenne pepper and lemon juice or vinegar to suit your taste.

If you are preparing the mayonnaise ahead of time, cover it with plastic wrap and refrigerate it, but bring it to room temperature before serving. Thin a little, if necessary, by stirring in hot water, a teaspoon at a time, until the sauce reaches the desired consistency.

Black Olive Sauce

Makes about 2 cups

¾ cup pitted oil-cured olives, finely chopped
⅓ cup extra-virgin olive oil
¼ cup tomato juice
⅓ cup peeled shallots
Freshly ground black pepper to taste
5–7 medium-size fresh sage leaves (if not available substitute ¼ cup fresh Italian parsley leaves with no stems)

Puree ¼ cup chopped olives with the olive oil, tomato juice, shallots, pepper, and sage or parsley. Mix in the rest of the chopped olives. Serve at room temperature.

Garlic Bread

Serves 6

5 medium-size garlic cloves, peeled and minced
Salt
¼ cup extra-virgin olive oil
Black pepper, coarsely ground
2 long crusty loaves Italian bread, split lengthwise
4 tablespoons grated low-fat cheese

Using a mortar and pestle, crush the garlic with a sprinkling of salt. Add 1 tablespoon olive oil and work until pureed. Work in the remaining oil. Cover the cut surfaces of the bread with the garlic mixture, sprinkle with cheese, and grill or broil until golden brown.

Seasonal Fruit with Yogurt Cheese

Here's one cheese that is not only extremely tasty, but low in calories as well as cholesterol. Since yogurt cheese can go it alone or partner with an infinite variety of ingredients, I make sure to keep a supply on hand at all times. You'll be amazed how tasty this is spread on halved ripe strawberries or apple slices or garnishing the center of pitted peach, plum, or apricot halves.

Yogurt cheese also stores well when chilled and is extremely versatile, so prepare a double recipe well in advance of your party.

Makes 1 cup

2½ cups plain low-fat yogurt
Salt and black pepper (optional)
Lemon juice or 2 teaspoons olive oil
Seasonal fruits

Place the yogurt in a cheesecloth-lined sieve and place the sieve in a bowl large enough so that its bottom is at least 2 inches from the bottom of the sieve. Let stand 2–3 hours. Season to taste with salt and pepper if desired.

For a zestier cheese, add a squeeze of lemon juice. For a sweeter cheese, sprinkle with granulated sugar. For a richer cheese, mix in the oil. Press the cheese into a small, well-oiled bowl and chill. Unmold the cheese in the center of an attractive plate or platter and surround with fruit.

A Rustic Monday-Night Supper

MENU

Zucchini Pancakes with Dill and Salmon Roe

Soy Noodles with Veal Neckbone and Vegetable Sauce

Warm Spinach and Radicchio Salad

Lemon Ice and Sliced Kiwi in a Puddle of Fresh Raspberry Sauce

---

SUGGESTIONS

A quick, wholesome meal that is easier to present if you omit the appetizer or substitute for it half an avocado filled with a few tablespoons jellied consommé topped with a teaspoon of low-fat French dressing.

The Neckbone Sauce should be waiting in the refrigerator, merely to be reheated; the green and red leafy salad fixings pre-washed; the raspberry sauce defrosted and drained of frozen berries.

To save time when preparing the Veal Neckbone and Vegetable Sauce, substitute canned chicken or beef stock for the home-cooked variety.

Zucchini Pancakes with Dill and Salmon Roe

Salmon roe is wonderful for enhancing both the appearance and flavor of these little cakes. It's also worth its weight in Omega-3 fatty acids. A tasty tidbit to offer with drinks.

Zucchini pancakes freeze well for a few days if they are double-wrapped in foil and defrosted in the refrigerator. Reheat them in the same package.

Makes 2 dozen

4 medium-size zucchini, scrubbed, trimmed, and finely grated
1 small onion, peeled and minced
½ cup (4 ounces) egg substitute equivalent to 2 eggs
¼ cup all-purpose flour
2 tablespoons each grated Parmesan and fine bread crumbs
Salt and coarsely ground fresh black pepper to taste
Vegetable oil for frying
1 cup plain low-fat yogurt
2 tablespoons minced fresh dill
Salmon roe

Use your hands to squeeze out and discard as much moisture as possible from the zucchini. Press between paper towels to drain away any remaining juices. Mix the zucchini and onion with the eggs, flour, cheese, bread crumbs, and salt and pepper. If the mixture is too runny to hold its shape, add a few more bread crumbs; if it is too dry, add a little yogurt.

Heat one teaspoon oil in a large non-stick skillet and add the zucchini batter a tablespoon at a time, pressing down gently with the back of the spoon to form small pancakes. Lightly brown on both sides, turning once. Add another teaspoon or two of oil, if needed. Mix the yogurt, dill, and salt and pepper to taste. Serve pancakes warm, each topped with half a teaspoon of yogurt and a few grains of roe.

Soy Noodles with Veal Neckbone and Vegetable Sauce

Serves 6

1–2 tablespoons olive oil
1 cup coarsely chopped sweet onion
3 medium-size cloves garlic, peeled
1 tablespoon each minced fresh sage, thyme, and marjoram (or 1 teaspoon dried of each)
Salt (optional)
Freshly ground black pepper to taste
1 cup tomato juice
1 recipe Veal Neckbone Sauce (recipe follows)
Hot soy noodles
Blanched walnuts
Sautéed Sweet Orange or Yellow Peppers (pages 214)

Heat 1 tablespoon of the oil and lightly brown the onion, garlic, herbs, salt, if desired, and pepper. Add the tomato juice and Veal Neckbone Sauce, lower the heat, and simmer until nicely integrated. Serve hot over soy noodles; sprinkle with blanched walnuts and strips of Sautéed Orange or Yellow Peppers.

Veal Neckbone and Vegetable Sauce

Not a very flattering name for a soothing sauce that provides the flavor and substance of meat with very little cholesterol; sweet red pepper lights up the color and flavor. This is really "down-homey," and satisfying with mashed potatoes or noodles, on fettuccini, or spaghetti squash with coarsely chopped blanched walnuts and Greek olives.

Veal neckbones are seldom in stock where I shop, so when they do appear, I buy quite a few. (The bones themselves freeze quite well, but the finished sauce does not.) The sauce does take quite a while to bake but there is little effort involved. Prepare it several days in advance of serving and refrigerate until needed.

Makes 1½ to 2 quarts

2 tablespoons olive oil
2 pounds meaty veal neckbones, with no fat included
4 medium-large onions, peeled and cut into ½-inch slices
3 medium carrots, scraped, cut into 1-inch slices
1 pound mushrooms, wiped clean and sliced
1 red sweet pepper, with stem, seeds, and pith discarded, sliced
3 quarts Homemade Chicken Broth, Rich Beef Broth, or Vegetable Stock (pages 186, 187, and 184) or canned broth
2 tablespoons minced fresh parsley
1 tablespoon minced fresh sage
Salt and freshly ground black pepper to taste
Gravy Master (optional)

Preheat the oven to 375° F.

In a heavy, ovenproof kettle, heat the olive oil over medium heat on top of the stove. Brown the neckbones on all sides in the oil, then remove them with a slotted spoon and set aside. Discard the fat in the pan. Brown the vegetables on all sides in the same pan. Return the neckbones to the pot, place in the oven, and bake, uncovered, for 1 hour. Add the broth or stock and seasonings and lower the heat to 325° F. Bake for at least 2 hours, stirring occasionally and adding broth or water, if necessary, to keep the vegetables covered with liquid. The meat should be very tender.

Use a slotted spoon to remove the neckbones and set them aside. Puree the broth and vegetables, return them to the kettle, and simmer until nicely thickened. (If you like, stir in a few drops of Gravy Master to produce a rich brown sauce.) Remove the meat from the bones, chop it finely, and add it to the sauce. Serve hot.

Warm Spinach and Radicchio Salad

Serves 6

1 pound fresh spinach
1 small head radicchio
3 tablespoons olive oil
2 tablespoons red wine vinegar
4 flat anchovies, drained and finely chopped (optional)
Generous sprinkle of freshly ground black pepper
1 tablespoon chives, minced

Pretty, pink radicchio makes this dish much lovelier to look at, but if this imported lettuce is not available, you'll find the salad is extremely tasty if you substitute cooked beets and/or scatter with pine nuts. Serve as an appetizer or salad.

Rinse the spinach thoroughly, discard any tough stems, and wrap the leaves in paper towels to dry. Cut the radicchio in quarters and cut away and discard the core, then separate the leaves and pat them dry. In a large skillet, sauté the radicchio in the oil until it just begins to wilt. Add the vinegar, quickly bring to a boil, then remove from the heat and let stand 2–3 minutes. Place the spinach leaves in a bowl large enough to hold them and toss them with the anchovies and warm dressing. Sprinkle with pepper and the minced chives and serve immediately.

Lemon Ice and Sliced Kiwi in a Puddle of Fresh Raspberry Sauce

Serves 6

Raspberry Sauce (recipe follows)
1 pint storebought lemon ice (or boysenberry or orange, if lemon is not available)
30 paper-thin slices ripe kiwi, peeled

At serving time, spoon a puddle of the Raspberry Sauce in the center of each of 6 dessert plates, place a scoop of lemon ice in each, and surround with slices of kiwi. Serve at once, topped with whole berries.

Raspberry Sauce

1 pint clean fresh raspberries, if available
1 box frozen raspberries in syrup

Set aside 36 of the most perfect fresh raspberries. Puree the remaining fresh berries and the frozen ones in a food processor or blender. Press through a sieve and discard the seeds. Serve cold. The sauce is pleasant even without the fresh berries.

Tori-Suki Dinner

MENU

Warm Scallions in Clam Sauce

Tori-Suki with Spring Herbs and
Vegetables

Sesame-Asparagus Salad

Champagne Snow

SUGGESTIONS

Substitute vermicelli noodles for the shiratiki, candied nuggets of sweet potato for the chestnuts, and prettily cut Carrot Flowers (page 192) or Radish Roses (page 193) for the squash flowers if these are nowhere to be found. For an even easier repast, omit the appetizer. Dinner will still be elegant.

Warm Scallions in Clam Sauce

Nothing could be nicer than scallions, poached until barely tender, then served with a warm, lemony clam sauce. This is different and delicious.

Serves 6

36 pencil-thin scallions, with roots trimmed
  Salt (optional)
2 tablespoons olive oil
1 6½-ounce can minced clams or 1 cup fresh minced clams, simmered for 2 minutes in ¼ cup each water and white wine
2 tablespoons lemon juice
8 pimiento strips, each 3 inches long and ¼ inch wide

Arrange the scallions side by side, with their roots lined up. Use a large sharp knife to cut off all the roots at one time, then cut the tops off evenly, including about 3 inches of the green part. The trimmed scallions should all be the same length.

Place 5 cups water and salt, if desired, in a skillet large enough to hold the scallions without bending them, add the scallions, and simmer for 2 minutes, or until barely tender. Do not overcook. Carefully transfer the scallions to paper towels to drain for a few seconds. Arrange the scallions neatly on a serving plate with the roots and tops lined up and set aside in a warm place.

Heat the oil in a small skillet. Spoon the clams from the can without disturbing any sand that may be in the bottom. Let the clam juice left in the can settle, then spoon off and add to the skillet all but the last ¼-inch (which probably will be sandy). Add the lemon juice and simmer the ingredients in the pan until they are reduced and somewhat thickened. Using a slotted spoon, spoon just the clams in a band across the middle of the warm scallions. Spoon the remaining sauce across the bulbs and the tops of the scallions. Garnish the clams with crisscrossed strips of pimiento and serve warm.

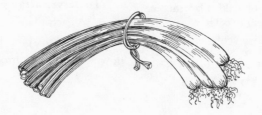

Tori-Suki with Spring Herbs and Vegetables

The well-known Japanese beef dish, sukiyaki, is supplanted here by its not-as-well-known chicken counterpart. I've chosen chicken breasts here pounded until thin, served side-by-side, because I thought it would be pleasant to top them with candied chestnuts (marron glacé).

This recipe also includes three additional palate pleasers: hot-spicy shirataki (clear filaments made from the starchy root of devil's-tongue plant), sour vinegar-tossed spinach with celery root, and fresh squash flowers.

Serves 6

3 boned chicken breasts, halved
3 tablespoons vegetable oil
3 tablespoons sesame oil
2½ cups Homemade Chicken Broth (page 186) or canned broth
¾ cup light soy sauce
⅓ cup mirin or 3 tablespoons each sherry and sugar
6 sweet chestnuts or marron glacé, halved (optional)
2 leeks, well rinsed, cut into 2-inch lengths and tied in bundles (page 209)
1½ pounds spinach leaves, well-rinsed, with stems removed (about 6 cups)
2 cups matchstick-thin pieces of peeled celery root
3 tablespoons balsamic vinegar
8 ounces shirataki filaments or vermicelli noodles
Hot vegetable oil
6 squash flowers, Carrot Flowers (page 192), or Radish Roses (page 193)

Discard the skin from the chicken and pound lightly between waxed paper. Do not tear the meat. In a heavy pan or skillet, heat 1 tablespoon each vegetable oil and sesame oil and lightly brown chicken pieces. Set the chicken aside and add the broth, soy sauce, mirin (or sherry and sugar), chestnuts, and leeks to the skillet. Simmer until the leeks are tender (about 20 minutes), turning several times, adding broth as needed to keep the leeks covered.

Meanwhile, carefully wrap the spinach in paper towels and refrigerate. Toss the celery root with the vinegar and refrigerate until the chicken is tender. If you are using the shirataki, cook it in the liquid in the pan following package directions (this takes only 2 to 3 minutes). If you are using the vermicelli, cook it until al dente, drain it well, and toss it with a little broth from the pan. Warm the bean curd in the broth in the pan. Toss the shirataki or noodles with hot vegetable oil to taste. Toss the spinach with the celery root and the remainder of the vegetable oil and sesame oil.

To serve, arrange one chicken piece topped with two chestnut halves on each plate with a small pile of shirataki or noodles on its left and a mound of spinach and celery root on the right. Decorate with the "flowers." Pass hot broth separately.

Sesame-Asparagus Salad

This is a crunchy combination of nicely undercooked asparagus and toasted sesame seeds mellowed with sesame oil. Used here as a salad, this also is superb heated quickly and served as a vegetable.

Serves 6

24 slender asparagus spears, scraped (page 199)
 1 tablespoon dark soy sauce
 1 tablespoon sesame oil
 1 teaspoon rice wine vinegar
 1 teaspoon granulated sugar
 1 teaspoon Toasted Sesame Seeds (page 192)

Break off and discard the woody ends from the asparagus. Cut the spears on the diagonal into ½-inch pieces and place them in a wire basket with a long handle, such as a fry-basket. Plunge the basket into 1 quart of rapidly boiling water. (The asparagus can be cooked directly in the water if you have no such basket.) After 1 minute, remove, drain, refresh under cold water, and drain again.

Mix the soy sauce, sesame oil, vinegar, and sugar. Toss with the asparagus. Sprinkle the Toasted Sesame Seeds over the asparagus and serve.

Champagne Snow

For a festive occasion, make a soft sherbet from a bottle of inexpensive champagne or other sparkling wine. Top with a few fresh or canned lychee nuts to preserve the delicate white aura, or, if you wish to heighten the drama with a splash of color, top with a few pomegranate seeds.

Serves 6

 1 cup granulated sugar
 ¼ teaspoon salt
 1 cup freshly squeezed orange juice
 1 tablespoon lemon juice
 1 egg white, lightly beaten
 1 bottle champagne or other sparkling wine

Boil together the sugar, 1 cup water, and salt until the mixture reaches the soft-ball stage (234–240° F. on a candy thermometer). Stir in the orange and lemon juices and bring to the boil again. Beat in the egg white and champagne and freeze until mushy. Stir and then continue freezing for 4 hours, stirring frequently. Heap into champagne glasses and top with fruit, if desired.

An Elegant Boardroom Lunch

MENU

Spring Watercress and Scallion
Soup with Toasted Sesame Seeds

Oven-Poached Salmon Petals
with Asparagus Essence and
Garnish of Pickled Ginger and
White Radish

Oriental Noodle Cakes

Strawberry-Marmalade
Pie

SUGGESTIONS

Prepare the soup as much as 48 hours in advance of serving.

Twenty-four hours prior to your party, clean and refrigerate the asparagus, cook the noodles, and prepare the pie crust.

Substitute canned broth for homemade when preparing the soup.

Substitute your favorite commercial Italian dressing for the White Wine Vinaigrette.

Spring Watercress and Scallion Soup with Toasted Sesame Seeds

Dispatch the winter doldrums with a simple-to-prepare, fresh-tasting sip of this soup. If the day is mild, anticipate spring by serving the soup chilled. On a blustery evening it might be more soothing served steaming.

Serves 6

1 pound potatoes, peeled and quartered
2 bunches slender young scallions, trimmed and thinly sliced (include 4 inches of green top)
3 celery ribs, trimmed and cut into 2-inch pieces
8 cups Homemade Chicken Broth or Vegetable Stock (pages 186 or 184) or canned broth
2 bunches well-washed watercress
3 tablespoons low-fat cream cheese
1 tablespoon fresh lemon juice
  Salt (optional)
  White pepper to taste
  Skim milk (if needed)
1 tablespoon Toasted Sesame Seeds (page 192)

Bring the potatoes, half the scallions, and the celery to a boil in the broth or stock, skim off and discard any froth, and lower the heat. Simmer, partially covered, for 40 minutes. Discard the tough stems from the watercress, add the leaves to the soup, and simmer for 5 minutes more. Using a food processor, puree the mixture along with the cream cheese and lemon juice; add salt, if desired, and pepper to taste. Chill well and thin with a little skim milk if necessary. Serve hot or cold, garnished with the remaining sliced scallions and sesame seeds.

Oven-Poached Salmon Petals with Asparagus Essence and Garnish of Pickled Ginger and White Radish

Salmon is not only among the most succulent and prized of fish, but it is also one of the most healthful. Here, salmon steaks are halved and shaped to form attractive "petals," poached briefly in a hot oven and served with asparagus tips and a sauce of asparagus "essence." Piquancy is added with a pickled ginger and radish garnish.

NOTE

This and other cold-water marine fish are rich in Omega-3 fatty acids, which are believed to prevent the likelihood of clotting in the coronary arteries. A diet rich in salmon oils was shown to have a beneficial effect in one study at the Oregon Health Sciences University, where volunteers experienced a decline in total blood cholesterol levels from 188 to 162.

Serves 6

  3 1-inch salmon steaks, with skin removed
 ½ teaspoon each black peppercorns and dried whole coriander seeds
 ½ cup mild white vinegar
 ½ cup white wine
     Salt (optional)
24 slender young asparagus
     Boiling water
 ½ cup White Wine Vinaigrette (page 189)
 ¼ cup well-drained bottled pickled ginger
 ½ cup finely grated daikon or other radish, peeled
  1 tablespoon commercial low-fat mayonnaise

Neatly cut each steak in half by sliding a sharp knife along both sides of the backbone and then cutting through the bones at the bottom. Use pliers to pull out any bones that remain. Handle the fish carefully so it does not tear. Press each piece gently with the palm of your hand into a nicely shaped petal. Arrange the salmon in a shallow ovenproof dish large enough to hold them without overlapping (a 9-inch glass pie plate is fine).

Crush the peppercorns and coriander seeds with a mortar and pestle; add the vinegar and wine and salt to taste. Pour the marinade over the fish. Cover with plastic wrap and let stand in a cool place for an hour or two, turning once.

Preheat the oven to 425° F.

Remove the plastic wrap and cover the dish with lightly oiled aluminum foil cut to fit just inside the dish. Place in the preheated oven 8–9 minutes; remove and allow the fish to cool in the dish.

Break off and discard the woody ends from the asparagus (page 199). Plunge the asparagus into boiling water, remove the pot immediately from the heat, and let stand 1 minute. Drain and cover with cold water to stop the asparagus from cooking further. Drain again. Cut off the asparagus tips on the slant and set them aside. Coarsely chop the asparagus stems and place them, along with ¼ cup of the cooking liquid from the salmon, in a blender or food processor fitted with a steel blade; puree this mixture. Line a strainer with 4 thicknesses of cheesecloth and set it over a bowl. Spoon in the puree and let it drain for 15 minutes; squeeze all the moisture from the cheesecloth and discard what's left. Mix with the White Wine Vinaigrette.

Slice the ginger into find shreds and mix with the grated radish and mayonnaise. Divide evenly among 6 well-oiled small molds or other holders (the bottoms of shot glasses or small demitasse cups, for example). Press the mixture down firmly.

To assemble the dish, carefully wipe the top of each salmon "petal" and arrange it across the middle of a plate—I like this on plain white. Arrange 4 asparagus tips around the bottom of each plate and unmold the ginger-radish garnish at the top. Spoon a small puddle of the asparagus essence between the two. Arrange the Oriental Noodle Cakes prettily on the other side of the plate. Serve at room temperature.

Oriental Noodle Cakes

Thin noodles such as vermicelli, morocco sheriya, soba, and Korean naeng myon also respond well to this treatment.

Serves 6

1 package Soy Noodles (see package directions)
1 egg white
2 tablespoons minced scallion with
  green top
2 tablespoons Toasted Sesame
  Seeds (page 192)
¼ cup sesame seeds
  Vegetable oil for frying

Prepare the noodles, drain them, and while they are still warm, mix in the egg white and then the scallion and Toasted Sesame Seeds. Use a well-oiled 2½- to 3-inch mold or custard cup to firmly press the noodles into 6 round shapes, then turn out and fry briefly in 1-inch hot oil, turning once. Drain on paper towels. Serve hot.

Strawberry-Marmalade Pie

Serves 6 to 8

1 Three-Grain Pie Crust (page 43)
3 pints fresh ripe strawberries,
  rinsed, hulled, and drained
¼ cup granulated sugar
3 tablespoons cornstarch
½ cup cold orange juice
⅓ cup orange marmalade

Prepare the pie crust.

Slice those berries that are imperfect or overripe (you'll need at least 2 cups) and place them in a small saucepan along with the sugar. Stir the cornstarch into the cold orange juice until completely dissolved. Add to the saucepan and stir continuously over medium heat until thick and glossy. Cool to room temperature and pour into the prepared crust.

Arrange the perfect berries attractively in concentric circles, stem ends down, over the pie. Stir the marmalade and 1 tablespoon water over low heat until melted, and while it's still warm, drizzle over the tops of the berries. Chill for 2 hours or overnight. Serve cold.

Hot and Sweet Pepper Chicken Dinner

MENU

Foil-Baked Asparagus

Vinegar-Soy Sauce

Hot and Sweet Peppers and
Chicken with Bananas

Fried Wild Rice with Vegetables

Gingered Fresh Figs

SUGGESTIONS

If you prefer to serve an uncooked vegetable with drinks rather than a cooked one, prepare fresh vegetable strips and a double recipe of Vinegar-Soy Sauce.

Omit the chicken and shrimp from the wild rice recipe. Substitute brown rice for wild rice.

Prepare the ginger syrup for the dessert 24 hours early. Substitute canned figs for fresh ones.

Foil-Baked Asparagus

If the oven is hot anyway, I usually opt for baking rather than steaming asparagus. This method is practically foolproof.

Serves 6

36 asparagus spears, scraped (page 199)
3 tablespoons Vinegar-Soy Sauce (recipe follows)
1 tablespoon each minced chives and dill

To serve hot: Preheat the oven to 425° F.

Rinse the asparagus. Divide in groups of 6. Wrap each group in 2 sheets of aluminum foil, crimping the edges to tightly seal. The packages should be flat enough so that the spears are only 2 rows deep. Bake 25 minutes. Unwrap the packages and serve immediately, sprinkled with dressing, chives, and dill.

To serve cold: Proceed as above, but while the asparagus are still warm, sprinkle them with dressing, chives, and dill, and chill well.

Vinegar-Soy Sauce

A traditional Oriental condiment, and one that is more interesting than soy sauce alone, this makes a fine dipping sauce for nearly any vegetable: cooked (potato, squash, mushrooms, Brussels sprouts), blanched (asparagus, broccoli, cauliflower), or fresh (snow peas, endive leaves, carrot sticks, celery). I find the chopped pine nuts add delicate flavor and an interesting crunch, particularly to cooked vegetables.

Makes ¾ cup

½ cup soy sauce
1 tablespoon granulated sugar
3 tablespoons rice vinegar (or other mild vinegar)
1 tablespoon finely chopped pine nuts (optional)

In a small bowl, combine soy sauce, sugar, and vinegar and stir until well mixed. Sprinkle the nuts over the top of the sauce. Serve at room temperature.

Hot and Sweet Peppers and Chicken with Bananas

Bold strokes of red hot spices deepen the satisfaction of meals that don't rely on meat. This one is fiery! But if you can't tolerate the heat, it's perfectly all right to omit the hot pepper and enjoy the sweet anisey flavor that is so well complemented by the bananas.

Serves 6

- 2 chicken breasts, skinless and boneless
- 1 teaspoon aniseed
- 1 1-inch-long piece hot chili pepper or 1 teaspoon dried red pepper
- ½ stick cinnamon
- ¾ cup soy sauce
- 2 tablespoons light olive oil
- ⅓ cup sherry
- 7 scallions, each with 6 inches green top, finely chopped
- 2 tablespoons honey
- 2 tablespoons fruity olive oil
- 6 sweet red peppers, cut in eighths, with pith, seeds, and stems discarded
- 3 large, slightly green bananas, peeled
- ½ teaspoon ground cinnamon
- ½ teaspoon turmeric (optional)
- 1 small head lettuce, with core and outer leaves discarded
- 1 recipe Fried Wild Rice (recipe follows) or 4 cups plain

Trim away and discard any fat or gristle from the chicken, and dry the breasts with paper towels. Tie the aniseed, hot chili pepper, and cinnamon stick in a double-thick square of cheesecloth to form a small spice bag.

Heat the soy sauce, light oil, and sherry in a large, heavy non-stick skillet. Add the chicken, half of the scallions, and the spice bag. (Make sure the spice bag is resting in the liquid on the bottom of the pan and not on the chicken.) Simmer, covered, for 15 minutes, turning the breasts several times and pressing the spice bag to extract the flavor.

Add the remaining scallions to the pan along with the honey and simmer for 10 minutes more, turning the chicken once. Meanwhile, heat the fruity olive oil in a non-stick skillet, sauté the sweet pepper pieces until they are not quite tender, then remove them and set them aside.

Cut the peeled bananas on the diagonal into 1-inch sections, sprinkle with the cinnamon and turmeric, if desired, and fry until lightly browned on all sides, adding a little more oil if needed.

Remove the chicken breasts and cut them into ¼-inch shreds. Discard the spice bag and return the chicken and sweet pepper pieces to the pan along with the bananas. Bring to a boil for 2 or 3 minutes or until syrupy, and serve immediately on shredded lettuce with the rice.

Fried Wild Rice with Vegetables

The small quantity of chicken and shrimp called for in this recipe are meant to add flavor and texture, but even so, they are expendable. The essential ingredients are the vegetables and that star performer, wild rice. This is most often served as a company dish, since wild rice is so pricey, but prepare it with white or brown rice for your family and you'll still get raves.

Serves 6

5 tablespoons vegetable oil
¼ cup uncooked shrimp, finely chopped, peeled, and deveined
¼ cup skinless, uncooked chicken breast, finely chopped
½ cup (4 ounces) egg substitute equivalent to 2 eggs
½ teaspoon salt
1 cup wild rice, cooked according to package directions
1 large red onion, peeled and cut into ⅓-inch-thick vertical slices
6 each medium-size fresh mushrooms and wild mushrooms, cut into ¼-inch-thick slices
1 5-inch zucchini, trimmed and thinly sliced
10 snow peas with strings removed, cut into ¼-inch-thick slices
6 young slender scallions, trimmed of all but 3 inches of green tops and cut on the diagonal into 1-inch pieces
1 cup shredded Chinese cabbage
2 teaspoons Vinegar-Soy Sauce (page 61)

Heat 1 tablespoon oil in a small skillet. Stir the shrimp and chicken over medium heat for 2 minutes, then lower the heat and add the lightly beaten egg substitute. Cook until the eggs are just set, turning once. Remove the omelet from the pan and cut it into strips 1½ inches long by ¼-inch wide and set aside.

In a large non-stick pan, heat 2 tablespoons of the oil with the salt, and when the oil begins to smoke, add the rice and fry for 5 minutes, stirring continuously. Remove from the pan and set aside.

Add the remaining oil to the pan, stir in the onion, and sauté until lightly browned. Add the remaining vegetables and sauté together for 3 minutes. Gradually stir in the rice until heated and then add the omelet strips. Serve at once with Vinegar-Soy Sauce.

Gingered Fresh Figs

Prepare the ginger syrup and serve it with fresh plums or apricots when figs are not available, which unfortunately is most of the time. Pressed fresh ginger juices may be added to the ginger marmalade if you like. Use this syrup sparingly.

⅓ cup ginger marmalade
3 tablespoons Cointreau or freshly squeezed orange juice
⅓ teaspoon fresh ginger juice (press peeled fresh ginger in a garlic press), optional
1–2 ripe fresh figs per person
2 tablespoons chilled low-fat sour cream

Heat the marmalade with the Cointreau and mix well. Cover and store at room temperature for up to a day, or longer in the refrigerator. Bring to room temperature before serving. Squeeze in the optional ginger juice and stir.

Cut the figs in halves and arrange on individual dessert plates (glass ones are most attractive). Spoon a scant teaspoon of syrup over each half, top each with ½ teaspoon sour cream, and serve immediately.

Summer

A Prepare-Ahead Curry Dinner for Weekend Guests

MENU

Celery Victor Salad

Biryani with Tomato Curry,
Young Peas, and Fresh-Cut Corn

Indian Fry Bread

Cranshaw Granité

SUGGESTIONS

Prepare and assemble Celery Victor Salad in advance. The Biryani appears to be more difficult than it actually is. Don't let the long list of ingredients put you off. The seasoned rice and the curry can be prepared and the corn cut from the cob a day early.

If you're really pressed for time, the peas and corn could be frozen rather than fresh.

All that's left to do before the guests arrive is to assemble the dish and bake it. It needn't even be served piping hot.

The Indian bread freezes well, but a good toasted French bread takes its place very nicely.

The granité should be frozen ahead in ice-cube trays and whirled in the food processor until soft enough to spoon into dishes just before serving.

Celery Victor Salad

Cooked celery as a salad? Of course! This is a classic, famed throughout the Western world. Here it is presented as an hors d'oeuvre.

Serves 6

3 bunches celery
½ cup white vinegar
16 large, perfect spinach leaves, well washed and with the bottoms of the tough stems removed
24 pimiento strips, each 3 inches long and ¼ inch wide
14 pimiento-stuffed olives, cut crosswise in half
½ cup Vinaigrette Dressing (page 189)
1 tablespoon minced fresh dill

Remove the large outer ribs from the celery bunches and reserve them for another use. Cut away and discard most of the leafy tops. Cut each of the remaining celery hearts lengthwise into 4 pieces and arrange without overlapping in a large skillet or pan. Add the vinegar and 6 cups water and simmer until barely tender (the water should just cover them). Drain well and chill.

To serve: Arrange 4 medium-size spinach leaves attractively in each corner of a pretty plate or platter. Over them arrange the celery in a fan shape, bases together, tops pointing outward. Crisscross the base of each with 2 pimiento strips and tuck the olive halves in between. Spoon the dressing over and sprinkle with dill. Serve chilled.

Biryani with Tomato Curry, Young Peas, and Fresh-Cut Corn

In case you have never experienced biryani in one of its many forms, prepare yourself for the most wonderful one-dish summer meal. It's a many-layered kind of thing, in this case one that alternates between a highly seasoned rice and a fresh-tasting tomato curry. Once, on a whim, I included two additional layers, one of corn fresh cut from the cob, and another of tender young peas. Whenever these vegetables are in season I include them still. Their "crunch" further enlivens what is already a lively dish.

Incidentally, each part of this unusual recipe can go it alone very nicely. The curry is easy, inexpensive, and very pleasing over plain rice for a light lunch or supper. The seasoned rice is excellent with fish or chicken.

Onion and Orange Marmalade adds zest when served with the Biryani; however, bottled chutney could be used if you are pressed for time.

Serves 6

SEASONED RICE

3 medium-size onions, peeled and coarsely chopped
2 tablespoons vegetable oil
2 cloves garlic, peeled and minced
4 whole cloves
¾ cup seedless raisins
½ teaspoon each ground cinnamon and cardamom
1 teaspoon paprika
1 teaspoon chili powder
½ teaspoon salt (optional)
1 tablespoon peeled and minced fresh ginger
2½ cups rice
4¼ cups Homemade Chicken Broth or Vegetable Stock (pages 186 or 184), or canned broth

SEASONED RICE

In a large, heavy pot, sauté the onions in the oil until lightly browned. Add the garlic, cloves, raisins, seasonings, and rice, and sauté for 2 minutes more. Add the broth, stir once, then cover and bring to a boil over medium-high heat. Lower the heat and cook the rice for 10 minutes. Let stand, covered, while you prepare the curry.

TOMATO CURRY

¼ cup vegetable oil
3 large onions, peeled and thinly sliced
3 cloves garlic, peeled and minced
12 medium-size ripe tomatoes, peeled, seeded, and cut in quarters
1 teaspoon anchovy paste (optional)
  Salt (optional)
  Freshly ground black pepper to taste
½ teaspoon ground turmeric
1 teaspoon Garam-Masala (page 192)
1 tablespoon chopped cilantro or basil
  Minced hot fresh red pepper to taste (optional)
⅓ cup Homemade Chicken Broth or Vegetable Stock (pages 186 or 184) or canned broth
3 cups fresh corn, cut from the cob
3 cups shelled fresh young peas
½ cup seedless golden raisins
⅓ cup chopped cashew nuts or pecans
1 tablespoon vegetable oil
1½ cups plain yogurt
⅓ cup finely chopped mint leaves

TOMATO CURRY

Heat the oil in a large, heavy skillet, add the onions and sauté until soft but not brown. Add the garlic and sauté 1 minute more. Add the ingredients up to and including the broth. Simmer over low heat, stirring frequently, for 15 minutes.

Preheat the oven to 375° F.

Generously oil a large ovenproof baking dish, preferably glass so that the multicolored layers can be seen. Spread half the seasoned rice over the bottom of the dish, top with half the curry, and then half the corn and half the peas. Cover with the remaining rice, remaining corn, and the peas, and then the remaining curry. Decorate the top with raisins and nuts, sprinkle with oil, and cover tightly with aluminum foil. Bake for 20 minutes, then uncover and bake 10 minutes more, or until nuts are nicely browned. Mix the yogurt with the mint. Serve the biryani hot or at room temperature and pass the yogurt.

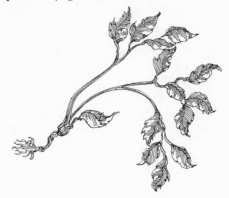

Indian Fry Bread

Quick and easy to prepare, and delicious with soups, vegetables, honey, or jam.

Makes three 10-inch breads

5 cups all-purpose flour
1½ tablespoons baking powder
1 teaspoon salt (optional)
1½ tablespoons vegetable oil
2 cups warm water
  Vegetable oil for frying

Sift together or otherwise thoroughly mix the flour, baking powder, and salt, if desired. Combine the 1½ tablespoons vegetable oil and water and mix into the dry ingredients. When the dough becomes too stiff to stir, turn it out and knead in any remaining flour. Continue to knead until the dough is smooth and elastic or use the steel blade of your food processor or a mixer with a dough hook.

To freeze: Divide the dough into 3 pieces and place each in a Ziploc plastic bag. Remove from freezer as needed; defrost in refrigerator. Roll out into circles about ⅛-inch thick and 10 inches in diameter. Heat 3 tablespoons oil in a 10-inch skillet and fry each bread until crisp, turning once if necessary, to lightly brown on both sides. Serve hot or reheat and serve.

Cranshaw Granité

Any sweet, ripe melon makes a wonderful fruit ice, but cranshaw is particularly exotic.

Serves 6

7–8 cups cranshaw melon, peeled, seeded, and cubed
¾ cup granulated sugar
¼ cup freshly squeezed lemon juice
1 teaspoon rosewater or almond extract (optional)
2 tablespoons vodka (optional)

Puree the melon with the sugar and lemon juice and freeze in ice cube trays until fairly firm but not solid. Beat until fluffy, beat in the flavorings and vodka, if desired, and return the mixture to the freezer just until firm enough to hold its shape. Serve in compotes or parfait glasses.

White Puchero Dinner

MENU

Polenta, Black Olives, and Wild Mushrooms in Peppery Consommé

White Puchero with Vegetables, Fruits, Almonds, and Soft Garlic Sauce

Peaches in Almond Sauce

SUGGESTIONS

As presented in the pages that follow, this is an unusually complex and sophisticated party repast. Not at all difficult to comprehend or execute, but time consuming. And well worth that time and effort. Most of the preparation may be accomplished one or several days prior to party day if you prefer or omit several ingredients and refinements and you'll be able to accomplish it with relative ease.

Prepare the pepper strips and the peppery broth one day in advance of your party.

Substitute canned chicken broth for the Homemade Chicken or Vegetable Broth when preparing the puchero, but do not neglect to strengthen that broth with additional bones (or chicken wings), onions, celery, and a head of garlic.

Use canned black-eyed peas if fresh or frozen ones are not available.

Wash, cut, and refrigerate the kale ribbons a day in advance.

Omit the zucchini sautéed in oil.

Substitute sweet potatoes for the whites ones; boil and sauté several days in advance.

Sauté the banana slices.

Polenta, Black Olives, and Wild Mushrooms in Peppery Consommé

This is a wonderful soup; the slightly chewy qualities of the oil-cured olives and wild mushrooms make it uniquely satisfying. The distinct flavors work well with the sweetness of roasted red pepper, a shaped turban of polenta, and a clear peppery broth.

Serves 6

½ pound oil-cured black olives
1 large red sweet pepper
1 cup shiitake mushrooms
1 tablespoon extra-virgin olive oil
  Squeeze of lemon or lime juice
1 recipe Basic Polenta (page 183) shaped into turbans
1 recipe Peppery Consommé (page 188)

Cut the flesh from the olive pits into ¼-inch-wide strips. Charbroil the pepper following the directions on page 214 and cut into strips ½ inch wide by 2 inches long. Cut the mushroom caps into ¼-inch strips, saving the stems to flavor the broth. Sauté the mushrooms in the oil in a non-stick pan. Squeeze a little lemon or lime juice over them.

To serve, place hot polenta turbans in the centers of 6 flat soup plates, arrange the olives, sliced mushroom caps, and sweet pepper strips attractively around them, ladle just enough hot consommé over, to half-way cover the turbans. Serve immediately.

White Puchero with Vegetables, Fruits, Almonds, and Soft Garlic Sauce

Conventional puchero is a flavorful combination of meats, vegetables, and fruit, similar to a Latin pot-au-feu imaginatively put forward with a variety of cooked and fresh fruits, a lime wedge to squeeze over all, and a dollop of guacamole to help marry the flavors. In the authentic version, ham, lamb, beef, chicken, and a split veal knuckle are simmered with vegetables to produce a delicious but rich and fatty stew. In this version, meat bones flavor a broth prepared hours or days in advance of serving, so that the fat can rise to the surface and be discarded. The broth is simmered with an entire head of garlic which is later combined with ground almonds to produce a pale, mellow sauce. Small mounds of black-eyed peas, sautéed ribbons of kale, zucchini, slices of sweet and white potatoes flavored with coriander, fried banana or plantain, fresh pear and guacamole complete the dish. Small succulent bits of meat that fall from the cooking bones or a few ounces of chicken breast cut in thin shards may be added to the surprisingly delicate sauce.

Serves 6

1 split veal knuckle or 1 veal shin cut for osso bucco or 1 ham bone with most of the meat and all of the fat removed or ½ pound chicken wings

2 quarts Homemade Chicken Broth or Vegetable Stock (pages 186 or 184) or a combination of the two or canned broth

2 large onions, peeled and quartered

2 large carrots, scraped and quartered

2 ribs celery, cut into 2-inch pieces

1 medium-size head garlic

1 cup fresh (or frozen) black-eyed peas

2 each small white and small sweet potatoes, each no more than 2 inches in diameter

3 tablespoons vegetable oil

2 small zucchini, thinly sliced

1 large bunch fresh, young kale

½ cup blanched almonds

2 limes, cut in wedges

2 large slightly green bananas or half-ripe plantain

1 tablespoon light soy sauce Tabasco to taste

1 Anjou pear

1 small head radicchio, separated into leaf cups

1 recipe Guacamole (page 100)

Rinse the bones or wings, place them in a heavy pot, and cover them with the broth. Add the onions, carrots, and celery. Bring to a boil and use a slotted spoon to skim off and discard any froth that accumulates on the top. Lower the heat and simmer for 1 hour. Discard the excess papery outside skins from the head of garlic (do not remove too much; the garlic head should remain intact), submerge it in the broth, and continue to simmer 30–40 minutes. Add 1 or 2 cups of water if necessary to keep the broth level constant. Remove the bones and garlic and strain the broth. Cool all of these to room temperature. Refrigerate the broth until the fat rises to the top and solidifies.

Bring the black-eyed peas to a boil in water to cover, cover, and simmer 35–45 minutes or until barely tender (or follow package directions). Do not overcook. Drain well and refrigerate.

Meanwhile, in separate pans, boil all the potatoes in their jackets until they are barely tender. Refrigerate.

Heat 1 tablespoon oil in a non-stick pan and sauté the zucchini slices over medium-high heat only until they are lightly browned on the outsides, still crisp on the insides. Refrigerate.

Wash the kale and use kitchen scissors or a knife to cut the leaves into ½-inch ribbons, discarding the stems and veins as you go along. Spin or pat the kale ribbons dry and refrigerate them, or, if the leaves are not as young and tender as might be desired, simmer them in broth 15–20 minutes before draining, cooling, and refrigerating them.

An hour or so before serving, remove the pan with the broth from the refrigerator and carefully remove and discard the congealed fat. Take out the garlic head and place it in a small bowl. Discard the carrots (their nutrients are now in the broth). Puree the broth, along with the onions, celery, and almonds. Separate the garlic cloves and, one by one, squeeze the soft garlic into the sauce. Heat the sauce; if it is watery, simmer until it reduces to the consistency of heavy cream.

Peel the potatoes and cut them into ½-inch-thick slices. Sauté them in 1 tablespoon oil in a non-stick skillet until they are lightly browned on both sides. Squeeze a wedge of lime over them.

Peel the bananas, cut them on the slant into 2-inch wedges, and sauté them in 1 tablespoon oil in a non-stick pan until they are light brown on all sides. Sprinkle with lime juice, and set aside. Reheat the black-eyed peas in the soy sauce. Then reheat the zucchini in a little oil. Set it aside and sauté the kale for a few seconds in a little oil. Sprinkle to taste with the Tabasco and keep warm over very low heat.

To serve, spoon enough hot sauce on each plate to barely cover the center. Arrange on each a small mound of black-eyed peas, kale, zuc-chini, several slices each of white and sweet potato, fried banana, a pear slice, a wedge of lime, and a radicchio leaf cup filled with 1 generous tablespoon Guacamole. Serve immediately.

Peaches in Almond Sauce

Serves 6

9 medium-size ripe peaches
3 tablespoons fresh lime juice
2 tablespoons blanched, slivered al-
    monds
⅓ cup Amaretto
2 tablespoons low-fat cream cheese

Spear a peach at the stem end with a fork and dip into boiling water for a few seconds. Pull off and discard the skin. Cut the peaches in half, then slice and toss with lime juice. Repeat this process with the remaining peaches. Puree the remaining ingredients in a blender or food processor, using the steel cutting blade. Toss this sauce with the peach slices and chill for no longer than 30 minutes. Serve cold.

Jambalaya Supper

MENU

Bulgur-Stuffed Mushrooms

*Vegetable Jambalaya with
Seafood and Cornmeal
Dumplings*

*Fresh Fava Beans with
Artichokes in Rosemary
Vinaigrette*

*Green Gage Plums with
Praline Powder*

SUGGESTIONS

Bake the stuffed mushrooms a day early and serve them chilled.

Prepare the jambalaya the day before the party, omitting the fish and the shrimps and doubling the onion and fennel. Reheat to bubbling before adding the cornmeal dumplings.

Substitute canned broth and canned artichoke bottoms for homemade.

Substitute 3 cups drained canned tomatoes for the fresh ones.

Bulgur-Stuffed Mushrooms

Serve these hot or cold, as a side dish or an hors d'oeuvre. They have a nice crunch and are extremely low in calories as well as cholesterol.

Serves 6

18 large mushrooms
2 tablespoons light olive oil
3 scallions, each with 3 inches green top, trimmed and finely chopped
3 tablespoons Basic Bulgur (page 183) or bread crumbs
5 tablespoons tomato sauce
1 teaspoon granulated sugar (optional)
¼ cup finely chopped blanched almonds
32 small slivers of sweet red pepper Homemade Chicken Broth or Vegetable Stock (pages 86 or 84) or canned broth
½ lemon

Carefully remove the mushroom stems without breaking the caps. Finely chop the stems. Wipe the caps with a damp cloth to clean if necessary.

Preheat the oven to 350° F.

Heat the oil and sauté the scallions and minced mushroom stems for 4 minutes, stirring frequently. Remove from the heat and stir in the bulgur or bread crumbs, tomato sauce, sugar, if desired, and almonds. Use this mixture to stuff the mushroom caps. Top each with a crisscross of red pepper. Set the caps in an ovenproof dish just large enough to hold them without touching.

Pour in enough broth to reach halfway up the mushroom caps, but do not let it spill over onto the mushroom stuffing. Squeeze lemon juice over the caps and broth. Bake for 30 minutes. Remove the pan from the oven and, using a slotted spoon, carefully transfer the mushrooms to a serving plate. (Save the broth for soup.) Serve the mushrooms hot, warm, or cold.

Vegetable Jambalaya with Seafood and Cornmeal Dumplings

You're sure to enjoy the glowing red color and rich, spicy-sweet flavor of this classy vegetable stew. The cornmeal-dumpling topping provides additional crunch and down-home goodness (and may be prepared in star-shapes to make the dish more attractive). This is thoroughly satisfying as is, but should you feel the need for a more festive dish, by all means add the shrimp and fish. Incidentally, when red peppers and good-quality tomatoes are unavailable, you may substitute green peppers and additional tomato puree without loss of impact. The bacon, while not essential, does deepen the flavor and adds only a minuscule amount of fat per portion. If you have a "hot tooth," add razzle-dazzle by including the entire hot pepper. If not, eliminate it altogether.

Serves 8

3 tablespoons olive oil
3 large cloves garlic, peeled and minced (or more to taste)
1 large sweet red onion, peeled and quartered
3 medium-size sweet red peppers, quartered, with seeds, pith, and stem removed
4 large ribs of celery, trimmed
1 medium-size bulb fennel
4 medium-size ripe red tomatoes, peeled, quartered, and seeded
2 cups Sacramento tomato juice
2 cups chicken broth
2 cups tomato puree
2–3 tablespoons granulated sugar (or to taste)
½ teaspoon dried thyme leaves
1 tablespoon chili powder
¼ teaspoon each dried fennel seed and rosemary
1 bay leaf
 Salt and freshly ground black pepper to taste
 Fresh or jalapeño pepper to taste, minced (optional)
1 large sweet potato, peeled
1 large rutabaga, peeled
2 cups whole okra pods, 2½ inches long
½ pound small shrimp (optional)
1 pound monkfish, skinned, fileted, and cut into 1-inch cubes (optional)
1 recipe Cornmeal Dumplings (recipe follows)

Heat the oil in a deep, heavy, 12-quart stockpot. Sauté the garlic for 2 minutes over medium heat. Cut the onion, sweet peppers, celery, and fennel (bulb only), into 1-inch-square pieces. Add these to the kettle and sauté until the onion is lightly browned.

Add the tomatoes, tomato juice, chicken broth, and tomato puree and bring to a boil. Skim and discard any froth. Add the sugar, seasonings, and minced hot pepper; lower the heat and simmer, uncovered. Meanwhile, cut the sweet potato and rutabaga into 1-inch cubes. Add to the pot and cook, stirring occasionally, until the sweet potato is barely tender (about 30–40 minutes). Add additional tomato juice if necessary to keep the liquid just covering the vegetables.

Preheat the oven to 400° F.

Adjust the seasonings, stir in the okra and seafood, and bring back to a boil. Remove the kettle from the heat and immediately drop the dumpling batter, 1 tablespoon at a time, around the edges of the bubbling stew. (If you prefer star-shaped dumplings, stir in additional flour, 1 tablespoon at a time, to produce a soft dough that will hold its shape, Pat out on a floured surface and use a small cookie cutter to produce the shapes you like.) Place the kettle, covered, in the preheated oven and bake for 15 minutes. Uncover and bake until the bottoms of the dumplings are cooked (this is important so check carefully) and the tops are golden brown. Serve immediately.

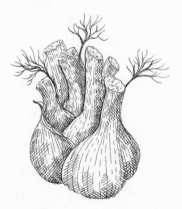

Cornmeal Dumplings

Ideally, it's best to cook the dumplings in the pan with the jambalaya so that the cornmeal has a chance to thicken and flavor the sauce. If this seems impractical, dumplings may be simmered separately in tomato juice; you can then add the somewhat thickened juice to the jambalaya if desired.

Serves 8

1 cup yellow cornmeal
¼ cup all-purpose flour
1 teaspoon baking powder
½ teaspoon salt (optional)
1 egg and ¼ cup (2 ounces) egg substitute equivalent to 1 egg
½ cup milk
2 teaspoons sesame oil (optional)
Tomato juice (optional)

Thoroughly mix dry ingredients in a large bowl. Beat egg, egg substitute, and milk lightly together and stir into dry ingredients only enough to barely mix. Stir in sesame oil, if desired. Drop dumpling batter, 1 tablespoon at a time, into boiling jambalaya. Cover pan tightly, lower heat to medium and cook 15 minutes. Uncover and bake until bottom of dumplings look flaky when tested with a fork and tops are golden brown.

If there is not sufficient liquid on top of the jambalaya to allow dumpling batter to sink to a depth of at least ¾ inch, bring tomato juice to a boil in a separate skillet, drop in the dumpling batter, cover tightly, and continue recipe as directed.

Fresh Fava Beans with Artichokes in Rosemary Vinaigrette

Sweet artichoke hearts, briefly simmered in stock and then sliced, prove an ideal foil for mellow fresh fava beans.

Serves 6

6 medium-size artichokes with tops removed
Homemade Chicken Broth or Vegetable Stock (pages 186 or 184) or canned broth
1 tablespoon lemon juice
3 cups shelled fresh fava beans (about 5 pounds unshelled)
⅔ cup Rosemary Vinaigrette (page 189)

Follow directions for preparing artichokes on page 198. Simmer the artichoke bottoms until tender in acidulated broth or stock. Drain the artichokes, bring them to room temperature, and remove the leaves and chokes. Use a spoon to scrape the leaves and reserve the pulp. Thinly slice the artichoke bottoms.

Meanwhile, steam the fava beans until tender (about 15 minutes). Toss with the sliced artichokes and vinaigrette. Marinate for 15 minutes before serving at room temperature.

Green Gage Plums with Praline Powder

Try this unusual presentation of plums on other poached fruits. The poaching syrup is reduced and served over the fruit with praline powder passed on the side.

Serves 6

⅔ cup granulated sugar
⅓ cup Sauternes
½ stick cinnamon
4 whole cloves
2 pounds ripe green gage plums, rinsed
⅓ cup Praline Powder (recipe follows)

Bring the sugar, 1⅓ cups water, and Sauternes to a boil, add the spices, and boil for 5 minutes. Add the whole plums and simmer for 5 minutes or until tender. Do not overcook. Remove the fruit and reduce the syrup to the consistency of thin honey. Return the fruit to the syrup; chill. Remove cinnamon stick and cloves before serving. Serve the chilled fruit with a little syrup and pass the Praline Powder.

Praline Powder

Excellent sprinkled over most fresh or stewed stone fruits.

Makes about 2 cups

¾ cup granulated sugar
¼ cup water
¼ teaspoon cream of tartar
⅓ cup each blanched slivered almonds and pecan meats

Combine the sugar, water, and cream of tartar and bring to a boil in a heavy saucepan. Add the nuts and cook without stirring until the syrup is a deep amber. Do not let it get too dark. Pour the praline into a shallow buttered cake pan and cool to room temperature. Crack the praline and pulverize it in a food processor, or mortar and pestle. Store in an air-tight jar.

Summer-Vegetable Tempura Lunch

MENU

Nasturtium Flower Soup

Summer-Vegetable Tempura

Bulgur with Soy Sauce and Chives (page 183)

Carrot Rapée

Honeydew Marinated in Rum and Pernod

SUGGESTIONS

If nasturtium flowers are not in bloom where you shop, substitute finely chopped green and purple basil or red and yellow sweet peppers, in fact almost any garnish that provides texture and color. The soup can be prepared a day in advance using canned broth.

Prepare the Bulgur with Soy Sauce and Chives and the Carrot Rapée 24 hours in advance of your dinner.

Marinate the melon slices 6 hours before serving.

Nasturtium Flower Soup

Prepare this delicate chilled soup when you have a spare minute, then refrigerate it overnight. It's even tastier the second day. Nasturtium flowers are not only beautiful to look at but they sparkle with peppery crispness that enlivens any dish they garnish.

Serves 6

3 small yellow summer squash
1 large potato, peeled and sliced
1 large onion, peeled and sliced
  Generous pinch each saffron and ground nutmeg
  Salt and freshly ground white pepper to taste
  Homemade Chicken Broth or Vegetable Stock (pages 186 or 184) or water
3 cups plain low-fat yogurt
12 nasturtium flowers (if these are not available, use finely chopped green and purple basil or red and yellow sweet peppers, in fact, almost any garnish that provides a little crunch and color)

Place the squash, potato, onion, saffron, nutmeg, and salt and pepper in a medium-size saucepan and add just enough chicken broth, vegetable stock, or water to cover. Boil gently until the vegetables are tender. Puree in a blender or food processor and mix with yogurt. Chill well. To serve, ladle into bowls, chop 6 of the nasturtiums and sprinkle them over the soup, then top each serving with a whole blossom.

Summer-Vegetable Tempura

Occasionally we all have the urge to indulge. When that craving strikes nothing could be finer than this casual, devour-as-you-go summer lunch. At their leisure, guests dip pre-cut bits of vegetable (and shrimp or scallops if desired) into batter and then, briefly, into hot oil.

NOTE

It's important to handle the ingredients as directed, rather than washing them in water, so that the oil won't splatter dangerously. If you desire you may include thin slices of parboiled well-dried sweet potato and turnip, florettes of broccoli and cauliflower. Fondue pots—ideally one for every 2 guests—and forks work beautifully here. Tag sales are good sources for inexpensive fondue pots.

Serves 6

1 recipe Tempura Batter (recipe follows)

2 each 4-inch-long zucchini and yellow summer squash, rinsed, thoroughly dried, then cut on the diagonal into ½-inch slices

18 small mushrooms, wiped (not rinsed) clean

1 each red, green, and yellow sweet pepper, wiped clean with a damp cloth, then cut into 1-inch squares, discarding seeds and pith

18 small sugarsnap peas, wiped clean with a damp cloth

24 young, slender green beans, each no more than 3 inches long, wiped clean with a damp cloth

12 shelled scallops and/or butter-flied shrimp (optional) Vegetable or peanut oil for frying

Prepare the Tempura Batter. Blot the vegetables and shellfish one final time to make sure they are perfectly dry. Dip the pieces in batter, one at a time, drain off excess, and fry until golden. Serve over small plates of Bulgur with Soy Sauce and Chives. Pass the Carrot Rapée.

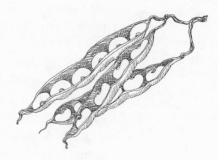

Tempura Batter

1 egg

1 cup cold water plus 3 tablespoons (optional)

1 cup all-purpose flour, sifted

Beat egg in a medium-size bowl (large, wooden chopsticks are best for beating, since they mix lightly). Beat in the water. Mix in the flour lightly, without overmixing. There should be a few lumps. Add additional cold water for fish tempura.

Carrot Rapée

Makes about 2 cups

4 medium-size carrots, scraped and finely grated

2 tablespoons extra-virgin olive oil

1 tablespoon lemon juice Salt (optional) Freshly ground black pepper

Mix together the carrots, olive oil, and lemon juice. Season to taste with salt and pepper.

Honeydew Marinated in Rum and Pernod

This dessert is based on my favorite summer drink—rum punch with a thin float of Pernod. If you are not a rum aficionado, just use the Pernod; its lovely color and exotic flavor brings out the very best in chilled honeydew. Very refreshing.

Serves 6

1 good-size ripe, sweet, honeydew
¼ cup each white rum and Pernod
  (or ½ cup of either)
1–2 tablespoons honey (optional)

Peel the melon, cut it in half, and scoop out and discard the pith and seeds. Cut each half in 1-inch-thick slices and arrange without overlapping in a flat glass dish. Handle gently so the slices do not break or bruise.

Mix together the rum, Pernod, and 3 tablespoons water. Taste a sliver of the melon. If it is not as sweet as you would like, stir a tablespoon or 2 of honey into the rum mixture until it is completely dissolved. (If the melon seems sweet enough, omit the honey.) Pour the marinade over the melon slices, cover with plastic wrap, and refrigerate from 3 to 6 hours. Remove the melon from the dish, arrange on a chilled platter, and serve at once.

Red-Vegetable Curry Dinner

MENU

Sautéed Cucumber with Sweet Herbs

Red-Vegetable Curry

Brown Rice (page 183)

Turnip Kimchi

Lemon Ice and Sliced Kiwi in a Puddle of Raspberry Sauce (page 51)

SUGGESTIONS

Prepare the Red-Vegetable Curry and cook the beets 1 day in advance of your party.

Make the dry curries and heat the red curry on party day. Substitute canned beets for home-steamed ones if necessary.

Prepare the Turnip Kimchi 2 weeks prior to party day.

Sautéed Cucumber with Sweet Herbs

Few people think of serving cooked cucumbers, but these are among the most subtle and delicious of vegetables. Here, fresh herbs enhance the finished product, but if these are not at hand, a pinch of the dried variety will do. Cucumbers are always available in your market, they store well, are easy to prepare, and are burpless when cooked.

Serves 6

6 medium-size cucumbers, peeled
2 tablespoons light olive oil
1 teaspoon each minced fresh thyme, marjoram, and basil (or those available to you)
1 teaspoon granulated sugar
Salt (optional)
1 teaspoon minced chives

Cut the cucumbers in half lengthwise and use a spoon or melonballer to remove the seeds. Slice the cucumbers into 1-inch pieces, cover with boiling salted water, and boil for about 4 minutes.

Heat the oil in a large skillet. Drain and dry the cucumbers thoroughly and sauté until they reach a light golden color on all sides, sprinkling with the minced herbs and sugar as they cook, reserving the chives. Transfer to a serving dish, season with salt, if desired, and sprinkle with chives. Serve hot.

Red-Vegetable Curry

My all-time favorite vegetable dish is this one. It contains no meat, fish, eggs, milk, cream, or cheese, and yet few people ever suspect that it's vegetarian. Although the recipe appeared in my last book, *That's Entertaining,* this is so full-flavored, so satisfying, and so ideally suited to the theme of this book I can't resist including it (and I don't want you to miss it!).

A lot of peeling and slicing goes on here, but much of this can be accomplished in advance without destroying the finished product completely. This is a hot curry, but if you prefer, you can omit the red chili pepper and cut back just a little on the curry and chili powder. And, obviously, this is a party meal, not something you'd whip up for a quiet little supper for two. If you take it one step at a time, it's basically simple to prepare, and I've never encountered anyone who wasn't thrilled with the results.

When most Westerners think of curry, they automatically associate the food with the brilliant, yellow-gold shimmer of saffron and turmeric. Actually, many Indian curries are tomato-based, as is this sizzler, but this recipe carries the red curry theme a step further to include only red-vegetable ingredients. The result is a dish that glows on the plate while it incinerates the palate.

Serves 10

1 large sweet potato, peeled, quartered lengthwise, parboiled 2 minutes in 1 tablespoon lemon juice and water to cover, and then drained
3 tablespoons vegetable oil
4 large cloves garlic, peeled and minced
3 medium-size red onions, peeled and quartered and cut lengthwise into fine shreds
2 medium-size carrots, scraped and cut lengthwise into very fine shreds
¼ cup red basil, cut into fine shreds
Salt to taste
2 teaspoons hot curry powder or paste (or more or less, to taste)
1 teaspoon chili powder
1 teaspoon Garam-Masala (page 192)
8 large, fully ripe tomatoes, peeled, seeded, and coarsely chopped
3 tablespoons lemon juice

Cut the sweet potato into strips ¼ inch by ¼ inch by 2 inches long.

Heat the vegetable oil in a large heavy skillet. Add the garlic, onions, sweet potatoes, carrots, and basil, and sauté for 2 minutes. Add the salt, curry powder, chili powder, and Garam-Masala, and stir-fry until the onions are transparent, but not browned. Remove from the pan with a slotted spoon and set aside. Add the tomatoes to the pan and sauté until soft, stirring occasionally, then mash with a fork. Simmer until the sauce is nicely thickened; add the lemon juice. These elements of the curry may be made to this point a day in advance of your party and then tossed together and reheated just in time to be spread in a shallow bowl, topped with Dry-Curried Red Vegetables (recipe follows), and edged with Dry-Curried Cabbage and Beets (page 87).

Dry-Curried Red Vegetables

Not all the vegetables contained herein are actually red, of course, but all are "hot" in color as opposed to "cool." All are also "dry-curried" and arranged over the "saucy" curry just prior to serving. Since the red cabbage and beets tend to bleed color onto the other vegetables, those two are prepared last and then used as a garnish around the edge of the dish.

5 large sweet red peppers, cut into quarters lengthwise, with pith and seeds discarded

2 large golden peppers, cut into quarters lengthwise, with pith and seeds discarded

4 medium-size carrots, scraped and quartered lengthwise

2 cloves garlic, peeled and minced

1 small fresh hot red chili pepper, with seeds discarded, minced (or more or less to taste)

¼ cup red basil, cut into narrow shreds

1 large red onion, peeled and coarsely chopped

3 tablespoons vegetable oil

1 teaspoon ground turmeric

1 teaspoon chili powder (or more to taste)

Salt to taste

2 large sweet potatoes, peeled, cut lengthwise into strips ¼ inch by ¼ inch by 2 inches, and parboiled 2 minutes (in 1 tablespoon of lemon juice and water to cover, and then drained)

1 teaspoon Garam-Masala (page 192)

1 teaspoon arrowroot

2 tablespoons mild red wine vinegar

¾ cup canned chicken broth

Cut the red peppers, golden peppers, and carrots into strips ¼-inch thick by about 2 inches long. Sauté the garlic, red chili pepper, basil, and onion in the oil until the onion is transparent. Stir in the turmeric, chili powder, and salt. Add the peppers, carrots, and sweet potato strips, sprinkle with Garam-Masala, arrowroot, and vinegar and toss with the seasonings in the pan. Pour the chicken broth over all, then bring to a boil over medium heat while you continue to toss the vegetables for about 3 minutes. Do not overcook. When ready to serve, arrange the hot red vegetables over the center of the red curry sauce and edge with the Dry-Curried Cabbage and Beets.

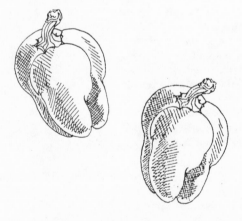

4 medium-size beets, steamed until barely tender and then peeled (or use canned)

2 medium-size red cabbages, quartered and cored, with limp outer leaves discarded

2 medium-size onions, peeled, halved lengthwise, and cut into fine shreds

2 tablespoons vegetable oil

1 teaspoon chili powder

Salt to taste

2 teaspoons Garam-Masala (page 192)

Dry-Curried Cabbage and Beets

Steam and trim the beets, and then run them through the coarse grater of a food processor or cut them into matchstick julienne. Cut the cabbages into long shreds, each no more than ¼-inch thick. Fry the onions in 1 tablespoon of the oil until golden, then stir in the chili powder and salt. Add the cabbage all at once then cover and cook it over medium heat for 5 minutes without stirring. Slip a spatula under the cabbage and carefully turn it over so that the uncooked portion is nearest the heat. Continue to cook, uncovered, a minute or 2 until the excess moisture is absorbed, then lower the heat, cover, and cook several minutes until the cabbage is barely tender. Finally, remove the cover once more, add 1 tablespoon oil, raise the heat slightly, and stir-fry until the vegetables lose most of their moisture but not their color. Toss them with the Garam-Masala. Immediately arrange the cabbage and beets around the edge of the shallow bowl containing the Red-Vegetable Curry and serve.

Turnip Kimchi

Unusual, to say the least, but an interesting accompaniment for curry. A little bit goes a long way.

Makes 1 pint

8 firm white turnips, peeled and cut in quarters

2 tablespoons salt

1 small red chili pepper, chopped

1 tablespoon finely chopped candied ginger

Place the turnip quarters in a deep bowl, sprinkle with 1 tablespoon salt and one cup water, and let stand for 48 hours at room temperature. Remove the turnips (save the water) and cut into ¼-inch slices. Place the turnips in a jar, add the pepper, ginger, and the remaining salt. Add enough water to the reserved soaking water to make 2 cups, pour this over the turnips, mix thoroughly, cover, and refrigerate for 2 weeks, turning the jar once a day.

Vegetable Croquettes on Fried Greens with Salsa Cruda

MENU

Eggplant and Mushrooms with Miso

Assorted Vegetable Croquettes on Flash-Fried Greens Tossed with Salsa Cruda

Deep-Fried Leek Threads

Herbed Cherry Tomatoes

Melon Baskets Filled with Fruit Ice and Papaya and Raspberries in Peach Schnapps

---

SUGGESTIONS

Whip up the Eggplant and Mushrooms with Miso several days early. Refrigerate.

Prepare the croquette mixture 24 hours in advance and refrigerate overnight. Two hours prior to serving, shape the mixture into croquettes and then chill again.

The vegetables can be washed and pre-cooked well in advance of final preparation. In fact, this is recommended to be sure they are as dry as possible before going into the skillet or wok.

Make the Salsa Cruda several days in advance of serving.

Omit the leek threads and substitute sprouts.

Cut the melons in half rather than preparing the baskets and omit the fruit ice.

Eggplant and Mushrooms with Miso

Serves 6

- 3 small or 2 large eggplants, peeled and cut into ¾-inch cubes
  Salt
- 3 tablespoons walnut oil
- ½ lemon
- ½ pound fresh mushrooms, sliced
- ⅓ cup canned chicken broth
- ⅓ cup red miso
- ⅓ cup granulated sugar
- 10 scallions, each with 3 inches of green top, trimmed and finely chopped

Arrange the eggplant cubes on paper towels, sprinkle lightly with salt, and allow to drain for 10 minutes. Pat the cubes dry. Heat half the oil in a non-stick skillet. Add the eggplant, toss with the oil, then cook over medium heat for 5 minutes, stirring occasionally. Remove the eggplant and set aside.

Squeeze lemon juice over the mushroom slices. Wipe out the skillet, heat the remaining oil, and sauté the mushroom slices until the moisture cooks away and the slices are lightly browned. Return the eggplant to the pan.

Mix the broth, miso, and sugar until the sugar is dissolved, then pour the mixture over the vegetables and cook over low-medium heat 4–5 minutes, stirring continuously. Add the scallions and continue to stir for 5 minutes more. Serve hot, at room temperature, or chilled.

Assorted Vegetable Croquettes

Serves 6

- 4 tablespoons light olive oil
- 3 cloves garlic, peeled and minced
- 8 tablespoons all-purpose flour
- ⅔ cup skim milk
- ⅔ cup canned chicken or vegetable broth
- 2 tablespoons peeled fresh ginger, minced
- 2 teaspoons MBT instant chicken or vegetable broth mix
- 1 medium-size potato, peeled, quartered, cooked until tender, and drained well
- ¼ cup soft tofu
- ½ small avocado, peeled and cut into ¼-inch dice
  Juice from ½ lime
- ½ cup radicchio, cut in very fine julienne and then coarsely chopped
- ⅛ teaspoon dried thyme
  Salt and freshly ground Szechwan pepper to taste
  White or yellow cornmeal, finely ground
  Fine bread crumbs (optional)
  Vegetable oil for frying

Quite simply, delicious! And barely a hint of cholesterol in an entire batch.

These do take a little time to prepare so try to accomplish the preliminary steps a day in advance. Try these also as bite-size hors d'oeuvre.

Heat the olive oil in a medium-size non-stick pan and sauté the garlic over medium heat for 1 minute. Stir in the flour, pressing out any lumps with the back of a spoon. Remove the pan from the heat and stir in milk and broth, again pressing out any lumps with the back of a spoon or with a whisk. Cook, stirring continually, over medium heat until the sauce thickens. Add the ginger, instant broth powder, potato, tofu, avocado, lime juice, radicchio, and seasonings. Remove from the heat and lightly mash mixture with a fork. Chill for at least one hour or even overnight.

About 2 hours prior to dinner, spread the cornmeal on a paper towel.

If the croquette mixture seems too moist to form croquettes or patties, add a few bread crumbs. Drop a heaping tablespoon of chilled croquette mixture onto the cornmeal, flip it over, then either roll it into a cone shape (this is a little tricky), or pat it between your palms into a small cake. Refrigerate. Just prior to serving, heat ½ inch of vegetable oil to bubbling in a non-stick skillet large enough to hold the croquettes without letting them touch (or do them in two batches). Cook over

YVONNE YOUNG TARR'S LOW-CHOLESTEROL GOURMET

medium-high heat until golden brown, carefully turning them until all surfaces are browned. Serve immediately on a plate of Flash-Fried Greens Tossed with Salsa Cruda (recipe follows).

VARIATIONS

These croquettes are sensational with an ounce or two of crabmeat or minced cooked chicken breast mixed in, but in no way are they dependent upon these added ingredients.

For a change of pace, substitute one of these tasty optional ingredients for the radicchio (ingredients to equal ½ cup each):

Fresh young corn cut from the cob (or frozen corn defrosted, well-drained. Slightly chop in food processor using the steel cutting blade)

Carrot, scraped, grated and cooked a minute or 2, or until barely tender

Mushrooms, finely chopped and sautéed in a few drops of oil until the liquid disappears

Fresh young asparagus tips covered with boiling water for 2 minutes, then well-drained and finely chopped

Flash-Fried Greens Tossed with Salsa Cruda

For this, a single green or a combination may be used. They are tossed in olive oil over searing heat for a few seconds only and served warm, topped with one or two spoonfuls of room-temperature Salsa Cruda. Here, I've chosen two of my favorites, spinach, which needs no pre-cooking, and kale, which does, simply because the latter lends a bit of "tooth" to the texture of the "wilty" but flavorful spinach. The quantity called for may seem excessive, but greens cook down substantially.

Serves 6

2 pounds spinach
1½ pounds fresh young kale
3 tablespoons olive oil
2 large cloves garlic, peeled and minced
Salt and coarsely ground black pepper to taste
1 cup Salsa Cruda (page 80)

Rinse the greens in several changes of cold water (they are apt to be sandy). Tear or cut away the leaves from the tough stems. Discard the stems and any wilted or discolored leaves. Drain the spinach in a colander, then roll in kitchen towels to dry.

Cut the kale into ½-inch-wide ribbons. Cook in a large pot of lightly salted boiling water for 10 minutes or less—it should not be quite tender. Place in a colander, rinse with cold water, drain well, then roll in kitchen towels to dry.

In a large skillet or wok, heat the oil and garlic until the garlic is golden. Add the kale and toss over high heat for 2 minutes. Push the kale to one side, add the spinach, and toss until it begins to wilt. Toss the vegetables together for 1 minute, then season and divide among 6 plates. Spoon a little Salsa Cruda on the side of each and serve immediately.

VARIATION

Pasta with greens? Of course. Just double the Flash-Fried Greens recipe, spoon it over your favorite pasta, and top with Salsa Cruda and grated low-fat cheese.

Deep-Fried Leek Threads

These crisp, flavorful threads of deep-fried leeks turn almost any entrée into a special-occasion dish. Wash the leeks thoroughly (page 209); they are frequently sandy inside.

3 medium-size leeks, including 3 inches of green top
Vegetable oil for frying

Trim the tops and the roots of the leeks. Split them in half lengthwise, and rinse well without completely separating the leaves. Use a very sharp knife to cut the leeks into long, grass-blade-thin threads, each 3–4 inches long. Pat thoroughly dry between paper towels. Fry until crisp in hot, deep oil. Use immediately.

VARIATION

When time is short, vary the crunch of the topping. Cool, fresh sprouts take the place of Deep-Fried Leek Threads.

Herbed Cherry Tomatoes

These add a splash of color and a fresh sweetness to any meal.

Serves 6

30 red or yellow cherry tomatoes (or half red and half yellow)
2 teaspoons each minced fresh basil, marjoram, and thyme
2 tablespoons best-quality fruity extra-virgin olive oil
Salt and freshly ground black pepper to taste

Rinse and carefully dry the tomatoes. Stir the herbs into the hot olive oil for 1 minute over low heat. Add the tomatoes and shake the pan gently until tomatoes are heated through (2–3 minutes). Turn into a serving dish, sprinkle with salt and pepper, and serve immediately.

VARIATION

Follow directions for the above recipe, but add a large, peeled, and minced garlic clove before you add the herbs. If the other dishes in your meal are already heavily herbed, you may omit the herbs and increase the garlic.

Melon Baskets Filled with Fruit Ice and Papaya and Raspberries in Peach Schnapps

Almost any combination of fruits will fill the bill when marinated and tucked into these attractive melon "baskets." I've included a variation utilizing those irresistible small golden watermelons available in August and September. If you can't find really small melons, use slightly larger ones, but you'll have to sacrifice the handles on the "baskets" and simply cut the melons in half (see illustration, page 65).

A lovely touch is to prepare your own sherbet from the scooped-out melon if you have the time or equipment, but the dessert is very special even with store-bought lemon ice.

Serves 6

6 4- to 5-inch golden watermelons or cantaloupes
   Watermelon or cantaloupe sherbet or store-bought lemon ice
2 medium-large papayas, halved and peeled (reserve the seeds)
4 nectarines, cut into ½-inch slices with the skin
¾ cup peach schnapps
   Juice of 1 lime
½ pint red raspberries
   Sprig of mint

Pick out the most attractive, most evenly rounded side of one melon, turn the melon over, and cut a thin slice from the bottom to ensure that the fruit basket will stand evenly. With a small, sharp knife, cut a 2-inch-wide handle over the top, then, beginning at the base of each handle, cut the edges on each side into small points. Use a spoon to carefully scoop out and set aside the melon pulp, leaving ½-inch-thick sides. Repeat this process with the remaining 5 melons. Turn the cantaloupe baskets upside down to drain.

Puree the scooped-out watermelon or cantaloupe pulp and use it to prepare the melon sherbet.

Blot the hollowed-out melon baskets dry with paper towels.

Cut the papayas into slices ½ inch by 2 inches and place in a large bowl. In a strainer, rinse 2 tablespoons of the seeds, discarding all traces of fruit. Add the seeds and the nectarine slices to the papaya slices and toss the fruits with the schnapps and the lime juice. Let stand, unrefrigerated, for 30 minutes, then chill for at least 1 hour.

To serve, fill the baskets with the chilled fruit, and arrange each on a small plate (cut glass is nice). Top each with a small scoop of sherbet, sprinkle with berries, and garnish with mint. Serve immediately.

Autumn

A Simple Supper to Enjoy with Friends

MENU

Spinach Mullagatawny

Carrot and Ginger Bread

Pasta–Sweet Basil Frittata

Sautéed Broccoli di Rape

Autumn Pudding

SUGGESTIONS

The soup can be made ahead using canned broth if you are rushed. The frittata is served warm or at room temperature and will hold for an hour or 2. Only the Broccoli di Rape is best served hot.

The bread freezes beautifully. Defrost it in the refrigerator, reheat it in the oven, and serve it with the soup.

Prepare the Autumn Pudding 48 hours in advance of serving.

Spinach Mullagatawny

The classic method calls for a whole chicken to enrich the broth of this soup, but I've included skinless breast meat only to eliminate most of the cholesterol but save the flavor. The amount of cholesterol in 1 tablespoon coconut (which lends such unique flavor), is next to nothing, but eliminate it if you prefer. Spinach, although not traditional to this dish, blends so well with the other flavors it actually makes this version richer and smoother. This recipe may look complex, but is actually just a matter of coarsely chopping the ingredients, browning the chicken breast, simmering, and then pureeing the soup.

Serves 6

- 1 chicken breast, including bone, with skin removed
- 2 tablespoons vegetable oil
- 1 medium-size onion, peeled and coarsely chopped
- 2 medium-size carrots, scraped and coarsely chopped
- 1 green pepper, blanched in boiling water for 2 minutes, then seeded and coarsely chopped
- 2 tart green apples, peeled and coarsely chopped
- 2 tablespoons curry powder
- 2 tablespoons all-purpose flour
- 6 cups Homemade Chicken Broth (page 186) or canned broth
- 1 heaping tablespoon unsweetened dried or fresh grated coconut
- 1 tablespoon granulated sugar
- 1 teaspoon salt
- 4 whole cloves
- 2 cups fresh spinach leaves, with coarse stems removed
- 1 large tomato, peeled, seeded, and coarsely chopped
- 1 tablespoon finely chopped fresh parsley
- 1½ cups cooked rice

In a heavy soup kettle, lightly brown the chicken breast in the oil. Remove and set aside.

Add to the pan the onion, carrots, pepper, and apples and cook, stirring occasionally, until the onion turns golden. Blend in the curry powder, flour, and 1 cup broth, stir for 3 or 4 minutes, pressing out any lumps as you go. Mix in the rest of the broth and coconut and stir continuously over low heat until the mixture comes to a boil. Add the sugar, salt, cloves, spinach leaves, tomato, parsley, and chicken, and simmer for 15–20 minutes or until the chicken is cooked through but still tender. Remove the chicken from the kettle and set aside to cool. Puree the soup in a food processor or blender.

To serve, cut the cooled chicken into cubes, discarding the bone. Return the soup to the heat, add the cubed chicken, and bring to just under a boil. Serve piping hot, with several spoonfuls of rice added to each serving.

Carrot and Ginger Bread

This is neither a sweet carrot bread, nor a gingerbread, but rather a yeasty whole oat loaf made with carrot juice and spiraled with crunchy minced carrots and fresh ginger. It is unusual, and unusually tasty.

Makes 1 giant or two medium-size loaves

2 cups fresh or canned carrot juice, at wrist* temperature
2 packages dry active yeast
2 teaspoons salt (optional)
1 tablespoon melted margarine
1 tablespoon honey
½ teaspoon ground cumin
2 cups whole oat flour
1 cup whole wheat flour
4–5 cups white flour (or more or less as needed)
½ cup cracked wheat, plain or with honey added
1½ cups finely minced fresh carrots
2 tablespoons peeled and finely minced fresh ginger root
Oil or butter for greasing baking pans or cookie sheet

Place the carrot juice in a large mixing bowl and add the yeast, salt, if desired, margarine, honey, and cumin. Stir and let stand for 10 minutes until the yeast begins to bubble. Add the oat flour and thoroughly mix. Stir in the whole wheat flour all at once and then add the white flour, a little at a time, until the dough comes clean from the sides of the bowl. Follow directions for Mixing, Kneading, Forming, and Baking Yeast Breads, pages 194 to 196.

Preheat the oven to 350° F.

To form the loaf, roll out the dough into 2 equal rectangles or 1 long rectangle about 10 inches wide. Sprinkle the cracked wheat and minced carrot and ginger over the center of the dough to within 2 inches of the edges. Roll the dough up tightly from the long side, pinch the edges closed, and place it in greased loaf pans or on a greased baking sheet. Bake until the breads are golden brown and sound hollow when the bottom of the pans are tapped with the finger. Cool on a wire rack.

NOTE

A note about leaving out the salt in home-baked bread: Salt adds flavor to bread just as it does to other foods, but here it also regulates the yeast and consequently slows the rising of the bread, promoting the enzyme action that gives bread its earthy flavor, satisfying texture, and superior keeping quality.

Two teaspoons per large loaf (or 2 small ones) is the least you can get by with if you don't want to end up with a bland loaf lacking in character. This figures out to approximately 1 generous pinch of salt per slice—and to my mind well worth every grain.

---

* A few drops on the inside of your wrist will feel comfortably warm.

Pasta–Sweet Basil Frittata

Frittata is usually thought of as a type of omelet incorporating various ingredients bound together with lots of eggs. This version keeps eggs to a bare minimum. Choose your favorite dried pasta shape—the more fanciful it is, the more attractive the finished product will be when you cut into it but, of course, avoid any made with eggs.

Serves 6

2 tablespoons olive oil
1 cup sweet red or green basil leaves (or combination of both), with stems removed (substitute Italian parsley if basil is out of season)
1 large clove garlic, peeled and minced
1 cup soft bean curd, drained and crumbled (or substitute left-over cooked potatoes)
3 cups cooked pasta, well drained
  Salt and coarsely ground fresh black pepper to taste
1¼ cups (10 ounces) egg substitute equivalent to 5 eggs*
1 recipe Salsa Cruda (page 80) (optional)

Turn the oven to broil.

Heat the oil in a medium-size non-stick skillet. Add the basil and garlic and sauté for 1 minute. Add the bean curd (or potato), pasta, and salt and pepper to taste, and toss over medium heat until heated through (about 3–4 minutes). Beat the egg substitute and stir it into the paste mixture. Remove the pan immediately from the heat and slide it under the broiler until it is very lightly browned. Cover the pan with a plate large enough to hold the frittata, let it stand away from the heat for 2 to 3 minutes or until the egg has set. Carefully loosen the edges with a pliable spatula. Invert the pan and turn the frittata onto the plate. Cut into 6 pie-shaped wedges and serve at room temperature. Pass Salsa Cruda.

Sautéed Broccoli di Rape

Serves 6

2 slices good Italian bread, dried out in a slow oven
3 tablespoons olive oil
½ small hot pepper (with seeds and veins discarded), sliced (optional)
3 cloves garlic, peeled and minced
1½ pounds broccoli di rape, rinsed and wrapped in towels to drain
  Salt and freshly ground Szechwan pepper to taste
  Plain low-fat yogurt, cold (optional)

The marvelous, slightly bitter taste of this vegetable needs little enhancing. Omit the hot pepper if you prefer.

Crumble the bread into crumbs. In a small skillet, heat 1 tablespoon oil and sauté the pepper, if using, for 1 minute. Add crumbs and sauté until very lightly browned. Transfer to a small bowl.

Add the remaining oil and the garlic to the skillet. Discard any broccoli di rape stems larger than your little finger and add the vegetable to the pan. Cover and cook over medium heat until wilted and tender. Sprinkle with salt and pepper, divide among 6 plates, and top each serving with the crumbs. Top with a spoonful of yogurt, if desired.

---

* The yolk of a whole egg enriches the flavor and helps to firm and bind the ingredients, adding about 1 gram of fat and 21 mgs. of cholesterol per serving. It's your decision if you want to mix in a whole egg with the egg substitute.

Autumn Pudding

A beautiful, deep-purple fruit pudding. When using mostly cranberries, add additional sugar to taste.

Serves 6

3 pounds mixed autumn ber-
    ries (blueberries, raspber-
    ries, cranberries), well
    rinsed and drained
½ cup granulated sugar
⅛ teaspoon each ground nut-
    meg and cloves
    Soft margarine
10–12 slices good white bread
    (home-baked is best),
    trimmed of crusts

Bring the fruit, sugar, and spices to a boil, then lower the heat and simmer, stirring frequently until syrupy. Generously grease a 1-quart pudding mold or bowl with margarine and line it neatly with 7 or 8 of the bread slices, trimming them to fit exactly. There should be no spaces between the slices. Pour in the fruits and top with the remaining bread slices, again fitting them neatly so that there are no spaces. Cover with aluminum foil and a small plate that fits comfortably just inside the mold. Weight the plate down with an unopened 16-ounce can and refrigerate the pudding overnight.

An hour or so prior to serving remove the can, the plate, and the foil. Loosen the sides of the pudding carefully with a dull knife. Drain off any excess fruit juice. Place a serving plate over the mold and quickly flip it over to turn the pudding onto the plate. Refrigerate until ready to serve.

Mexican Dry-Soup Supper

MENU

Guacamole

Mexican Dry Chicken-and-Garlic Soup

Tortillas or Crêpes de Maiz Filled with Grilled Red Onions, Mashed White Beans, Wilted Spinach, and Soft Garlic Sauce

Creamy Sweet Potato Pudding/Pie

SUGGESTIONS

Prepare the soup early as directed in the recipe.

Cook the chicken for the soup, julienne the meat, and puree the soup base 1 or 2 days in advance.

Make Crêpes de Maiz ahead of time.

Prepare the Sweet Potato Pudding/Pie 2 to 8 hours prior to serving.

Use good-quality store-bought corn tortillas.

Guacamole

Serves 4–6

2 large, ripe avocados, peeled, pitted, and sliced (keep the pit)
2 cloves garlic, peeled and minced
2 green chilies, with seeds discarded, minced
1 medium-size ripe tomato, peeled, seeded, and finely chopped
1 small onion, peeled and finely chopped
¼ teaspoon chili powder (or more to taste)
  Salt and freshly ground black pepper to taste
½ lime
2 tablespoons chopped fresh coriander

Guacamole tastes best when freshly made. If you must prepare it ahead, place the pit in the center of the dip and refrigerate for up to 60 minutes. The pit helps keep the dip from darkening.

Mash all ingredients together except the lime, a few coriander leaves, and the pit. Turn the guacamole into a bowl, place the pit in the center, and squeeze the juice from the lime over to keep it from darkening. To serve, remove and discard the pit and garnish with the reserved coriander leaves.

Mexican Dry Chicken-and-Garlic Soup

Serves 8

1 large or two small whole chicken breasts, including bone (about ½ pound meat)
8 cups Homemade Chicken Broth (page 186) or canned broth
1 medium-size head of garlic, peeled
2 tablespoons vegetable oil
1 large onion, peeled and chopped
4 ounces mild green chilies, chopped, or 2 2-ounce cans, drained
3 cups cooked chick-peas, or 2 15-ounce cans, rinsed and drained
2 cups thinly sliced radishes
2 cups coarsely chopped scallions
½ cup coarsely chopped avocado tossed in lime juice (to prevent darkening)
2 medium-size ripe tomatoes, seeded
½ cup grated low-fat cheese (optional)
2 cups plain low-fat yogurt, cold
2 limes, cut into wedges

In Mexico, soups don't stick to the same old soup rules. Sometimes they're dry rather than soupy, sometimes they're soup and salad rolled into one satisfying dish. This one is both.

Remove and discard the skin from the chicken breast. Bring the broth to the boil, add the chicken breast and the garlic, then immediately lower the heat and simmer at lowest setting until the breast meat is just tender (about 15–20 minutes). Do not overcook or the meat will be rubbery. Cool to room temperature. Remove and discard the chicken bones. Blot the chicken meat dry and cut into thin julienne.

Heat the oil in a small skillet, add the onion and half the chilies, and stir until the onion is translucent (about 5 minutes). Puree these along with the garlic, half the chick-peas, and 1 cup broth. Stir these back into the rest of the broth. The soup may be prepared to this point, the elements separately wrapped and stored in the refrigerator for 1 or 2 days.

About 30 minutes prior to serving, heat the chicken broth mixture to steaming over low heat. In a small skillet, heat the chicken meat, remaining onion and chilies, and divide among 8 small bowls. Ladle the soup over and divide the remaining toppings—radishes, scallions, avocado, tomato, and grated cheese, if desired—over each. Pass yogurt and lime wedges.

Tortillas or Crêpes de Maiz Filled with Grilled Red Onions, Mashed White Beans, Wilted Spinach, and Soft Garlic Sauce

This is not precisely a burrito, wrapped as it is in a corn flour crêpe, but it is bound to be one of the most popular meals you've ever presented. Sweet red onions are included for crunch, slightly mashed white beans smothered in soft garlic sauce provide melt-in-your-mouth beany goodness, and barely wilted fresh spinach completes the partnership.

Serves 6

1 recipe Tortillas de Maiz or Crêpes de Maiz (recipes follow)
1 recipe Soft Garlic Sauce (recipe follows)
2 large red onions, cut in half, brushed with oil, then broiled or grilled and then peeled; or peeled and fried
3 cups cooked white beans (or canned, rinsed and well drained)
1 pound spinach, well washed

Heat the tortillas or crêpes as directed in their recipes. Prepare the garlic sauce. Broil or grill the halved onions until tender and then peel and cut them into ⅓-inch-thick slices. (Or cut the raw onions into ⅓-inch-thick slices and fry in a non-stick pan, stirring constantly for 4 minutes.) Use a fork to lightly mash the beans (they should still retain some texture).

Discard the tough stems from the spinach and place it in a heavy pot. Cover and cook in the water clinging to the leaves until just slightly wilted, then place on paper towels to drain.

To assemble a Crêpe de Maiz: Place a few onion slices in the center of the warm crêpe, top with beans, sauce, and spinach. Fold in three sides of the crêpe, then roll it over to secure the fourth side.

Tortillas de Maiz

In previous times, the small corn tortilla and the larger flour tortilla always seemed to me to be ideal vehicles for creating vegetable meals that were out of the ordinary, yet extraordinarily delicious. It's hard to feel deprived when these satisfying Mexican treats are on the table. It wasn't until I began to experiment in earnest with the low-cholesterol aspect of reduced-meat meals that I remembered that flour tortillas, which had always seemed so benign, were, at worst, usually prepared with lard, or, at best, with solid vegetable shortening.

On the other hand, corn tortillas, while not as large and therefore not able to support such a varied load of fillings as those popular "little burros," or burritos, are prepared with water and masa harina, a very finely ground cornmeal flour. Masa harina is also called harinilla and is commercially produced and available in markets in the Southwest and in gourmet food stores in other parts of the country, and by mail order.

I've included the recipe here, just in case you have the time or the interest to experiment. To be really first rate, corn tortillas should be rolled or patted paper-thin, no simple task for a beginner.

Here follow recipes for Tortillas de Maiz and Crêpes de Maiz. This last name is a bastardization, but the finished product has an ethereal quality most cooks never achieve with tortillas. An additional advantage is that the larger crêpe has a larger capacity for fillings.

Makes about 14–16 6-inch tortillas

2 cups masa harina (Quaker brand Masa Harina is available across the country)
1¼–1½ cups warm water

Mix masa harina with 1¼ cups of warm water to make a dough that will cling together but is not sticky. This is not difficult, but a food processor fitted with a plastic blade makes it even easier. If the dough is too dry, knead in additional water, a little at a time, until it has the proper consistency. Cover lightly and let stand for 15 to 20 minutes.

Knead for a minute, then pull off a piece about the size of an egg, or roughly 1¾ inches in diameter, and roll into a ball. Pat the dough flat on a lightly floured surface, and roll out between waxed paper or in a 6-inch plastic baggie (or pat it between your hands) until paper-thin. Come as close as you can to a perfect circle; cut off any really raggy edges with kitchen scissors.

Cook on a moderately hot griddle or cast-iron skillet for 15 to 20 seconds on each side until flecked with brown. Adjust the heat as necessary—if it is too intense the tortillas will brown before they are cooked through. If the tortilla puffs up here and there, flatten it gently with a spatula. As it comes off the heat wrap each tortilla in paper towels and place in a serving basket lined with a slightly dampened (not wet) towel, or slip it into a Ziploc plastic baggie where it will remain moist and hot. Serve warm.

To keep: Seal the finished tortillas in Ziploc plastic bags and refrigerate up to 5 days or freeze them for 3 to 6 months, perhaps longer.

To reheat: In a microwave oven, covered, on a dry, moderately hot griddle or skillet, turning each several times, or wrapped in double-thick aluminum foil in a 325° F. oven.

Crêpes de Maiz

There is no getting away from the fact that all varieties of crêpes begin with eggs. In this case, however, half the normal amount needed is replaced with egg substitutes, so we end up with only one-third an egg for a 4-crêpe portion per person. Use your own requirements to decide if the results are worth the small transgression. This recipe also includes healthful corn flour.

Makes 20–24 crêpes

1 egg
1¼ cups (10 ounces) egg substitute equivalent to 5 eggs
1½ cups masa harina (corn flour)
¼ teaspoon salt
2 cups low-fat milk
    Vegetable oil or vegetable spray

Beat the egg and egg substitute lightly, then continue to beat as you gradually add the flour and salt. When the mixture is smooth, beat in the milk until the batter is smooth once again. Press out any lumps with the back of a spoon. The food processor makes this child's play. Refrigerate the batter for 2 to 3 hours.

Season a 6-inch skillet by rubbing lightly with oil or spraying with vegetable spray. Set over low heat for a minute, then remove from the heat and wipe the pan. Repeat the process.

Heat the skillet, stir the cold crêpe batter, and pour 3 tablespoons batter all at once into the pan, rotating it quickly so the mixture spreads thinly over the surface. When small bubbles appear on the top of the crêpe, loosen it with a spatula, then turn it over to lightly brown it on the other side. Wipe the pan with oil or spray it if the crêpes begin to stick. Stack the crêpes as you finish each one, and keep them warm in a plastic bag until serving time.

To freeze: Stack the crêpes with plastic wrap in between. They usually don't stick, but this way you can remove any number without defrosting the rest. Slip the crêpes into a 6-inch Ziploc plastic bag, seal closed, and place in freezer for up to 2 weeks.

Soft Garlic Sauce

Makes about 4 cups

3 cups Chicken Broth or Vegetable Stock (pages 186 or 184) or canned broth
1 small whole head garlic
1 large carrot, scraped and coarsely chopped
2 ribs celery, coarsely chopped
1 large onion, peeled and coarsely chopped
½ cup slivered blanched almonds
2 tablespoons low-fat sour cream

Place all ingredients except the sour cream in a medium-size saucepan and bring to a boil (there should be enough liquid to almost cover the whole garlic head).

Lower the heat and simmer until the vegetables are tender.

Remove the garlic and squeeze each clove to extract the soft garlic. Discard the papery garlic skins. Puree all ingredients except the sour cream in a food processor using the steel blade. Add the sour cream and whirl for a few seconds to mix.

Creamy Sweet Potato Pudding/Pie

Who says that all desserts are taboo? Not anyone who tries this spicy potato pudding with graham cracker crumbs, wheat germ, and the lingering aftertaste of orange and honey. Since each serving contains less than ⅛ egg yolk and ½ tablespoon milk, I've chosen to include a whole egg and whole milk. The low-fat substitutes don't set the pudding quite as well, but use them if you prefer. If you dare, a tablespoon of vanilla ice milk is an excellent garnish.

Serves 8

2 pounds sweet potatoes, boiled until tender and peeled
2 tablespoons melted or liquid margarine
1 egg
¼ cup (2 ounces) egg substitute equivalent to 1 egg
Strained juice of 1 small orange
½ cup honey
½ cup light brown sugar
¼ cup milk
4 tablespoons molasses
¼ teaspoon each ground allspice, nutmeg, and aniseed
½ teaspoon almond extract
1½ tablespoons soft margarine
¾ cup graham cracker crumbs
¾ cup toasted wheat germ

Preheat the oven to 325° F.

Mash the sweet potatoes and place them in the large bowl of an electric mixer along with the melted or liquid margarine, egg, and egg substitute. Beat at low speed until thoroughly mixed. Add the juice, honey, sugar, milk, molasses, spices, and almond extract, and beat until the batter is smooth.

Grease the bottom and sides of a 10-inch pie plate with the soft margarine and sprinkle first with graham cracker crumbs and then with the wheat germ. Press these down firmly into the margarine. Carefully spoon the batter over the crumbs and bake for 1¼ to 1½ hours or until the center is set. Cut into wedges and serve warm (not hot) or cold.

Red, Hot, and Pasta Dinner

MENU

Chilled Tuna, Chicken, Shrimp, and Buttermilk Soup

Pasta with Fiery Tomato–Shiitake Mushroom Sauce

Celery Root in Capered French Dressing

Date Pie

SUGGESTIONS

Prepare the soup 24–48 hours in advance, the taste actually improves as the flavors meld.
Both the salad and the dessert can be made ahead without compromising flavor.
Additional tuna may replace any or all of the chicken or shrimp, if you prefer.

Chilled Tuna, Chicken, Shrimp, and Buttermilk Soup

Serves 6

3½ cups plain low-fat yogurt
3½ cups buttermilk
2½ tablespoons lemon juice
1 cup coarsely chopped cooked fresh tuna (or first-quality, well-drained water-packed canned)
½ cup coarsely chopped shrimp
½ cup skinless, boneless white meat chicken (or 1 cup of either shrimp or chicken)
2 medium-size cucumbers, peeled, seeded, and coarsely chopped
2 small dill pickles, peeled and coarsely chopped
6 scallions including 3 inches of green tops, trimmed of their roots
¼ cup each finely chopped fresh parsley and dill
Salt (optional)
Freshly ground black pepper to taste

Very few summer soups are as satisfying as this one with its chilly dill flavor backed up with tart yogurt and buttermilk and treasures of shrimp, chicken, and fish. This can begin a meal luxuriously, or be served as a meal-in-a-bowl when coupled with a crunchy salad and a thick, wholesome slice of home-baked bread brushed with extra-virgin olive oil rubbed with cut garlic.

Thoroughly mix together the yogurt, buttermilk, and lemon juice, then stir in the tuna, shrimp, chicken, cucumbers, pickles, scallions, and half the herbs. Season to taste with salt, if desired, and a generous grind of pepper. Refrigerate for at least 4 hours or overnight. To serve, add as much buttermilk as necessary to bring the soup to the consistency you prefer, ladle into bowls, and garnish with the remaining herbs and freshly ground pepper.

Pasta with Fiery Tomato–Shiitake Mushroom Sauce

Serves 6

1½ cups sliced shiitake mushrooms (or other mushrooms)
2 tablespoons fine, fruity olive oil
1 clove garlic, peeled and minced (optional)
4 large ripe tomatoes, peeled, seeded, and coarsely chopped
Minced fresh serrano or other hot peppers to taste
1 tablespoon fresh thyme leaves, or 1 teaspoon dried
Pinch each ground mace, granulated sugar, and marjoram
Salt and pepper to taste
3 tablespoons vodka
6 cups cooked hot pasta (not egg pasta)
1 cup fresh sprouts or well-washed watercress (leaves only)

Actually, any variety of boletus mushroom—shiitake, porcini, or cepes—takes admirably to this treatment. Fresh tomatoes, partnered with fresh hot peppers, are most effective for the base. Spike all with vodka and serve over pasta topped with your favorite fresh sprouts (mine are sweet wheat sprouts) or watercress.

If it seems necessary, wipe the mushrooms with a damp cloth to clean. Cut into thin shards and sauté in the olive oil for 2 minutes with the garlic. Add the tomatoes, minced hot pepper, thyme, and seasonings and simmer until the sauce is no longer watery.

Just before serving, stir the vodka into the tomato sauce. Arrange a 1-cup mound of pasta in the center of each plate; top with sauce and sprouts or watercress leaves.

Celery Root in Capered French Dressing

Serves 6

6 cups peeled and coarsely grated celery root
1 cup Capered French Dressing (page 189)
  Salt and pepper to taste
2 tablespoons capers, rinsed, well drained, and coarsely chopped

Toss the celery root, dressing, and seasonings to thoroughly coat the vegetable strands. Chill 2 hours or until serving time. Place in a clean, chilled bowl and sprinkle with capers. Toss lightly again at table and serve.

Date Pie

Serves 6–8

1 recipe Three-Grain Crust (page 43)
2 cups chopped seedless dates
¼ cup (2 ounces) egg substitute equivalent to 1 egg
½ cup low-fat sour cream
¼ cup plain low-fat yogurt
2 tablespoons brandy
  Pinch each salt, ground cloves, nutmeg, cardamom, and mace
¾ cup light brown sugar
½ cup coarsely broken walnuts

Bake the crust as directed and cool to room temperature.
  Preheat the oven to 425° F.
  Gently but thoroughly stir together all remaining ingredients except the nuts. Spoon the mixture into the pie crust, sprinkle with the walnuts, and bake for 10 minutes, then lower the heat to 325° F. and bake for 30 minutes longer or until the filling is set in the center. Cool to room temperature, then chill.

Scandinavian Harvest Dinner

MENU

*Fresh Sweet Pea Soup with Wild
Mushrooms*

*Fish "Frikadeller" and Hot
Pickled Vegetables with Dilly
Cider/Mustard Sauce*

Hasselback Potatoes

*Swedish Limpa Bread with Rye
and Oats*

Cranberry Orange-Rye Pudding

SUGGESTIONS

The soup is not difficult to prepare but could be made even easier by preparing it in advance and adding frozen peas at the last minute.

You can prepare the dill sauce and vegetables a day in advance.

The fish mixture waits nicely refrigerated overnight prior to shaping and sautéing at the last moment.

The beauty of this intriguing dinner is its variety and unique bouquet of flavors. To simplify, you could omit the pea soup and home-baked bread but that would mean losing two exquisite taste treats.

This meal is on all levels a Scandinavian repast. I didn't intend it that way, it just happened. That's the best way, it seems to me, to make certain a largely vegetarian meal doesn't become humdrum. Choose each recipe because of its sparkle, and the entire dinner is likely to shine.

You'll never believe how sweet a sweet pea soup can be until you try this lovely green brew. There's a mysterious taste hidden in the stock—lettuce and leek to be exact. The texture is provided by chewy sautéed wild mushrooms and thinly sliced scallions. The pungent flavor of coriander deepens the pleasure.

To the Danes, "Frikadeller" is synonymous with meatballs, and very popular they are, either as tiny hors d'oeuvre or in their larger version as an entrée. Fish "Frikadeller" serves also as a tidbit with drinks or as an entrée that falls somewhere between a fish cake and a quenelle. However they are presented, fish "Frikadeller" are excellent, particularly when accompanied by a dill-scented cider and mustard sauce.

Another uncommon feature of this menu is vegetables served hot and lightly pickled rather than steamed in the traditional manner. The meal is rounded out with the inclusion of a Swedish favorite, Hasselback Potatoes. These are most often baked in the pan with the roast, causing them to turn a lovely dark brown as their thin center slices soak up pan juices plus cupfuls of the roasting fat that elevates our cholesterol. Once, the results seemed worth the risk. Today we know it isn't, particularly when it's possible to obtain much the same results by cutting the spuds in the attractive, traditional method that allows the oil to penetrate the potato, rubbing with a meat extract, dribbling with a light olive oil, and allowing them to bake to a crisp, dark, golden brown.

For "closers" there is a unique warm cranberry pudding served with ice milk and peach schnapps.

Fresh Sweet Pea Soup with Wild Mushrooms

Serves 6

1 medium-size leek, split lengthwise, trimmed, and washed thoroughly (page 209), trimmed of root and all but 3 inches of green top
1 cup coarsely chopped lettuce
2 tablespoons vegetable oil
¾ cup coarsely chopped wild or other mushrooms (I usually use shiitake)
2 cups small fresh peas, shelled
1 small potato, peeled and cut in fine dice
½ teaspoon ground ginger
¼ teaspoon whole allspice
1 teaspoon dried marjoram
  Salt (optional)
  Freshly ground black pepper to taste
  Water or Vegetable Stock (page 184)
¼ cup low-fat milk
3 pencil-thin scallions, trimmed of roots and all but 2 inches of green top
2 tablespoons finely chopped coriander

In a heavy saucepan, sauté the leek and lettuce in the oil until the leek is transparent. Transfer the vegetables to a bowl. Sauté the mushrooms in the remaining oil for several minutes or until tender. Transfer to a small bowl; add ½ cup peas and set aside.

Add to the saucepan the leek, lettuce, potato, seasonings, the remaining peas, and water or stock to barely cover. Bring to a boil and boil for 4 minutes. Puree the soup with the milk and return it to the saucepan. Add the reserved peas and mushrooms and simmer the soup for 3 minutes or until the peas are just tender. Serve the soup hot, topped with the sliced scallions and coriander.

Fish "Frikadeller"

Serves 6

2 slices Swedish Limpa with Rye and Oats (page 112) or Arnold's or Pepperidge Farm Oat Bread, crumbled
1 tablespoon milk
1 medium-size onion, peeled and cut into eighths
  Salt to taste
  White pepper to taste
1 teaspoon baking powder
1 teaspoon curry powder
1½ pounds cod, cut into 1-inch pieces
¼ cup soft bean curd or leftover mashed potatoes
  Vegetable oil for frying

Soak the bread in the milk until all the liquid has been absorbed. Use the steel blade in your food processor or blender to whirl the bread until it becomes a paste. Add the onion, salt, pepper, baking powder, curry powder, and 2 pieces of the fish. Puree. With the motor running, drop in 2 more pieces of fish, one at a time, until pureed.

Add the remaining fish and this time turn the motor on and off a few times only until the fish is coarsely chopped. Add the bean curd or potatoes and turn the machine on and off 2 or 3 times. The fish should be coarsely chopped and most of the bean curd or potatoes should still be in ⅓-inch pieces. Chill for at least 30 minutes.

Dip 2 tablespoons in ice water, shake off most of the water, and use the moistened spoons to shape the fish mixture into six 3-inch ovals. Heat 2 tablespoons oil in a large non-stick pan and arrange the ovals in it so they do not touch. Flatten the top of each cake slightly with the back of a spoon. Sauté over medium-low heat about 5 minutes on each side, or until the cakes are soft but cooked through the center. Add another tablespoon of oil if needed. The cakes should be golden on both sides. Serve immediately with Hot Pickled Vegetables and Dilly Cider/ Mustard Sauce (recipe follows) passed separately.

Hot Pickled Vegetables

Pungent, not sweet, these could become a regular feature at your table.

Serves 6

1 small whole cauliflower
6 small white onions, peeled
⅔ cup granulated sugar
¼ cup salt
1 cup white vinegar
6 small carrots, trimmed and scraped
1 small bunch broccoli, cut into 6 stalks, each peeled

Drop the cauliflower and onions into a large pot of boiling water to which has been added the sugar, salt, and vinegar. After 15 minutes, add the carrots and broccoli and cook, testing each vegetable and removing it when it is slightly underdone. Arrange the hot vegetables on a platter.

Dilly Cider/Mustard Sauce

The idea here is that the combination of dill, cider, and mustard makes not only the fish but the slightly pickled vegetables that are served with it really sing. I love a sweet/hot combination, but if your tastebuds rebel at sweets with dinner, use less cider and more mustard and dill.

Makes 2½ cups

1½ teaspoons cornstarch
3 cups apple cider
3 tablespoons Dijon mustard
⅓ cup molasses
½ cup minced fresh dill

Use the back of a spoon to work the cornstarch into ¼ cup of the cider until smooth. Add the mustard and molasses and work them in, in a similar fashion. Transfer the mixture and the remaining cider to a small saucepan and bring to a boil, stirring constantly until the mixture thickens slightly. Stir in the dill and serve hot.

Hasselback Potatoes

Serves 6

6 large baking potatoes, peeled
  Gravy Master (or other meat
  concentrate)
¼ cup vegetable oil
  Salt to taste
¼ cup fine dry bread crumbs made
  from rye bread

Preheat the oven to 425° F.

Rinse the potatoes and place them in ice water. One by one, remove each potato, dry, and place in a large deep spoon. Cut each potato into slices, ⅛ inch thick, careful not to slice completely through the potato. (The rim of the spoon should stop the knife about ¼ inch from the bottom of the potato.) Replace the potato in the ice water, remove the next and repeat the process.

Place the potatoes, cut sides down, on paper towels to drain. Mix Gravy Master and oil. Dry each potato, rub it with the oil mixture, pulling the slits apart a little so the oil can drip down inside. Sprinkle with salt.

Arrange in an ovenproof dish, cut sides up, and bake for 35 minutes, or until tender, turning every 10 minutes. (If the potatoes seem to be browning too quickly, lower the heat 25 degrees.)

Remove the dish from the oven and arrange the potatoes cut sides up. Sprinkle the potatoes with the bread crumbs and drizzle them with a little oil, then return them to the oven for 15 minutes or until well browned. Serve immediately.

Swedish Limpa Bread with Rye and Oats

Usually, this superb bread is made primarily with rye flour flavored with orange zest and caraway and anise seeds. Here the same flavors remain but oats are added for additional fiber and nutrition. The result is a wonderful loaf that is ideal toasted for breakfast or brunch, or makes an outstanding accompaniment for soups, salads, and/or cheese.

Makes 2 large loaves

3½ cups water
 ¾ cup light brown sugar
  2 tablespoons vegetable oil
  2 teaspoons caraway seeds
  2 teaspoons anise seeds
  1 tablespoon orange zest (thin
    outerskin), grated
1½ packages dry active yeast
  3 cups 100-percent rye flour
  2 cups rolled oats (not instant)
  2 teaspoons salt
6–7 cups unbleached white flour

In a saucepan combine the water, sugar, oil, caraway and anise seeds, and orange zest. Bring to a boil and boil for 3 minutes. Cool to tepid, sprinkle the yeast over, wait 5 minutes, and then stir.

Stir in the rye flour, rolled oats, and the salt and let stand 15 minutes. Stir in enough white flour to make a soft dough that will hold its shape. Place the dough in a clean, well-greased bowl, turn it over to grease the top, cover it lightly with a kitchen towel, and allow it to rise for 1½ hours in a warm, draft-free place.

Divide the dough into two equal portions. Put each piece in a separate bowl, grease the top, and allow to rise again for 2 hours in a warm, draft-free place.

Preheat the oven to 350° F.

Knead each portion for five minutes (page 195), shape into loaves (page 196), and place into 2 greased loaf pans. Cover and let rise again for 30 minutes or until doubled in bulk.

Bake 50–60 minutes or until the loaves test done (page 196). Remove immediately from the pans and cool on wire racks.

Cranberry Orange-Rye Pudding

On cold, blustery evenings this nutritious pudding bolsters spirits in Finland. It's a dessert you can actually feel righteous, rather than guilty, about eating. This recipe is changed a bit from the original "Ruismarjapuuro" Finnish version. The freshly squeezed orange juice and brandy-soaked raisins heighten the fruit flavor, and peach schnapps and ice milk add the finishing touches.

Serves 8

¾ cup rye flour
¼ cup all-purpose white flour
2 tablespoons cornstarch
¼ cup granulated sugar
¼ cup light brown sugar
½ teaspoon salt
3 cups cranberry juice
1 cup freshly squeezed orange juice
¼ cup plus 1 tablespoon dark corn syrup
2 tablespoons pearl sugar (or substitute granulated)
¾ cup muscat raisins
¼ cup orange juice
¼ cup brandy
1 cup whole-cranberry sauce, canned
6 tablespoons peach schnapps (optional)
Good-quality commercial ice milk

Whirl the flours, cornstarch, sugars, salt, the first two juices, and ¼ cup corn syrup in food processor until well blended. Bring to a boil over medium heat, stirring constantly. Lower the heat to medium-low and continue cooking, stirring occasionally, until the pudding is nicely thickened, about 15 minutes. Sprinkle with the two tablespoons sugar and keep warm.

Simmer raisins, orange juice, brandy, cranberry sauce, and remaining corn syrup for several minutes over low heat. Sprinkle over the pudding. Serve immediately. Top each serving with a tablespoon peach schnapps and a scoop of ice milk.

Pink-Chili Chowdown

MENU

Green Herb Pie

Pink Vegetable Chili over Rice

Gingerbread with Sautéed Apple Slices

SUGGESTIONS

When preparing the pie, remove the thick stems from the spinach, wash and parboil the vegetables and herbs a day early. Or, if necessary, substitute finely chopped frozen spinach.

Omit the chicken from the chili and substitute canned beans for the home-cooked variety.

Prepare the cake and apples 24 hours prior to serving.

Green Herb Pie

Serves 8

1 pound fresh spinach, with all tough stems removed
½ pound Swiss chard (or use only spinach if chard is not available)
½ cup fresh parsley
¼ cup minced fresh chervil
½ cup low-fat milk
¼ cup currants (optional)
½ cup fresh soft bread crumbs
1 egg
¾ cup (6 ounces) egg substitute equivalent to 3 eggs
1 tablespoon granulated sugar
Generous pinch grated nutmeg
Salt and pepper to taste
2 tablespoons margarine
2 tablespoons ground almonds
¾ cup fine white dry bread crumbs

Preheat the oven to 425° F.

Parboil spinach, chard, parsley, and chervil in salted water to cover for 2 minutes, then drain well and coarsely chop. (Frozen spinach contains some tough stems and so should be finely chopped.) Boil the milk with the currants, if used, and soft bread crumbs until the mixture thickens, then remove from the heat and beat in the egg, egg substitute, sugar, nutmeg, and salt and pepper. Stir over very low heat until thickened somewhat; do not boil or the eggs will curdle.

Rub or cut the margarine into the almonds and dry bread crumbs. Press into the bottom and sides of a 9-inch pie plate and bake for 4 minutes. Remove the crust from oven. Stir the greens and add them to the milk–bread crumb–egg mixture. Pour the greens into the pie shell.

Bake in oven for 10 minutes, then lower the temperature to 350° F. and bake 30–40 minutes, or until the center of the pie no longer quivers when touched. Serve warm, not hot.

Pink Vegetable Chili over Rice

Serves 8

1 chicken breast, with skin discarded (optional)
1 tablespoon cornstarch
5 cloves garlic, peeled and minced
3 large onions, peeled and coarsely chopped
3 tablespoons vegetable oil
7 large red or golden tomatoes, peeled, seeded, and coarsely chopped
6 cups cooked pinto beans (or use canned beans, rinsed and drained)
3 cups rutabaga, cut into ½-inch cubes and parboiled until nearly tender
3–4 tablespoons chili powder
2 teaspoons each ground cumin and oregano
Salt and freshly ground black pepper to taste

When I began to put together a book of mainly vegetable recipes, the first dish that sprang to mind was a meatless version of the White Lightning Chili that was featured in my last book, *That's Entertaining.* White Lightning Chili was already on its way to becoming a vegetarian dish, substituting as it did chicken for beef. To carry out the color theme, white kidney beans replaced red ones and golden tomatoes stood in for the more common rosy variety.

This recipe takes that chili version the rest of the way by omitting the meat, sour cream, and high-fat cheese. Although I think the dish is excellent made with golden tomatoes, I've switched back to red ones because they're so much easier to find, but try the golden if they're available. If you do want a bit of meat, include the optional chicken breast in this for texture and for flavor. As this recipe serves 8, there would be but a trace of cholesterol in each portion.

(continued)

Homemade Chicken Broth or Vegetable Stock (pages 186 or 184) or canned broth
Rice (cooked according to package directions)

If you're including it, cut the chicken into ½-inch cubes and toss them with the cornstarch.

In a large, heavy non-stick pot, sauté the chicken cubes, garlic, and onions in the oil until they are all lightly browned, stirring from time to time. Add the tomatoes, beans, rutabaga, and seasonings and enough broth to cover. Heat the chili to just under a boil, then lower the heat and simmer, covered, for one hour or until the rutabaga is tender, stirring occasionally; add more broth if necessary. Adjust the seasonings. Serve hot over rice. Pass the bowls of cubed avocado, tomato, sweet onion, low-fat sour cream, and grated mild cheese.

Gingerbread with Sautéed Apple Slices

Serves 8

Oil
Flour
1 **cup dark brown sugar**
1 **egg**
¼ **cup (2 ounces) egg substitute equivalent to 1 egg**
¾ **cup molasses**
⅓ **cup liquid margarine (or soft margarine, melted)**
2½ **cups all-purpose flour**
½ **teaspoon baking powder**
1 **tablespoon baking soda**
2 **teaspoons each ginger and cinnamon**
½ **teaspoon each ground nutmeg and cloves**
1 **cup boiling water**
1 **tablespoon margarine**
3 **Granny Smith apples, cored and sliced**
¼ **cup light brown sugar**
2 **tablespoons dark rum**

Preheat the oven to 350° F.

Oil and lightly flour a rectangular cake pan and line it with waxed paper.

Beat together the sugar, egg, egg substitute, and molasses. Beat in the margarine. Sift together the dry ingredients. Stir one quarter of the dry ingredients thoroughly into the egg mixture, mix well, and repeat the process until all the dry ingredients have been incorporated. Beat in the boiling water and pour the batter into the prepared pan. Bake 35–45 minutes, or until a toothpick comes out clean.

Meanwhile, prepare the apple slices. Melt 1 tablespoon margarine in a non-stick pan and sauté the fruit for 3 to 4 minutes. Sprinkle the sugar and rum over the slices and stir over medium-low heat until they are barely tender. Serve gingerbread squares topped with warm apple slices.

A Cold-Weather Lunch

MENU

Tomato-Bluefish Aspic

Spaghetti Squash with Leek Sauce, Lemon Shrimp, and Browned Pumpernickel Crumbs

Scallion, White-Bean, and Pecan Pancakes

Red Wine and Cherry Soup in Cantaloupe Shells

SUGGESTIONS

Here's a menu with virtually no last-minute tasks involved. Prepare the aspic a day in advance; its flavor will improve overnight.

The leek sauce may also be prepared with canned broth and be chilled for a day or two. Only the spaghetti squash must be freshly baked or boiled for peak results.

The bean pancakes are child's play to prepare, particularly when you substitute rinsed and drained canned beans.

Tomato-Bluefish Aspic

When tomatoes are plentiful, it's wonderful to prepare this attractive hors d'oeuvre (or salad) with your own fresh tomato juice, but it's not in any way necessary. The fish may be omitted and minced cucumbers added, if you prefer a strictly vegetarian approach. Either way this is a cool and tasty summer something to spread on crackers.

Serves 4–6 as a salad, 8 as a cocktail accompaniment

- 4 cups fresh or canned tomato juice
- 1 small onion, peeled and finely chopped
- ¼ cup celery leaves, well washed and minced
- 1 tablespoon granulated sugar
- ¾ teaspoon salt
- 6 whole peppercorns
- 4 whole cloves
- 1 small bay leaf
- 3 tablespoons unflavored gelatin
- 1 tablespoon lemon juice (or more to taste)
- ⅓ cup plain low-fat yogurt
- 1 cup smoked bluefish (or any boned leftover cooked fish)
- ¼ cup finely chopped basil leaves
- ¼ cup finely chopped tender inside ribs of celery
- 2 scallions, each with 3 inches green top, finely minced
- 1 tablespoon minced fresh dill
- Crackers or Garlic Crusts (page 88)

Combine 3 cups of the tomato juice with the onion, celery leaves, sugar, and spices in a large saucepan. Bring the mixture to a boil, then reduce the heat, cover, and simmer for 15 minutes. Remove from the heat and strain into a large bowl.

Pour the gelatin over the remaining tomato juice, stir to mix well, and let stand for 3 minutes to soften, then dissolve in the hot tomato juice mixture. Add the lemon juice and yogurt and refrigerate until the mixture thickens slightly and begins to set. Fold in the fish, basil leaves, chopped celery, scallions, and dill. Rinse a 6-cup mold with cold water, shake out the excess, and spoon in the aspic. Refrigerate until thoroughly set. Unmold and serve as an hors d'oeuvre surrounded by crackers or Garlic Crusts, or as a salad on nicely arranged greens.

Spaghetti Squash with Leek Sauce, Lemon Shrimp, and Browned Pumpernickel Crumbs

- 4½ pounds medium-size spaghetti squash
- Olive oil
- Salt and pepper to taste

Wash squash, puncture the ends in several places, and bake in a preheated 325° F. oven for 1 hour (larger squash will take 15–20 minutes longer). Cool 15 minutes. Cut the squash in half, discard the seeds, and use two forks to toss and gently lift out the vegetable threads. Toss with the oil and salt and pepper to taste. Serve with Leek Sauce (recipe follows). Top with Lemon Shrimp (page 119) and Browned Pumpernickel Crumbs (page 119).

Leek Sauce

Very versatile. Those dark green discards, or leek tops, come into their own to form a puree that can also easily be expanded into a hot or cold soup.

Makes 2 cups

3 quarts leftover leek tops, well rinsed and cut into 2-inch lengths (or use whole leeks)
4 large cloves garlic, peeled and cut in half
Homemade Chicken Broth or Vegetable Stock (pages 186 or 184) or canned broth
Salt and freshly ground black pepper to taste
1 tablespoon fresh thyme leaves or 1 teaspoon dried

Place leeks and garlic in a 5-quart pot and cover with broth. Add salt and pepper and bring to a boil. Skim off and discard any froth, lower heat, add thyme, and simmer for 1 hour. Cool and puree.

Simmer puree until nicely thickened, but not dry. Refrigerate several days or freeze.

VARIATION

Prepare Leek Sauce as directed above. Stir in 2 cups each plain low-fat yogurt and skim milk. Chill well. To serve, ladle into bowls and top each with 1 tablespoon light cream, a sprinkle of nutmeg, and 1 teaspoon minced chives.

Lemon Shrimp

¾ pound medium-size shrimp, shelled and deveined
2 tablespoons olive oil
2 teaspoons grated lemon zest or 1 teaspoon commercially bottled lemon pepper
Salt (optional)

Blot the shrimp on paper towels. Heat the oil in a skillet and toss the shrimp over medium heat just until they are bright pink. Add the lemon zest (or pepper) and salt, if desired, and toss once more. Serve hot.

Browned Pumpernickel Crumbs

1½ cups soft pumpernickel crumbs
Olive oil

Toss crumbs in the oil over medium heat for 1 minute.

Scallion, White-Bean, and Pecan Pancakes

Whenever I need to enliven a menu with something quick and easy to put together, something everyone seems to enjoy, something inexpensive, nutritious, and out of the ordinary, I fall back on these sage-enhanced white-bean pancakes. The crunch of lightly browned scallion and coarsely chopped pecans makes them unique. I've included two variations that are equally pleasing.

Makes 8 pancakes

10 pencil-thin scallions, trimmed of roots and all but 2 inches of green top
2 tablespoons olive oil
1 cup coarsely chopped pecans
3 cups white kidney beans, cooked and well drained (or substitute well-drained canned beans)
2 tablespoons chopped fresh sage leaves or 1½ teaspoons dried
Salt and coarsely ground black pepper to taste
Pinch each ground nutmeg and cayenne pepper

Cut the scallions into pieces ½ inch long. Heat 1 tablespoon oil in a small non-stick skillet, and sauté the scallions over medium heat until lightly browned, stirring constantly. Add the pecans to the pan and stir over medium heat for 1 minute.

Use a potato masher or fork to coarsely mash the beans and transfer them to a deep dish. Stir in the scallions, nuts, and seasonings. Heat the remaining oil in a large non-stick skillet, form the bean mixture into 3-inch pancakes, and brown on both sides, turning once. Serve hot.

VARIATIONS

Follow directions for Scallion, White-Bean, and Pecan Pancakes but substitute well-drained pinto beans for the white beans and marjoram for the sage. Add ½ teaspoon grated orange zest, if you like.

Follow directions for Scallion, White-Bean, and Pecan Pancakes but substitute well-drained black beans for the white beans, cilantro for the sage, and walnuts for the pecans.

Red Wine and Cherry Soup in Cantaloupe Shells

Whatever the season, this is one of my favorite desserts. The color is magnificent, the flavor and icy consistency divine. Enjoy the soup, then eat the bowl.

Serves 6

3 small ripe cantaloupes
1 pound sweet cherries, pitted
½ cup granulated sugar
2 cups rich, full-bodied red wine
Half-stick cinnamon

Cut melons in half crosswise, scoop out and discard seeds and pith, and cut a thin slice from the bottoms to keep them from tipping. You may peel the melon shells or not, as you please. Scoop out each melon half leaving ½-inch-thick walls; reserve the melon flesh. Chill well.

Meanwhile, bring half the cherries to a boil with the sugar, wine, and cinnamon, then lower the heat and simmer for 10 minutes. Taste the liquid. If it seems sour, add additional sugar to taste. Remove the cinnamon. Mix together the wine and cherry mixture, the fresh cherries, and the melon scoopings, and place in the freezer. When quite slushy, puree the mixture in a food processor or blender, then return to freezer until 10–15 minutes before serving. Remove the puree from the freezer and refrigerate for a few minutes. Quickly fill the chilled melon shells and serve immediately in small bowls. A small dollop of whipped cream topped with a cherry makes the dessert even more appealing.

Red-Flannel Hash with Dash

MENU

Eggplant–White Bean Soup

Red-Flannel Hash with Dash

Batter-Dipped Baby 'Chokes

Green-Tomato Brown Betty

SUGGESTIONS

Prepare the soup (but not the meatballs) and refrigerate overnight. Continue the last two steps of the recipe several hours prior to serving.

Mix the hash, chill for 24 hours, then brown on both sides just prior to serving.

The cooked artichokes also reheat quite well when handled carefully.

The zesty ingredients in Green-Tomato Brown Betty actually mellow when the dessert is chilled overnight and reheated.

Eggplant–White Bean Soup

Imagine on a blustery day after a long, brisk walk that there is waiting for you a steamy thick soup fortified with succulent chunks of eggplant, white beans, tomatoes, tiny meatballs, and herbs, all topped off with crisp Garlic Crusts and minced chives. This solace can be yours if you take the care to prepare this soup before you begin your constitutional.

The soup is also excellent without the meatballs if you prefer not to include meat.

Serves 6–8

1   medium-size eggplant
    Salt
4   tablespoons vegetable oil
1   large onion, peeled and coarsely
      chopped
1   large clove garlic, peeled and
      minced
4   medium-size tomatoes, peeled,
      seeded, and coarsely chopped
1   bay leaf, crumbled
    Pinch marjoram
    A few threads of saffron
8   cups Rich Beef Broth (page 187)
    Freshly ground black pepper
⅓   pound ground veal
1   medium-size onion, peeled and
      finely chopped
⅛   teaspoon nutmeg
    Pinch dried oregano
    All-purpose or bran flour
1   cup cooked white beans
    Garlic Crusts (page 88)
2   tablespoons minced fresh chives

Peel the eggplant and cut it into ¾-inch cubes. Arrange in a single layer on paper towels, sprinkle lightly with salt, and set aside for 10 minutes to drain. Blot dry between several thicknesses of paper towel.

In a large saucepan, heat the oil and brown the eggplant cubes over medium-low heat for 15 minutes, stirring occasionally. Add the chopped large onion, garlic, tomatoes, bay leaf, marjoram, and saffron to the pan, and cook over low heat for 15 minutes, stirring occasionally. Add the broth, season with salt and pepper to taste and simmer the soup, covered, for 40 minutes more.

If you are including them, now is the time to prepare the meatballs. Mix together the veal, the chopped medium onion, nutmeg, oregano, and salt and pepper to taste. Shape the mixture into tiny meatballs, roll lightly in flour, and set aside.

Puree half the broth and vegetables, stir this puree back into the vegetables, bring the soup to a boil, drop in the meatballs, and add the cooked beans; then allow the soup to boil gently for 15 minutes, or until the meatballs are cooked. Add a little broth if the soup becomes too thick. Serve hot, topped with Garlic Crusts and minced chives.

Red-Flannel Hash with Dash

A flash of fresh jalapeño pepper, a dash of dill, and the substitution of yams for paler potatoes transforms this New England favorite.

Serves 6

1 cup coarsely chopped lean, cooked corned beef
1 medium-size onion, peeled and coarsely chopped
4 medium-size beets, cooked, peeled, and grated
2 large yams, cooked, peeled, and coarsely chopped
2 tablespoons plain low-fat yogurt
¼ cup minced fresh dill
1 jalapeño pepper, seeded and deveined (optional)
3 tablespoons vegetable oil

Thoroughly mix the beef, onion, beets, and yams. Stir in the yogurt and dill. Mince the jalapeño pepper, if used. Heat 2 tablespoons of the oil in a large non-stick skillet and sauté the pepper for 1 minute. Add the hash, flatten with a spatula, and cook over medium heat for 15–20 minutes, or until crusty brown on both sides, carefully turning once (so as not to break it) and adding a little more oil if necessary. To slip the hash out in one piece, set a serving plate upside down over the skillet, and flip both skillet and plate over quickly (take care to first blot up any excess oil with paper towels so you won't burn yourself). Cut into 6 wedges and serve hot with Batter-Dipped Baby 'Chokes (recipe follows).

Batter-Dipped Baby 'Chokes

Small artichokes are those that grow lower on the stalk. They are difficult to find, but when you do come across them, don't let them get away. You'll have a treat in store. If they are unavailable, substitute cooked and cleaned artichokes cut in quarters. The cornmeal batter lends an additional crunch.

Serves 6

24 small artichokes, trimmed of stems and dark outer leaves
Juice of 1 lemon
1 recipe Cornmeal Batter (recipe follows)
Vegetable oil

Cut away and discard the tops of the artichokes, leaving each bottom with about 1 inch of leaf above it. As they are cut, drop the bottoms into water to cover, to which has been added the juice of 1 lemon. Bring the water to a boil, then lower the heat, and simmer the artichokes for about 10 minutes, or until not quite tender. Drain well.

Arrange the artichokes, cut-side down, on an absorbent towel, pressing each down gently with the heel of your hand to spread and flatten them and remove any excess moisture. This is very important. The flat shape allows maximum fast cooking, and the elimination of all cooking moisture prevents dangerous splattering.

Line a cookie sheet with paper towels. Pick up the artichokes carefully without altering their shape (tongs work well here), dip in the Cornmeal Batter, and fry several at a time in hot oil. (Keep a lid handy to cover briefly just in case the oil splatters.) Drain on the cookie sheet. If necessary to prepare ahead, carefully remove the paper and replace the artichokes on the cookie sheet without breaking their crusts and reheat in a moderate oven for 3 or 4 minutes. Serve hot.

Cornmeal Batter

½ cup (4 ounces) egg substitute
    equivalent to 2 eggs
½ cup low-fat milk
1⅓ cups cornmeal
2 teaspoons baking powder
    Salt and pepper to taste
2 tablespoons minced parsley

Beat together the egg substitute and milk. Sift together the cornmeal, baking powder, salt and pepper and quickly mix into the egg-milk mixture. Stir in the parsley. Do not overmix.

Green-Tomato Brown Betty

Please don't sneer at a dessert made from green tomatoes. Remember, tomatoes are our fruitiest vegetable, and the green ones have much the same flavor, when cooked, of tart green apples. Select tomatoes that are beginning to lighten and turn white on the bottoms. The dark green ones will be bitter. Approach this tasty dessert without prejudice, and you're sure to love it.

Granny Smith apples substitute beautifully when green tomatoes are not in season.

Serves 6

5 large green tomatoes, seeded and
    chopped
1 teaspoon ground cinnamon
2 teaspoons lemon zest (the thin
    outer lemon skin without any
    of the bitter white underskin)
¼ teaspoon each ground nutmeg
    and cloves
2 tablespoons liquid margarine
3 tablespoons vegetable oil
1 cup light brown sugar
2 cups fine bread crumbs
2 tablespoons lemon juice
    Commercially prepared vanilla
    ice milk (optional)

In a heavy saucepan, simmer the tomatoes, cinnamon, lemon zest, nutmeg, and cloves in 1 tablespoon each liquid margarine and cooking oil for 5 minutes, stirring continuously to prevent browning. Add the sugar and continue stirring for 10 minutes over low heat.

Preheat the oven to 350° F.

Toss the bread crumbs with 1 tablespoon liquid margarine and 2 tablespoons of the oil until all are well coated. Use the remaining tablespoon of margarine to grease an 8-inch soufflé or glass baking dish. Firmly press one third of the crumbs into the bottom of dish, then carefully spread half the tomato mixture over them. Sprinkle with 1 tablespoon lemon juice and top with another third of the crumbs. Spread with the remaining tomato mixture, sprinkle with the remaining lemon juice, and top with the remaining crumbs.

Cover the dish with foil and bake for 40 minutes. Raise the oven temperature to 400° F., uncover the dish, and bake 10 minutes more or until the top is nicely browned. Serve warm with ice milk, if desired.

A Dinner with Italian Overtones

MENU

Grilled Red Onions and Peppers in Olive Oil and Balsamic Vinegar

Osso Buco with Gremolata

Galantine of Eggplant

Fruit Mincemeat

SUGGESTIONS

The onions and peppers may be prepared 4 or 5 days before you need them.

The Osso Buco and Galantine of Eggplant reheat well, and so may be cooked one day early (the eggplant actually slices more evenly when chilled).

Grilled Red Onions and Peppers in Olive Oil and Balsamic Vinegar

What's sweet and sour and red all over? These are! Dress up cold meat, poultry, or fish, or, for that matter, any picnic platter with these pretty vegetables. This recipe fills three large jars, which may seem like a lot, but they'll be empty before you know it. The quantity can easily be halved.

Makes 3 quarts

6 large sweet red onions, peeled and cut in half vertically
5 large sweet red peppers, halved vertically with seeds, pulp, and veins discarded
  Freshly ground black pepper
1 cup olive oil
1 cup balsamic vinegar

Arrange the onion halves, cut sides up, over medium-hot coals, cover, and grill for 15 minutes. Arrange the pepper halves, cut sides up, over the coals. Turn the onion halves over and grill all of the vegetables 10–15 minutes more. They should still have a bit of crunch. Cut the vegetables in 1½-inch (lengthwise) strips and fill quart jars with them. Sprinkle with black pepper and pour ¼ cup olive oil and ¼ cup vinegar into each jar. Cover and shake the jars to distribute the seasonings. Refrigerate until needed (up to 4 or 5 days), shaking the jars once a day. Serve at room temperature.

VARIATION

For indoor cooking, cut the vegetables as directed, arrange on baking sheets, cut sides up, and dribble a little olive oil over each. Broil under your indoor broiler until not quite done.

Osso Buco with Gremolata

There are times when nothing but meat will satisfy. When that urge is upon you, choose veal. And not just veal, but the most succulent meat of all, perfectly prepared veal shanks rich with marrow. They are child's play to prepare, but they must cook long and slow. Set them simmering the evening before you plan to serve them. They reheat gorgeously; one of those dishes that are even better the second day. And do choose small pieces. The flavor will be there in the sauce just waiting to be scooped up by bread and there's no need to have huge amounts of the meat. Incidentally, Gremolata is a must here. Your preference, either parsley, coriander, or basil.

Serves 6

  3 tablespoons olive oil
  6 3-inch-thick veal marrowbones for Osso Buco (pieces of meaty shanks of young veal with marrow intact), rinsed and dried
  2 cloves garlic, peeled and minced
  2 medium-size carrots, scraped and grated
  2 large onions, peeled and coarsely chopped
  4 ribs celery, coarsely chopped
  ¼ teaspoon each dried rosemary and powdered sage
  2 cups white wine
  2 tablespoons tomato paste
    Light beef, veal, or chicken broth
  1 recipe Gremolata (recipe follows)

In a large, heavy stew pot, heat the oil and brown the shanks on all sides, then turn them upright so the marrow won't spill out. Push the bones to one side and sauté the garlic 1 minute in the oil in the pan. Distribute the carrots, onions, celery, rosemary, and sage over the marrowbones. Cover and simmer for 15 minutes. Mix the wine with the tomato paste and pour it over the shanks and vegetables. Add enough water or broth (or combination of both) to not quite cover. Cover the pot and simmer for 1½ hours, adding a little additional liquid if necessary to keep the level about halfway up the sides of the meat pieces. The recipe can be brought to this point and successfully continued hours or even a day later. Return to room temperature before continuing.

Continue simmering. The meat should be very tender, almost, but not quite, ready to fall apart. If the meat is still chewy, cover and simmer until it is tender.

To serve, place one of the hot, meaty marrowbones upright on each of 6 good-size plates next to a slice of hot Gallantine of Eggplant (page 128). Pass the Gremolata separately.

Gremolata

I'm not one of those cooks who sprinkles garlic on everything but ice cream, but even I cannot resist the blaze of fresh garlic, lemon zest, and fresh herbs partnered with veal and eggplant. Gremolata is usually added to Osso Buco at table, as it is here, to allow guests the option of merely tasting or really indulging.

Makes about 1⅓ cups

  6 large lemons
  1½ cups finely chopped parsley, coriander, or basil
10–12 medium-size cloves garlic, peeled and minced

Use a grater or swivel-type vegetable peeler to remove the thin yellow skins or zest from the lemons. Mince the zest and mix it with the remaining ingredients. Cover and refrigerate for up to 1 hour prior to serving.

VARIATION

As very nearly everyone knows, classic Gremolata is prepared with parsley. However, for a change of pace, zesty coriander or basil adds zip.

NOTE

Parsley, coriander, and basil are easily chopped in a conventional food processor. Lemon zest and garlic are best finely minced in a mini-processor. If all ingredients are processed together, the herbs will practically disintegrate before the firmer lemon zest is the correct consistency.

Galantine of Eggplant

Well, no. This isn't actually a galantine. What it is really is an eggplant, stuffed in an interesting way, then simmered in sauce. I named it after the original idea I had for the dish, which involved meat. When I first tested this version, I had cut away the ends and the center, opened the eggplant up, filled it, and then rerolled it, galantinelike, only to realize that nature had already provided the perfect container: the hollowed-out vegetable itself.

This is very Italian, very hearty. It contains one egg and two tablespoons of grated Parmesan per eggplant, enough to serve 2–3. A reasonable amount, it seems to me. However, if your goal is a virtually fat-free diet, substitute egg beaters and low-fat cheese.

Serves 6

- 2 large eggplants
- 1 large onion, peeled and finely chopped
- ¼ teaspoon each thyme leaves and marjoram
- 2 tablespoons light olive oil
- 2 eggs (or ½ cup egg substitute)
- 1½ cups soft or custardy bean curd (firm will do in a pinch)
- 2 tablespoons grated Parmesan
- 2 tablespoons bread crumbs
  Salt and freshly ground black pepper to taste
- 1½–2 quarts Fresh and Easy Tomato Sauce (page 180)
  Finely chopped parsley

Cut off 2 inches from the stem end of each eggplant and set aside. Cut a thin sliver from the bottom end of each to help it stand up. Using a small sharp knife and a teaspoon, alternately cut away and scoop out the flesh from the two eggplants until you are left with two intact shells with walls about ½-inch thick. Take care not to scrape the shells too thin or puncture them.

Finely chop the eggplant pulp, add the onion and seasonings, and sauté in hot oil until the onion is translucent. Cool slightly and mix in the egg or egg substitute, bean curd, cheese, bread crumbs, and salt and pepper. Chill the mixture for at least 1 hour. Fill the eggplant shells with the mixture and cover with the reserved stem ends held in place with a few wooden toothpicks. Wrap each eggplant in cheesecloth tied at the top, and set each in a narrow pot (the top and bottom of a large double boiler, for example), so that they will not fall over. Thin the tomato sauce with 1 cup water and pour it into the pot to the point just beneath where the tops of the eggplants are attached. If the vegetables seem in danger of tipping over, arrange a rope of crumpled aluminum foil around them. Cover the tops of the double boiler tightly with foil so that steam cannot escape, and simmer over low heat for 1 to 1½ hours, or until the filling is set.

Remove the eggplants carefully to a platter, and let them cool to room temperature. Meanwhile, reduce the sauce if necessary to thicken it nicely. To serve, use an electric knife (or a very sharp single-bladed one) to cut each eggplant crosswise into round, 1-inch-thick slices. The centers should still be warm. Spoon a little piping hot sauce around the edges, sprinkle the eggplant slices with parsley, and serve.

Fruit Mincemeat

If anything, pure fruit mincemeat is fresher-tasting, more delectable than the old-fashioned variety that was made with beef and suet. You'll never again be satisfied with commercial meatless mincemeat once you've savored this. And there's no cooking until it's baked with the pie.

Makes 5–6 cups

- 3 Macintosh apples, peeled, cored, and coarsely chopped
- ⅓ cup finely chopped toasted almonds
- ¼ cup candied orange peel (substitute additional orange marmalade if candied peel is not available)
- ¼ cup orange marmalade (with any large pieces coarsely chopped)
- ⅓ cup dark raisins
- ⅓ cup golden raisins
- ½ teaspoon each ground cinnamon, allspice, and salt
- ¼ teaspoon each ground cloves and nutmeg
- 1½ cups granulated sugar
- ¼ cup lemon juice
- 2 tablespoons sherry
- 1 Three-Grain Pie Crust (page 43)

Mix all ingredients and seal in jars. Refrigerate 24 hours, turning the jars several times. The mincemeat will keep, refrigerated, for at least a week.

VARIATIONS

Fruit Mince Meat Relish

Add 1 tablespoon balsamic (or other mild) vinegar to the mincemeat prior to chilling it. Serve with poultry.

Boil 2 cups Fruit Mincemeat Relish with 1 pound shelled shrimp until shrimp are bright pink. Spoon over cooked rice. Serves 4.

Mostly Vegetable Lasagne Dinner

MENU

Tzatziki

Creamy Vegetable Lasagne

Fried Celeriac Petals

Fruit Medley

SUGGESTIONS

   Whip up the Tzatziki 24 hours early, but stir in 2 tablespoons plain low-fat yogurt just prior to serving to thicken the marinade somewhat.

Tzatziki

At only 80 calories per serving, you may want to double the recipe and save some for snack time.

Serves 6

2 large cucumbers, peeled and seeded
1 recipe Yogurt Cheese (page 47)
2 teaspoons each lemon juice and olive oil (omit these if you've already added them to the cheese)
  Salt and freshly ground black pepper to taste
6–8 small mint leaves (if available and if you like mint)

Thinly slice the cucumbers and spread them on paper towels to drain. Pat dry with additional towels. Thoroughly mix the cheese, lemon juice, olive oil, salt, and pepper and as many finely chopped mint leaves as suits your taste. Toss with the cucumbers. Serve cold.

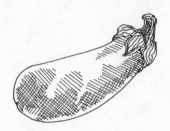

Creamy Vegetable Lasagne

There's something so satisfying about a layered pasta dish. It lends itself to an infinite number of variations and gives you the opportunity to nestle your favorite ingredients between delicate sheets of noodles.

This is a more healthful version of this Italian specialty. It is unique in that it uses low-fat products—ricotta, milk, yogurt, mozzarella, broiled vegetables, and just a touch of white, rather than red, meat. (The meat is optional, if a meatless version is desirable.) This new approach might just be the excuse (if you need one) for treating yourself and every one else to this outstanding, mostly vegetable treat. As is true in many one-dish meals, there are a few recipes within the major one. I always whip up the sauce, the vegetables, and the meatballs a day or two in advance to alleviate last-minute anxiety. Leave out the meatballs to reduce the work and cut down on the cholesterol. Substitute a good-grade bottled sauce for the Fresh and Easy Tomato Sauce.

There is no way to accurately predict how many this will serve. Presented with only a simple salad, bread, wine, and fruit, I've witnessed five healthy appetites very nearly demolish a quantity that I would normally consider enough to satisfy eight.

And, by the way, cooking time here may also fluctuate. The edges of the lasagna do firm up more quickly than the center. To my mind, optimum flavor and texture are reached when the center is still soft and creamy, even a little soupy. I deal with this by allowing the outside pieces to firm somewhat and then serve these to those who prefer them leaving the underdone center to myself and anyone else who prefers it. Return the unserved portion to the oven until seconds are called for. It works out just fine.

If you have prepared the dish early and refrigerated it, remove it 45 minutes prior to baking, and then bake it at 325° F. for 30 minutes and raise the heat to 375° F. for 15–20 minutes more. Use a fork to carefully separate the ingredients about 3 inches away from the side of the dish so that you can ascertain if the ricotta is beginning to set. Rearrange the ingredients to cover up the hole.

You may want to keep testing for doneness. If the top is a little pale, slide it under the broiler just a few minutes more to give it a nice, golden color.

Serves 6 to 8

TO PREPARE THE NOODLES AND SAUCE

15–18 cooked green eggless lasagne noodles (the number will depend on the size of the dish). Don't forget to keep the noodles moist and layered between sheets of plastic wrap if you aren't using them right away.
1 recipe Fresh and Easy Tomato Sauce (page 180) or 3 cups good-grade commercial tomato sauce
2 cups sliced mushrooms
1 jalapeño pepper
  Light olive oil
2 teaspoons lemon juice
¾ cup sweet basil, coarsely chopped

TO PREPARE THE VEGETABLES

2 medium to large eggplants, cut lengthwise into 1-inch-thick slices (with the skin)
  Salt (optional)
4 tablespoons light olive oil
1 large red pepper
1 large yellow pepper
3 large green peppers

TO PREPARE THE NOODLES AND SAUCE

Prepare the noodles. If you are making your own tomato sauce, prepare it now according to the recipe.

If you are using bottled sauce, place it in a large saucepot to simmer. In a separate pan, sauté the mushroom slices and the jalapeño pepper in a little oil until the mushrooms are not quite soft. Sprinkle immediately with lemon juice and stir into the sauce along with the basil; continue simmering until the sauce thickens. (Commercially bottled sauce will begin at a thick consistency and might need thinning with a little water or tomato juice.) Take a sip every once in a while to determine whether it is spicy enough. When it is to your taste, remove the jalapeño. Keep the sauce warm and continue.

TO PREPARE THE VEGETABLES

Sprinkle the eggplant slices lightly with salt and arrange between paper towels for 10 minutes. Brush the slices with olive oil and broil until brown on both sides. Broil the red, yellow, and green peppers as directed on page 214, rinse away any remaining seeds, and drain on paper towels. Set the vegetables aside.

TO PREPARE THE MEATBALLS

1 slice whole wheat bread
2 tablespoons skim milk
1 pound ground, uncooked, skinless
   turkey breast
¼ cup egg substitute
   Nutmeg
   Salt
   Garlic
2 tablespoons light olive oil

TO ASSEMBLE THE DISH

¼ cup plain low-fat yogurt
1 large clove garlic, peeled and
   minced
¼ teaspoon each salt and dried
   thyme leaves
3 cups low-fat ricotta
¾ cup (6 ounces) egg substitute
   equivalent to 6 eggs
   Olive or vegetable oil
¾ cup grated Parmesan
1 cup low-fat mozzarella, cut into
   ¼-inch cubes, and ¾ cup
   coarsely grated
2 cups White Sauce (recipe follows)
   Sprinkle of nutmeg
   Salt to taste

WHITE SAUCE

1½ tablespoons margarine
 2 tablespoons all-purpose flour
 2 cups cold skim milk
    Salt and white pepper to taste

TO PREPARE THE MEATBALLS

Crumble the bread slices and soak in milk for a few minutes. Drain off any excess milk and mix the moist crumbs with the meat, egg substitute, and the nutmeg, salt, and garlic. Form into 1-inch balls. Handle the mixture gently and do not overwork it. Fry the meatballs in 2 tablespoons oil until lightly browned on all sides. Drain on paper towels.

TO ASSEMBLE THE DISH

Mix the yogurt, garlic, salt, thyme, ricotta, and ¼ cup egg substitute, and set aside.

Use olive or vegetable oil to season a rectangular baking dish. Arrange a layer of the noodles so that they overlap, with the ends turning up the side of the dish. Spread with half of the tomato sauce, and then with half the ricotta mixture. Try not to mix the sauce and cheese mixture. Sprinkle with 2 tablespoons Parmesan and the mozzarella cubes. Top with another layer of noodles.

Preheat the oven to 325° F.

Spread the remaining ricotta mixture over the noodles. Cut the egg-plant and peppers into 1-inch squares (kitchen scissors are good for this), and arrange the vegetable pieces evenly over the cheese. Spread the remaining tomato sauce over all and sprinkle with 2 tablespoons Parmesan. Top with a final layer of noodles.

Beat the White Sauce with the remaining ½ cup egg substitute and season with nutmeg and salt, if desired. Spread this over the noodles and sprinkle with the grated mozzarella. Arrange the meatballs neatly in rows, pressing each down slightly. Sprinkle with 2 tablespoons Parmesan and bake at 325°F. for 30 minutes; raise the heat to 375° F. for 10 to 20 minutes more or until hot, bubbling, and lightly browned. Do not overcook. Let set slightly before cutting into serving sizes.

WHITE SAUCE

Melt the margarine in a small, heavy sauce pan. Stir in the flour, using the back of the spoon to smooth out any lumps. Remove the pan from the heat, add a little of the milk, and press out most of the lumps. Add the remaining milk and stir over medium heat, pressing out any remaining lumps of flour, until the sauce boils and thickens. Season with salt and pepper, if desired.

Fried Celeriac Petals

Makes 30 thin petallike slices

1 pound celeriac, peeled and trimmed to a smooth round or oval shape with no jagged edges
Salt
Juice of ½ lemon
1 egg white, lightly beaten
Cornstarch
Oil for frying
Sprinkle each of cayenne pepper and coarse salt

Thinly slice the celeriac and plunge into boiling, salted water into which has been squeezed the lemon juice. Immediately remove the pot from the heat, drain the celeriac, and cover with cold water. Drain well in a colander, then dry the slices with a kitchen towel.

In a large bowl, toss the slices with the egg white. Dust a double-thick paper towel lightly with sifted cornstarch. Lay the most perfect celeriac slices out on the cornstarch and very lightly dust the tops with additional sifted cornstarch.

Pour 2 inches of oil into a large skillet and heat to very hot. Shake the excess cornstarch from each slice of celeriac; test the heat of the oil by slipping in one slice; bubbles should immediately and actively surround it. Fry the slices, a few at a time, and keep them warm in a low oven. Sprinkle with a little cayenne and salt just prior to serving hot.

Fruit Medley

¾ cup plain low-fat yogurt
2 tablespoons low-fat sour cream
2 tablespoons maple syrup
⅛ teaspoon ground nutmeg
1 8-ounce can mandarin orange sections
1 banana, peeled
1 tablespoon fresh lime juice
1 cup purple grapes, halved and seeds removed
2 tablespoons slivered almonds, toasted

Thoroughly mix the yogurt, sour cream, maple syrup, and nutmeg. Chill the sauce well. Drain the orange sections. Cut the banana in ½-inch-thick diagonal slices and toss them with the lime juice. Combine all of the fruits and chill until serving time.

To serve, divide the fruit mixture among 6 small compotes or other small dessert dishes. Top each with sauce and sprinkle with almonds.

Winter

A Popular Dinner of Fried and Stuffed Potato Skins

MENU

Crunchy Fried Sweet-Potato Skins with Chicken Strips and Sautéed Vegetables

Cauliflower Salad in Creamy Dijon Dressing

Cranberry Ice with Meringue

SUGGESTIONS

The day before you intend to serve them, bake the sweet potatoes and carefully remove the thin outer skins as directed in the recipe.

Blanch and marinate the cauliflower several days early. Stir twice daily.

Prepare the dessert 48 hours prior to serving.

Crunchy Fried Sweet-Potato Skins with Chicken Strips and Sautéed Vegetables

Here, the original outside skins are removed and replaced with new ones that are tender, crisp, and more tasty. This is accomplished by brushing the whole baked sweet potato with egg white, rolling it in cornmeal, and frying it. Next, we scoop out some of the potato and replace it with a medley of choice tidbits: sautéed curried chicken strips, whole fried shallots, and green peppers. The result is something far beyond mere stuffed potatoes. Delicious. Try it.

Serves 6

6 large sweet potatoes
3 egg whites
2 cups cornmeal
  Vegetable oil for frying
12 shallots, peeled
½ pound skinless boned chicken breast
1 teaspoon curry powder
2 large green peppers, with seeds and pith removed
1 tablespoon heavy cream
6 thin slices of orange, cut in quarters

Preheat the oven to 350° F.

Bake the sweet potatoes until they are tender (at least 1 hour), place in a paper bag, and cool them 20 minutes. Carefully remove and discard the thin, papery brown outer skin. Brush all the sweet potatoes with 2 egg whites beaten with 1½ tablespoons water. Roll them in cornmeal and fry them in 1 inch of hot oil, turning them until they are brown on all sides. Set aside.

Discard the oil and cornmeal left in the pan and wipe the pan with a paper towel. Heat a tablespoon oil and fry the shallots for about 5 minutes, remove from the pan, and set aside. Trim off and discard any fat and gristle on the chicken, rub it with curry powder, and cut the breast into strips ¼ inch thick by 2 inches long by ¼ inch wide. Lightly beat the remaining egg white and dip the chicken strips first in it and then in the cornmeal. Sauté until golden brown on all sides. Set aside on paper towels to drain. Cut the peppers into ½-inch-wide strips, sauté for 1 minute, and set aside on paper towels to drain.

Cut the sweet potatoes in half lengthwise, and carefully scoop out the potato flesh to leave ½-inch-thick shells. Reserve the scooped out potato for another use.

Fill the sweet potato shells with equal amounts of shallots, chicken, and peppers. If necessary, reheat at 350° F. Garnish with orange slices and serve immediately.

Cauliflower Salad in Creamy Dijon Dressing

Snowy blanched cauliflower florets marinated in oil and vinegar are then tossed along with avocado in a creamy mustard dressing. Very piquant.

Serves 6

1 large head cauliflower
2 cloves garlic, peeled and crushed
2 tablespoons lemon juice
2 tablespoons olive oil
½ teaspoon salt
1 tablespoon light cream
1 tablespoon Dijon mustard
½ teaspoon granulated sugar (optional)
⅓ cup plain low-fat yogurt
½ avocado, peeled and cut into ½-inch cubes

Break medium-size florets from the cauliflower and plunge them in boiling water for 5 minutes, drain well in a colander, and dry with paper towels.

Meanwhile, mix the garlic, lemon juice, olive oil, and salt. Toss this marinade with the warm cauliflower and let it stand for at least an hour (or until ready to serve), tossing several times.

Thoroughly mix the cream, mustard, and sugar, if used, then stir in the yogurt gently so as not to break down the creamy texture. Toss this dressing with the cauliflower and avocado and serve at once.

Cranberry Ice with Meringue

When you've promised yourself you won't overindulge during the holidays, enjoy this dessert which is not only nutritious and low in fat, but festive as well.

Serves 6

3 large seedless oranges
2 apples, cored
2 cups fresh cranberries
¼ cup plain low-fat yogurt
⅓ cup honey
⅛ teaspoon each nutmeg and allspice
3 egg whites
½ cup granulated sugar
Pinch of cream of tartar

Cut the oranges in half, cutting zigzag rather than on a straight line. Separate and scoop out the pulp. When set upright, the shells will form small baskets with pointed edges (see illustration, page 65).

Puree the orange pulp along with the apples, cranberries, yogurt, honey, and spices. Freeze this puree until it is mushy, then stir with a fork and spoon it into the orange shells. Freeze until solid.

Beat the egg whites until they are foamy and gradually beat in the sugar and cream of tartar until the meringue no longer feels gritty when a little is rubbed between thumb and forefinger (about 5 minutes).

Top each frozen orange half with meringue, making sure that it touches the sides of the oranges to seal them all around. Bake at 400° F. until lightly browned. Serve immediately.

A Taste of India

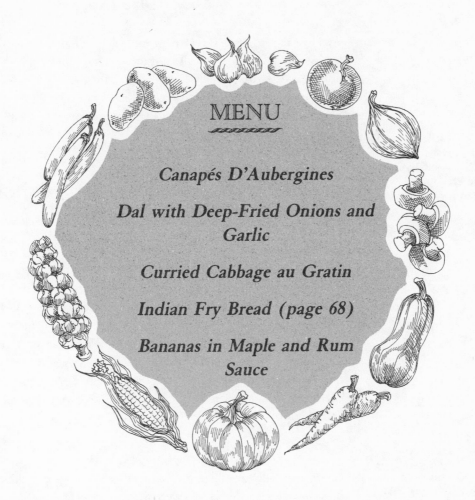

MENU

Canapés D'Aubergines

Dal with Deep-Fried Onions and Garlic

Curried Cabbage au Gratin

Indian Fry Bread (page 68)

Bananas in Maple and Rum Sauce

SUGGESTIONS

Prepare the dal 1 to 3 hours in advance, but do not chill.
Shred the cabbage and cook it in the broth. Refrigerate. Bake just prior to serving.

Canapés D'Aubergines

Serves 6

1 long, narrow Japanese eggplant, peeled and cut into 30 very thin slices
  Salt
  Toast rounds
1 recipe Basic Duxelles (page 183)
  Low-fat mayonnaise
  Olive oil, or a combination olive oil and vegetable oil
  Finely grated Parmesan or low-fat cheese

Arrange the eggplant slices on paper towels without letting them overlap. Sprinkle lightly with salt, and drain for 10 minutes. Blot dry (most of the salt will disappear). Meanwhile, cut the toast rounds the same size and number as the eggplant slices. Mix the duxelles with just enough mayonnaise to bind (don't let this get too moist) and spread it over the rounds.

Preheat the broiler.

Dip the eggplant slices into the oil, place over the duxelles mixture, and top with a light sprinkle of grated cheese. Broil until the cheese bubbles and lightly browns. Serve immediately.

Dal with Deep-Fried Onions and Garlic

This is the Hindi name given any legume, seed, or grain that is split into two halves. Dals come in a seemingly endless variety, each with its unique taste and texture. Rich in protein and probably the most popular food in India, they lend themselves to a host of dishes, from colorful soups and stews to desserts. This recipe is fairly typical, except that it is topped with highly flavored, crisp enhancements. Serve the Dal in a circle around a small mound of rice garnished with the onions, garlic, and daikon.

Serves 6

1 cup hulled and split yellow mung beans (mung dal)
½ teaspoon each ground turmeric and cardamom
1 teaspoon ground coriander seeds
  Minced red chilies to taste
1 bay leaf
  Salt to taste
3 tablespoons vegetable oil
3 medium-size onions, peeled, cut into thin slices, and separated into rings
12 cloves garlic, peeled and minced
1 cup peeled and thinly sliced daikon or small turnip
4½ cups hot cooked rice
  Indian Fry Bread (page 68)

Check carefully and discard any small stones or grit in the beans. Put them in a saucepan, cover with 6 cups water, turmeric, cardamom, coriander, chilies, and bay leaf, and simmer 25–30 minutes, or until tender. Beat with a wire whisk until fairly smooth, then stir in the salt.

Heat the oil in a large, non-stick skillet, and fry the onions and garlic until crisp and golden. Add a little more oil if necessary, and fry the daikon or turnip slices while you heat the rice and Dal. Arrange on plates as directed above. Top with the onions, garlic, and daikon, and serve immediately with Indian Fry Bread. Pass more Dal and rice and then bread to scoop them up with.

Curried Cabbage au Gratin

Serves 6

1 large head cabbage
3 cups beef broth
3 large cloves garlic, peeled and crushed
1 tablespoon curry powder (or to taste)
Pinch of sugar
1 tablespoon cornstarch
1 large bay leaf
½ cup plain low-fat yogurt
1 cup soft bean curd
¼ cup grated low-fat cheese
2 tablespoons wheat germ

Remove and discard the core of the cabbage along with any tough outer leaves or hard, thick veins. Cut the remaining leaves into thin shreds. Whirl 1 cup of broth, the garlic, curry powder, sugar, and cornstarch until smooth. Transfer to a large skillet, add the cabbage, the remaining broth, and the bay leaf and cook over medium heat, stirring continuously until the sauce thickens.

Preheat the oven to 350° F.

Stir the yogurt into the cabbage and transfer the mixture to an oiled dish. Discard the bay leaf. Crumble the bean curd over the cabbage, sprinkle first with the cheese, and then the wheat germ. Bake for 15 minutes. Serve hot.

Bananas in Maple and Rum Sauce

Serves 6

¾ cup maple syrup
½ cup dark rum
2 teaspoons margarine
⅛ teaspoon each ground nutmeg and cardamom
6 bananas
2 tablespoons fresh lime juice
6–12 tablespoons vanilla frozen yogurt (optional)

Bring the maple syrup, rum, margarine, and the spices to a full boil. Immediately lower the heat and cook at a low boil until the sauce is about the thickness of heavy cream.

Peel the bananas, cut on the diagonal into ¾-inch-thick slices, and toss with lime juice. Add the banana slices to the sauce and stir over medium-low heat for 2 to 3 minutes, or until heated through and nicely coated. Serve warm with dollops of frozen yogurt.

A Cozy Vegetarian Dinner

MENU

Welsh Potato-Onion Cake

White Turnips (and Turnip Greens) with Orange Sauce

Steamed Brussels Sprouts with Chestnuts and Scallions

Wheated Cloverleaf Rolls

Mulled Apple Slices

SUGGESTIONS

Cook, peel, and chop the chestnuts 2 days before your dinner. Or use canned.

Trim the Brussels sprouts and slice the turnips 5 to 6 hours prior to cooking and serving.

Prepare the rolls and bake until very lightly browned. Cool and freeze in the pan. Heat in a 350° F. oven until golden brown.

Welsh Potato-Onion Cake

Teisen nionod, or onion cake, lends a Welsh flavor to even a simple meal. Except for the fact that a good-quality oil is used rather than butter, and that the cake is baked in a heavy earthenware baking dish roughly the size and depth of a cake pan, this could almost double for *pommes boulangere.*

Serves 6

2 pounds (about 6) medium-size potatoes, peeled and thinly sliced
Olive oil
2 medium-size onions, peeled and finely chopped (not minced)
All-purpose flour
Salt, freshly ground black pepper, and sage (fresh is best) to taste
8 cups Rich Beef Broth (page 187)

Preheat the oven to 400° F.

Plunge the potato slices into cold water, rinse them for a minute or 2, then drain them well and blot them dry. Oil a heavy baking dish and cover the bottom with a layer of potatoes. Sprinkle with onions, 1 teaspoon flour, and seasonings and dribble with 1 tablespoon oil. Continue this layering until the dish is full, ending with potatoes. Press down firmly to compact the slices. Continue the layering until the dish is full, ending up with potatoes. Press down firmly once more and add enough broth to bring the level to ½ inch below the top layer of potatoes. Cover the dish tightly with foil.

Bake for 45 minutes. Remove the foil, raise the heat to 450° F., and bake 15–20 minutes more, or until the top is crisp. Let stand 10 minutes to allow the potatoes to absorb most of the broth, then sprinkle with chives and serve.

NOTE

If there seems to be too much broth left, or if it is too thin for your taste, cover with a plate just large enough to fit down over the potato slices, hold it in place to keep the slices from shifting, and carefully pour the broth off into a small saucepan. Reduce the broth over high heat until it is the consistency of heavy cream, pour it over the potato slices, sprinkle with chives, and serve.

White Turnips (and Turnip Greens) with Orange Sauce

If the turnips come with any small leaves, be sure to cook these too and serve all covered with the refreshing sauce.

Serves 6

2¼ pounds white turnips, peeled and thinly sliced

½ cup freshly squeezed orange juice
Chicken broth

½ teaspoon cornstarch mixed with 2 tablespoons cold water

½ cup small turnip leaves, cut into thin strips (or substitute other varieties of young greens)

1 teaspoon grated orange zest (thin outer skin of the fruit, with none of the bitter white underskin included)
Salt and freshly ground white pepper to taste

In a medium-size saucepan, place the turnips, orange juice, and enough chicken broth to barely cover. Simmer for 20–25 minutes, or until barely tender. Drain the turnips and keep them warm, reserving the liquid. Put the liquid and the cornstarch mixture in a small saucepan along with any turnip leaves and boil, stirring, until the sauce is reduced by half. Stir in the orange zest and salt and pepper. Place the turnip slices in a serving bowl and pour the sauce over. Serve immediately.

Steamed Brussels Sprouts with Chestnuts and Scallions

Serves 6

1 pound Brussels sprouts, trimmed of stems and any loose outer leaves

4 slim young scallions, trimmed of roots and all but 2 inches of green stems

2 tablespoons mild olive oil

½ cup coarsely chopped cooked and peeled chestnuts (page 194)
Pinch of nutmeg
Salt and freshly ground black pepper to taste

Steam sprouts until barely tender (page 217). Meanwhile, cut the scallions on the diagonal into ½-inch segments and sauté them for 1 minute in the oil. Add the sprouts, chestnuts, and seasonings, and toss over low heat for 2 minutes. Serve warm.

Wheated Cloverleaf Rolls

Makes about 3 dozen

   1 cup low-fat milk
  ½ cup liquid margarine
  ½ cup granulated sugar
   1 teaspoon salt (optional)
   2 packages dry active yeast
  ¼ cup lukewarm water
   1 cup whole wheat flour
4–5 cups all-purpose or unbleached
      flour
  ½ cup (4 ounces) egg substitute
      equivalent to 2 eggs
     Melted margarine

Scald the milk in a small saucepan, remove from the heat, and add the margarine, sugar, and salt, if desired; set aside to cool. Sprinkle the yeast over the lukewarm water and stir to dissolve. Measure the wheat flour and 2 cups white flour into a large bowl. Beat the egg substitute to a froth and blend into the flour along with the cooled milk mixture and dissolved yeast. The result should be a thick batter. Blend in enough of the remaining flour, a little at a time, to make a soft dough that will come clean from your hands.

Set the dough on a lightly floured board and knead until smooth and elastic, about 5–8 minutes (page 195). Oil a bowl lightly and put the dough into it, turning once to coat the top as well. Cover with a towel and set in a warm, draft-free place to double in bulk, about 1¼ hours (page 195). Punch the dough down and let it stand at room temperature 10–15 minutes. At this point, the dough may be refrigerated for up to 2 hours.

Divide the dough into 4 equal parts and shape each part into a 9-inch-long roll. Cut each roll into 9 pieces of equal size and then cut each of these pieces into thirds. Roll the thirds into small balls between your hands, and using a pastry brush, cover the balls on all sides with melted margarine. Grease muffin tins and arrange 3 balls in each well. Cover the muffin tins lightly with towels and set aside to rise in a warm, draft-free place for 1 hour, or until doubled in bulk.

Preheat the oven to 400° F. and bake for 15 minutes or until the rolls turn golden brown. Serve hot.

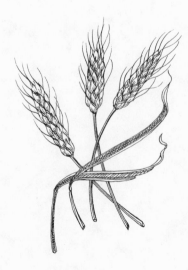

Mulled Apple Slices

The pale amber syrup that flavors the fruit becomes more piquant hour by hour. Chill it at least 4 hours or even overnight.

Serves 6

6 Granny Smith apples
½ lemon
2 cups sweet white wine or cider
1 teaspoon margarine
2 teaspoons minced fresh sage (or ¼ teaspoon dried)
  Sugar
½ cup muscat raisins
½ cup sliced pitted dates
½ cup broken walnut meats

Peel and slice the apples one at a time into a deep bowl and squeeze lemon juice over them as you go. When they are all peeled, squeeze the remaining juice over all.

Bring the wine or cider, margarine, sage, a 1-inch piece of lemon peel, and sugar to taste to a boil over low heat. Simmer for 3 minutes, then pour over the apple slices. Marinate until the slices come to room temperature, then add the raisins, dates, and walnuts and chill until ready to serve.

NOTE

The more attractive the serving dish, the more pleasing the dessert. Now's the time to unwrap Grandma's pretty cut-glass treasures.

Pre-Theater Sukiyaki Dinner

MENU

Stuffed Mushrooms with Walnuts

Beef Sukiyaki

Basic Brown Rice (page 183)

Eggplant Pickles

Orange Segments with Candied Ginger

SUGGESTIONS

Marinate the meat overnight. Prepare the vegetables and refrigerate each in its own plastic bag. Assemble the recipe just prior to serving.

Marinate the eggplant slices for 24 hours.

Stuffed Mushrooms with Walnuts

These are lovely. Rich and crunchy.

Serves 6

24 medium-size mushrooms
2 slices day-old bread
⅔ cup walnut meats
1 small onion, peeled and cut into quarters
1 tablespoon margarine
1 tablespoon vegetable oil
⅓ cup tomato catsup
Low-fat milk
Parsley for garnish

Preheat the oven to 350° F.

Wipe mushrooms with a damp cloth. Carefully remove the stems, taking care not to damage the caps. Mix the bread, walnuts, onion, and mushroom stems for a few seconds in food processor using the steel blade. The pieces should be the consistency of small peas.

Heat the margarine and oil in a non-stick skillet and sauté the mixture, stirring frequently, until the onion is transparent. Stir in the catsup. Mound the mixture in the mushroom caps and arrange them in an oblong oven-proof glass dish. Pour in equal amounts of milk and water, enough to reach halfway up the sides of the caps, and bake for 35 minutes. Remove the mushrooms from the dish and arrange on a heated platter, top each with a tiny bit of parsley, and serve hot or cold.

Beef Sukiyaki

Serves 6

½ pound lean, boneless sirloin, partially frozen
1 cup canned beef consommé
1 teaspoon cornstarch
1½ tablespoons granulated sugar
2 tablespoons sherry, vodka, or scotch
½ cup dark soy sauce
4 medium-size onions, peeled
4 ribs celery, trimmed, with all strings removed
10 small shiitake mushrooms, wiped clean and trimmed of stems
4 cups well-washed spinach leaves, with stems removed
6 scallions, each with 3 inches green top, trimmed
1½ cakes firm tofu (soybean curd)
½ pound shirataki filaments (if available)
2 tablespoons peanut oil
2 cups bamboo shoots
1 recipe Basic Brown Rice (page 183)

The flavor of beef definitely improves this dish, so the *flavor* is exactly what is left in. Instead of the 1½ pounds of meat normally used, half a pound serves 6 nicely. The meaty shiitake mushrooms substitute to some degree for the missing "tooth," and the soybean curd increases the satisfaction by providing protein. Served on brown rice rather than white, the dish is complete—at once nourishing and satisfying.

Slicing diagonally across the grain, cut the partially frozen meat into very thin slices and set aside. Mix together the consommé, cornstarch, sugar, sherry, and soy sauce, and pour it over the meat. Let this marinate while you prepare the remaining vegetables.

Thinly slice the onions and celery. Cut the mushrooms in half (if any are large, cut them into strips). Cut the spinach leaves into 1-inch ribbons. Slice the scallions diagonally into 1-inch pieces. Cut the tofu into ¾-inch cubes. Parboil the shirataki 1–2 minutes, uncovered, then drain well.

Heat the oil in a heavy skillet, electric frying pan, or wok, and quickly stir-fry (page 33) the onions, celery, mushrooms, scallions, and bamboo shoots; set them aside. Heat a little oil in the pan. Pick the meat out of the marinade with chopsticks, drop the slices into the hot oil, stir-fry for 1 minute, and set aside. Add the vegetables and the soy sauce marinade to the pan and bring to a boil, stirring continuously. Arrange the meat, bean curd, and shirataki over the top and simmer over low heat 2–3 minutes longer. Stir together and serve immediately with hot Brown Rice.

Eggplant Pickles

Yes! Uncooked. And delicious. And only about 1 calorie per piece.

Makes about 100 pieces

1 large eggplant, peeled and cut lengthwise into quarters
Salt
⅓ cup mild vinegar
2 tablespoons soy sauce
2 tablespoons granulated sugar
½ cup sweet onion, peeled and coarsely chopped
1 tablespoon dry mustard

Cut the eggplant into ½-inch- by ½-inch- by 2-inch-long "fingers" and place on paper towels. Sprinkle with salt and allow to drain for 10 minutes; pat dry with fresh paper towels.

Meanwhile, stir together the vinegar, soy sauce, sugar, onion, and mustard to form a smooth paste. Place the paste and the eggplant pieces in a 1-quart jar with a tight-fitting lid. Gently rotate until all the pickles have been coated with the paste. Refrigerate overnight, rotating the jar from time to time. Serve cold.

Orange Segments with Candied Ginger

Serves 6

6 large navel oranges, peeled and sliced, or 4½ cups canned mandarin orange segments, well drained and chilled
½ cup Cointreau
⅓ cup crystallized ginger, finely chopped

Toss the chilled orange slices or segments with the Cointreau and spoon into dessert dishes. Sprinkle with the ginger just prior to serving.

A Low-Calorie, Low-Cholesterol Lunch After Working Out

MENU

Tomato-Yogurt Pick-Me-Up

Takara-Mushi

Coffee Granité

SUGGESTIONS

Mix first 7 ingredients of Tomato-Yogurt Pick-Me-Up in advance. Refrigerate. Whirl with the ice just prior to serving.

Steam pumpkin 5 to 6 hours prior to filling them.

Tomato-Yogurt Pick-Me-Up

Serves 1

1 small ripe tomato, peeled, seeded, and coarsely chopped
¼ small onion, peeled and coarsely chopped
⅓ cup plain low-fat yogurt or buttermilk
½ cup vegetable broth or tomato juice
2 teaspoons wheat germ
4 mint leaves
½ teaspoon Oriental sesame oil
1 ice cube
Salt and freshly ground black pepper to taste

Combine all ingredients in a blender or food processor, and process until smooth. Serve immediately.

Takara-Mushi

Serves 6–8

6–8 small pumpkins or round acorn squash (or 2 2-pound pumpkins)
Salt
Sake or sherry for inside of pumpkin plus 2 tablespoons sake or sherry
2 ripe tomatoes, peeled and seeded (page 221)
1 teaspoon oil
3 cups Chicken Consommé (page 187)
12 dried mushroom caps, softened in warm water for 15 minutes, drained and finely sliced, stems discarded
1 chicken breast, cut into ½-inch cubes
6 shrimp, peeled and with veins removed, thinly sliced
¼ cup small green peas
2 tablespoons soy sauce
1½ tablespoons granulated sugar
1 cup soft bean curd, cut into 1-inch cubes

A particularly appealing way to serve an unusual lunch or light supper entrée. If individual-size pumpkins (¾-pounders) are available, these make the most attractive presentation. If not, choose large acorn squash and slice a piece from the bottom of each to make them stand upright. Or, 2 2-pound pumpkins may be used to serve 4.

Cut the tops from the pumpkins about 1 inch deep and reserve them. If the bottoms are uneven, even them by cutting away a thin slice. Scoop out and discard the seeds and strings. Cut away 1-inch strips of the skin at 1-inch intervals to give an attractive striped effect. Sprinkle the insides with a little salt and sake or sherry.

Arrange the pumpkins on a rack in a steamer or roasting pan, and add enough water to the bottom of the pan to steam but not touch them. Cover and steam over medium-low heat about 8–10 minutes for small ones, 12–14 minutes for medium-size ones.

Meanwhile, sauté the tomatoes in the oil until tender, and puree with the consommé. Mix with the mushrooms, chicken, shrimp, peas, soy sauce, sugar, and sake or sherry. Mash half the bean curd with a fork and add it, along with the remaining cubed bean curd, to the mixture.

Spoon equal amounts of the mixture into the pumpkins and steam over medium-low heat 20–25 minutes, following the same procedure as before. Be sure the heat is not too high or the pumpkins might crack. Serve hot. If you like, decorate with the reserved pumpkin tops stuck like parasols on toothpicks to one side of the filled pumpkin.

Coffee Granité

Serve with Seasonal Fruit and Yogurt Cheese (page 47). It's just as easy to prepare enough for 6 days as it is for 1 day.

Serves 6

Sugar to taste
6 cups strong decaffeinated coffee
Cognac

Stir the sugar into the hot coffee, bring to room temperature, and then freeze, stirring occasionally until softly frozen. Heap into small, fragile compotes into which have been spooned a little cognac.

Bulgur Frittata Dinner Before the Fire

MENU

Winter Squash and Black Bean Soup Served with Six Condiments

Bulgur Frittata

Char-Roasted Onions in Olive Oil

Wild Thyme–Cashew Custard

SUGGESTIONS

Several days prior to your dinner, prepare the Sweet Red Pepper Mayonnaise that accompanies the soup. Or if you are really pressed for time, omit it. Use frozen winter squash rather than fresh.

Prepare the bulgur for the frittata 24 hours prior to serving.

Save time by substituting canned broth for the home-simmered variety.

One cup leftover flaked fish is an excellent replacement for the shrimp.

Winter Squash and Black Bean Soup Served with Six Condiments

The soup itself is naturally smooth and thick and sweetened by winter squash that has gathered richness from the sun all summer long. The color is the saffron of an October moon, though it's not saffron but curry that adds a subtle warmth. This golden puree is partnered with ebony beans, the green of sage, and shreds of orange carrot, and is then served, steaming, with Sweet Red Pepper Mayonnaise to add depth and flavor, scallions for piquancy, salted pumpkin seeds and lettuce for additional texture, a teaspoon of grated low-fat cheese to melt and mellow the brew, and unflavored low-fat yogurt for cool contrast.

Serves 6–8

3 cups Squash Puree made with winter squash (page 182)
2 medium-size carrots, scraped and thinly shredded
4 cups Homemade Chicken Broth or Vegetable Stock (pages 186 or 184) or canned broth
1 cup minced onion
2 cups black beans, cooked and rinsed (see pages 199 to 201 for cooking directions) or canned beans
1 tablespoon mixed fresh herbs or 1 teaspoon dried
½ cup plain low-fat yogurt
Salt and freshly ground black pepper to taste

THE CONDIMENTS

1½ cups Sweet Red Pepper Mayonnaise (page 46)
1½ cups chopped scallions
1½ cups cold yogurt
1½ cups Toasted Pumpkin Seeds (page 192)
2 cups shredded lettuce
2–3 tablespoons grated low-fat cheese

Prepare the Squash Puree and place it in a heavy pot to heat. Simmer the carrot shreds in the broth or stock until they are not quite tender, then remove with a slotted spoon and set aside. Add the broth, onion, beans, and herbs to the squash and simmer until the onion is tender.

Stir in the yogurt and carrot shreds and adjust the seasonings. Serve steaming hot (so that the cheese will melt) with the condiments in small bowls on the side.

Bulgur Frittata

Whether you include the shrimp or not, this dish is delicious as well as healthful.

Serves 6

1 recipe Basic Bulgur (page 183)
1 tablespoon minced dulsa seaweed (optional)
1 tablespoon light soy sauce
2 tablespoons vegetable oil
2 scallions, trimmed and thinly sliced
1 tablespoon ginger root, peeled and minced
8 shrimp, shelled, deveined, and thinly sliced (optional)
1 egg
1 cup (8 ounces) egg substitute equivalent to 4 eggs
1 recipe Fresh Tomato Sauce with Orange (page 179)

Prepare the bulgur. Turn on the broiler.

Soak the seaweed in the soy sauce.

Heat the oil in a medium-size non-stick skillet, add the scallions, ginger, and the shrimp, and sauté for a minute or 2, until the shrimp turns bright pink. Stir in the bulgur. Stir in the drained seaweed. Toss the bulgur over low heat until it is hot. Beat together the egg and egg substitute and stir into the bulgur. Remove the pan immediately from the heat and slide it under the broiler until it is lightly browned. Cover the pan with a plate large enough to hold the frittata and let it stand away from the heat 2–3 minutes, or until the egg has set. Invert the pan and plate and turn the frittata out. Cut into 6 pie-shaped wedges and serve at room temperature. Pass Fresh Tomato Sauce with Orange.

Char-Roasted Onions in Olive Oil

When sweet onions are roasted over charcoal (or volcanic rocks) their sweetness is enhanced by the heat and smoke generated when the onion juices fall into the fire. Even so, I never can resist adding a twig of apple wood, during those few minutes when the top of the grill is down, to accentuate the woodsy flavor. If the season or the setting dictates oven roasting, however, the recipe is still effective.

Coating the cooked onions with a rich, fruity olive oil improves their flavor and increases their longevity. They partner beautifully with such a variety of foods that it's a good idea to prepare several jars at a time.

Makes 3 quarts

8 large sweet onions, peeled and cut in half vertically
¾ cup fruity olive oil
  Aromatic fruit wood or dried thyme leaves for adding flavor when grilling
3 teaspoons fresh thyme leaves (or 1 teaspoon dried)
  Freshly ground black pepper
¾ cup white vinegar
1½ teaspoons salt

Brush the onion halves with oil and arrange them, cut sides down, over medium coals in a covered outdoor grill. Grill for 15 minutes, then turn them cut side up. Add a twig of aromatic fruit wood or sprinkle the coals with dried thyme leaves. Close the grill top immediately so the smoke cannot escape. Grill 15 minutes more. *For indoor broiling:* Cut onions in quarters. Arrange on an oiled baking sheet, brush generously with oil, and grill. The onions should be partially cooked, but still have a bit of crunch.

Remove and cool on wire racks. Cut each half in half again (or in thirds if the onions are very large ones). Divide the onions among 3 quart jars. Add to each jar 1 teaspoon fresh (or ⅓ teaspoon dried) thyme, pepper to taste, ¼ cup vinegar, ¼ cup oil, and ½ teaspoon salt. Cover the jars and refrigerate until needed, shaking them once a day. Serve at room temperature.

Wild Thyme–Cashew Custard

A rich, nutritious dessert? One that doesn't make you feel guilty? This is it. You may substitute your own favorite for the natural wild thyme honey if you prefer. Buckwheat honey would be my second choice. Of course supermarket honey will suffice if that's what's on hand.

Serves 6

1 cup raw cashew nuts (or dry-roasted ones)
½ cup fresh goat's cheese
½ cup dried brown bread crumbs
½ teaspoon cinnamon
⅛ teaspoon nutmeg
1 cup plain low-fat yogurt
1 egg, lightly beaten
½ cup (4 ounces) egg substitute equivalent to 2 eggs
2 tablespoons light brown sugar
¼ cup wild thyme honey (or other type honey)
1 cup low-fat milk
1 tablespoon soft margarine

Preheat the oven to 350° F.

Grate the nuts and cheese and sprinkle half over the bottom of a well-oiled 8-inch glass pie plate or 6 individual oiled ovenproof custard cups. Sprinkle half the bread crumbs over the nuts and cheese, and season with cinnamon and nutmeg. Spread the yogurt carefully over all, taking care not to disturb the nuts and crumbs. Layer with the remaining nuts and cheese and bread crumbs.

Beat together the egg, egg substitute, brown sugar, and half the honey. Scald the milk with the margarine and add to the egg mixture a bit at a time. Pour carefully over the ingredients in the pie plate or custard cups without disturbing the layers.

Place the plate or cups in a baking pan filled with just enough hot water to reach halfway up the sides of the dishes. Bake 35–40 minutes or until a table knife comes out clean when inserted in the center. Serve warm or chilled topped with the remaining honey.

A Dinner Featuring Chou-Farci

MENU

Instant Fresh Tomato Soup

*Chou-Farci with Sweet Potato–
Cornbread Stuffing*

*Capered Carrot and Chestnut
Salad*

Hubbard Tea Bread

SUGGESTIONS

This entire menu may be prepared in advance, leaving only the actual stuffing and cooking of the cabbage to be accomplished on party day.

Prepare the cabbage for the stuffin, and refrigerate overnight.

Prepare the stuffing one day early, cool, and refrigerate overnight. Continue the recipe several hours before serving time. Bring the stuffing to room temperature before using, or add 15 minutes to cooking time.

The Hubbard Tea Bread refrigerates or freezes nicely. Prepare it well in advance.

Instant Fresh Tomato Soup

When the versatile tomato is in season, you'll want to whirl up this instant, no-cook soup. If you begin with chilled tomatoes and juice, this can be prepared and served within minutes.

In a food processor or blender, puree all ingredients except the yogurt, lemon slices, and a few marjoram leaves. Stir the yogurt into the puree. Adjust seasonings. Serve cold, topping each serving with a lemon slice and a few leaves of marjoram or a sprinkle of dill.

Serves 6

3 large ripe tomatoes, peeled and seeded
1 recipe Your Own Fresh Tomato Juice (page 178) or 1 quart canned
1 medium-size Vidalia or Texas sweet onion, peeled and coarsely chopped
2 cloves garlic, peeled
  Salt and freshly ground white pepper to taste
⅓ cup chopped fresh dill
2 tablespoons fresh marjoram leaves
3 cups plain low-fat yogurt
6 paper-thin lemon slices

Chou-Farci with Sweet Potato–Cornbread Stuffing

On frosty days when snow blankets meadows and rooftops, nothing will do as well as a hearty peasant repast simmering away, warming the kitchen, welcoming guests, and, finally, pleasing our palates.

Almost any cabbage may be stuffed, providing it is of good quality and size. My favorite for this purpose, I'll admit, is the ruffly, exquisitely designed Savoy cabbage. It's milder in taste and more attractive on the dish. You may also use just about any subtly flavored vegetable (or combination thereof) to fill it. The end result is bound to be tasty.

Prepare and set aside the stuffing. Rinse the cabbage and cut off its stem, so that it will not tilt or wobble. Simmer in lightly salted boiling water for 10 minutes to soften the outer leaves. Remove the cabbage from the pot and drain it well. When cool enough to handle, place the cabbage on the center of several layers of cheesecloth laid out on your workboard, and gently fold back the leaves without removing them from the stalk. When you reach the firm, more tightly curled center leaves, cut them away without disturbing the turned-back outer leaves.

Reserve 2 or 3 of the larger of these center leaves, then cut the rest of these into thin shreds. In the oil, sauté the bacon, if using, along with

Serves 6

1 recipe Sweet Potato–Cornbread Stuffing (recipe follows)
1 2½-pound Savoy cabbage, trimmed of any limp outer leaves
  Salt
2 tablespoons vegetable oil
2 slices lean bacon, minced (optional)
3 cloves garlic, peeled and minced
1 tablespoon minced Italian (flat) parsley
2 medium-size onions, peeled and coarsely chopped
2 medium-size carrots, scraped and coarsely chopped
2 ribs celery, coarsely chopped
1 bay leaf
  Water or chicken stock
  Tomato paste (optional)
  Cornbread crumbs (optional)
  Fresh and Easy Tomato Sauce (page 180)

the garlic and parsley. Add the shredded center leaves, and cook until these soften somewhat. Stir the mixture into the stuffing.

Transfer the cheesecloth with the whole cabbage on it to a large bowl. Make a ball of stuffing about the same size as the hollowed-out cabbage heart and set it in the cabbage center. Fit the large reserved center leaves over the stuffing and press the remaining stuffing over these. Fold the innermost leaves back over the stuffing, then continue to carefully replace all of the remaining folded-back leaves until the cabbage is as round and smooth as it was before. Tie up the tops of the cheesecloth layers.

Arrange the onions, carrots, celery, and bay leaf in the bottom of a pot just large enough to hold the stuffed cabbage. Lower the cabbage into the pot and cover with lightly boiling water or stock. Loosely cover the pot with foil, then turn the heat as low as possible and simmer for 2½–3 hours. Transfer the cabbage to a colander set in a pot large enough to hold it. Drain for 15 minutes. (You may keep it warm for an hour by covering the pot holding the colander with a second larger pot.)

To serve, transfer cabbage to a large, shallow bowl, stem side down, cut away the cheesecloth, and slip it out from under. The cabbage is ready to serve with sauce, or it can be finished in the oven.

Brush the top of the cabbage with tomato paste and sprinkle with crumbs. Bake in a 300° F. oven until crumbs are lightly browned, then cut in wedges and serve immediately with Fresh and Easy Tomato Sauce.

VARIATION

Top-grade commercial spaghetti sauce that does not contain palm oils can pinch-hit for Fresh and Easy Tomato Sauce. For a fresh taste, simmer one finely chopped fresh tomato in the sauce before serving it.

Sweet Potato–Cornbread Stuffing

Makes about 6 cups

1 large sweet potato
2 tablespoons vegetable oil
1 large onion, peeled and finely chopped
3 ribs celery, trimmed and finely chopped
½ cup finely chopped walnuts
1 teaspoon each dried marjoram and thyme leaves
½ teaspoon salt (optional)
⅓ cup hot chicken or vegetable broth
3 cups crumbled Cornbread Crumbs (page 188)
¼ cup (2 ounces) egg substitute equivalent to 1 egg

Boil the potato in its jacket until very tender. Meanwhile, heat the oil and sauté the onion, celery, walnuts, and seasonings until the onion turns golden. Remove from the heat and set aside. Peel the potato and cut into ¾-inch cubes. Sprinkle the hot broth over the crumbs, stir in the potato, and vegetable-nut mixture, and the egg substitute.

Capered Carrot and Chestnut Salad

This is a colorful, change-of-pace salad, where the sweetness of cooked carrots and mellow chestnuts are bound together by tart French dressing.

Serves 6

30 uncooked chestnuts in the shell or 1½ cups canned chestnuts, drained
4 cups scraped and sliced cooked carrots
⅔ cup Capered French Dressing (page 189)
1½ tablespoons minced chives

Preheat the oven to 350° F.

If you are using chestnuts in the shell, cut an x on the flat side of each and bake 15 minutes in the oven. Peel while hot (be sure to remove the brown underskin also).

Coarsely chop the peeled chestnuts and toss them with the carrot slices and dressing. Sprinkle with chives and serve at room temperature.

VARIATION

Use canned chestnuts in the salad and prepare it several days early, stirring once a day.

Hubbard Tea Bread

Hubbard squash makes this tea bread moist and nicely textured.

Serves 8

- 1 cup hubbard squash, peeled and seeded
- ½ cup egg substitute
- ⅓ cup granulated sugar
- ¼ cup honey
- 1 tablespoon melted or liquid margarine
- 1¼ cups all-purpose white flour
- 1 cup wheat flour
- 2 teaspoons baking powder
- ¾ teaspoon baking soda
- ¾ teaspoon salt
- ¾ teaspoon allspice
- ¾ teaspoon cinnamon
- 1 cup chopped dates
- ½ cup golden raisins
- ¼ cup currants
- ½ cup chopped walnuts

ICING:

- 1 cup confectioners' sugar
- 2 tablespoons lime juice (or a bit more as needed)

Preheat oven to 325° F.

Grate the squash. The fine grating blade of a food processor accomplishes this in seconds. Squeeze the grated squash dry between paper towels and place it in your food processor container fitted with the steel blade. Add the egg substitute, sugar, honey, and melted margarine. Turn the machine on and off quickly until the ingredients are well mixed and the squash is finely chopped. Transfer to a mixing bowl.

Sift together the flours, baking powder, baking soda, salt, and spices, and fold, a little at a time, into the squash mixture along with the dates, raisins, currants, and nuts. Transfer the batter to a well-oiled loaf pan and bake for 55 minutes, or until a toothpick stuck in the center comes out clean. Let stand for 10 minutes, then set on a wire rack to cool to room temperature.

Mix the confectioners' sugar with enough lime juice to make a glaze that is stiff enough to cling to the top of the cake but moist enough to drip over the edges a little. Chill briefly.

A Slightly South-of-the-Border Supper

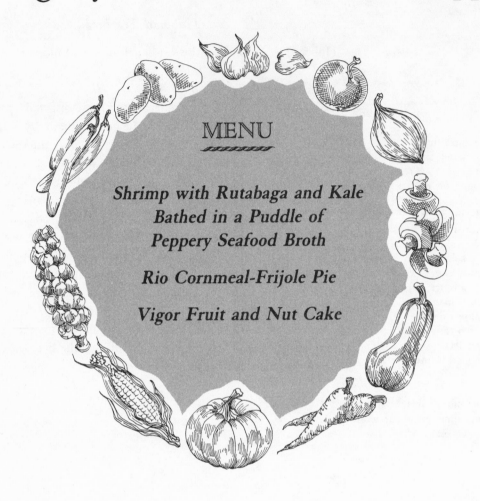

MENU

Shrimp with Rutabaga and Kale Bathed in a Puddle of Peppery Seafood Broth

Rio Cornmeal-Frijole Pie

Vigor Fruit and Nut Cake

SUGGESTION

For additional ease, the kale may be prepared and the broth boiled up to a day in advance.

Shrimp with Rutabaga and Kale Bathed in a Puddle of Peppery Seafood Broth

The crisp texture and potent flavor of the kale lends distinction to any menu.

What makes this dish extra-special is a fiery broth boiled up with the lobster and shrimp shells and half a hot cherry pepper. If you can't obtain a lobster shell, you might want to fortify the broth with prepared broth mix.

Serves 6

¾ pound medium-size raw shrimp in their shells
1 lobster shell (if you call your fish market in advance, they will most likely reserve one for you)
½ cherry pepper
Homemade Chicken Broth or Vegetable Stock (pages 186 or 184) or canned broth
MBT Instant Vegetable or Chicken Broth Mix (optional)
1½ pounds young kale leaves (those 5 inches long or less)
4 cloves garlic, peeled and minced
4 tablespoons extra-virgin olive oil
3 cups pureed rutabaga or winter squash

Remove the shells from the shrimp, rinse well, and place the shells in a pot with the lobster shell, the cherry pepper, and enough broth to cover. Refrigerate the shrimp meat itself. Bring the liquid to just under a boil, skim off any froth, partially cover, and continue to simmer for 1½ hours, adding additional broth as necessary to keep the shells covered. Taste the stock every 15 minutes to check that it is peppery enough to suit your taste. (If you did not use the lobster shell, the stock may taste a bit weak. Strengthen it with your favorite instant broth to taste.)

Meanwhile, rinse and drain the kale, and wrap it in paper towels. Just prior to serving, sauté the kale leaves in a large, non-stick frying pan with the garlic in 3 tablespoons olive oil.

Heat 1 tablespoon olive oil in a separate non-stick skillet, add the shrimp and sauté them just long enough for them to turn pink.

To serve, spoon a circle of warm rutabaga or squash puree around the edge of each of 6 shallow bowls. Place 2–3 tablespoons kale in the center, arrange the shrimp around the kale, and ladle ½ cup hot broth over each.

Rio Cornmeal-Frijole Pie

Serves 4–6

1¼ cups yellow cornmeal
  Salt to taste
5 cups cold water
3 tablespoons vegetable oil
1 large onion, peeled and coarsely chopped
1 large sweet pepper (your favorite color)
2 cloves garlic, peeled and minced
1 cup sliced mushrooms
1 teaspoon peeled and minced fresh ginger (optional)
3 cups cooked (or canned) frijoles, drained
2 cups tomatoes, peeled, seeded, and cut into ½-inch cubes
1 cup fresh corn cut from the cob or frozen, defrosted and drained
1 tablespoon chili powder (or to taste)
1 teaspoon crumbled sage leaves
  Coarsely ground black pepper to taste
2 tablespoons grated Parmesan

Serve this mellow Southwestern special either as a pie or baked in individual ovenproof dishes.

Mix the cornmeal and salt with the water, stir until smooth, and cook over low heat for 30 minutes, stirring frequently, until very thick.

Preheat the oven to 350° F.

Meanwhile, heat the oil in a medium-size saucepan and sauté the onion, pepper, and garlic for 2 minutes. Add the mushrooms and ginger, if desired, and sauté until the mushrooms are limp. Stir in the beans, tomatoes, corn, and seasonings, and simmer for 15 minutes or until most of the liquid is gone.

Spread half the cooked cornmeal over the bottom of a well-oiled casserole (or 6 individual ones), and top with the vegetable mixture. Spread the remaining cornmeal over, sprinkle with cheese, and bake for 40 minutes, or until nicely browned.

Vigor Fruit and Nut Cake

Serves 6

1 cup Vigor Cereal (recipe follows)
1 egg yolk
1 tablespoon plain yogurt
2 tablespoons honey
2 tablespoons Tiger Milk Powder (or wheat germ)
½ cup pecan meats
½ cup raisins
½ cup chopped pitted prunes
¼ teaspoon powdered cinnamon
⅛ teaspoon each ground nutmeg, cloves, and cumin

Good and good for you! All ingredients are available in health food stores. As I've mentioned, I don't freeze foods unless it's unavoidable. However, most breads and many cakes do freeze well. Fortunately, this Vigor cake is one of the latter and may be frozen for a week or so.

Preheat oven to 350° F.

Use a wooden spoon to beat all ingredients together (a food processor will chop the ingredients too finely). Spoon into a generously buttered loaf pan. Bake 45–55 minutes or until a toothpick comes out clean when stuck in the center of the cake. Cool to room temperature.

Vigor Cereal

Ingredients are available in health food stores. Great for breakfast!

3 cups

¼ cup wheat germ
¼ cup oat bran
½ cup rolled oats
2 tablespoons rice polish
¼ cup flaked wheat
¼ cup flaked rye
6 dates
¼ cup whole almonds
¼ cup sesame seeds
¼ cup sunflower seeds and kernels
1 tablespoon soy powder

Preheat the oven to 250° F.

Place the first 6 ingredients on a baking sheet and bake for 10 minutes, stirring once. Heap this mixture, the dates, and the almonds on a chopping board and, using a large knife, reduce to a coarse powder (a food processor accomplishes this with just a few pulses). Stir in remaining ingredients. Spoon into a jar with a tight-fitting lid and refrigerate until needed.

A Dinner of Cross-Cultural Influences

MENU

Mexican Tomato-Oatmeal Soup with Corn

Pakistani Spiced Peas and Potatoes with Marinated Turkey Breast

Rosé-Poached Ginger Pears

SUGGESTIONS

The soup may be prepared the day before you plan to serve it, but add the corn during the reheating.
If you add an extra teaspoon lemon juice and spoon the juices over the pears every few hours, the dessert may also be prepared in advance.

Mexican Tomato-Oatmeal Soup with Corn

Using oatmeal to thicken soup may seem trendy, even outlandish, but people all over the world have been doing it for centuries. This version is based on a hearty Mexican warm-me-up.

Serves 6

1¼ cups rolled oats (not instant or flavored)
3 tablespoons light olive oil
1 medium-size onion, peeled and finely chopped
3 large cloves garlic, peeled and minced
2 large tomatoes, peeled, seeded, and finely chopped
10 cups Homemade Chicken Broth (page 186), or canned
½ teaspoon salt
½ teaspoon light brown sugar
½ teaspoon powdered sage
1½ cups fresh corn cut from the cob

In a heavy saucepan, brown the oats lightly over medium heat, stirring continuously to keep them from scorching. Remove from the heat and set aside in a bowl.

In the same saucepan, heat the oil, add the onion, garlic, tomatoes, broth, salt, sugar, and sage. Bring the mixture to a boil, add oatmeal, and cook over medium heat for 3 minutes. Lower the heat, add the corn and simmer 3 minutes or until barely tender. Adjust the seasoning, if necessary. Serve immediately.

Pakistani Spiced Peas and Potatoes with Marinated Turkey Breast

Serves 6

2 tablespoons light olive oil
1 large clove garlic, peeled and minced
3 pounds potatoes, peeled and cut into ½-inch cubes
1½ cups fresh green young peas (or 1 10-ounce package frozen peas)
2 medium-size ripe tomatoes, coarsely chopped
½ teaspoon chili powder
¼ teaspoon each ground cumin, turmeric, and dried ginger
Salt to taste
6 turkey scallopini (optional)
½ cup Vinaigrette Dressing (page 189)
3 scallions, each with 3 inches of green top, thinly sliced
2 tablespoons minced parsley

It's always interesting to discover how those in other cultures approach the foods that are staples here. In this recipe, potatoes are handled in a manner unique to Pakistan, but with a slant that is valid in this country as well. With the marinated turkey breast the dish constitutes a pleasant lunch or light supper. Without it, the dish serves as a vegetable that can practically carry the meal.

In a large non-stick skillet heat 2 tablespoons oil, sauté the garlic for 1 minute and stir in the potato cubes. Lightly brown. Cover the potatoes and cook, stirring frequently, until they are fork tender. Stir in the peas and cook for 5 minutes more, then spoon the vegetables into a large bowl and set aside.

Add the tomatoes to the skillet along with the spices and salt, and continue to stir over medium heat for 3 minutes. Return the potatoes and peas to the pan, and cook over low heat for 5 minutes.

Meanwhile, if you are including the turkey, marinate the scallopini for 30 minutes in the Vinaigrette Dressing. Drain well. Sauté or grill for several minutes on each side or until just cooked through.

Spoon the vegetables into 6 large, shallow bowls or onto plates, top each with a scallopini, if used, garnish with the sliced scallions and parsley, and serve immediately.

Rosé-Poached Ginger Pears

Here, pears are cut into fan shapes and then prettily poached in rosé wine and orange. This elegant dessert is always well received.

Serves 6

- ¾ cup rosé wine
- 3 tablespoons orange marmalade
- 2 teaspoons lemon juice
- ⅛ teaspoon ground nutmeg
- ¼ teaspoon ground cinnamon
- 3 medium-size pears
- 18–24 rose petals (optional)

In a non-stick skillet, thoroughly mix all ingredients except the pears and rose petals with 2 tablespoons water. Bring to a boil. Cut the pears in half, lengthwise, leaving the stem attached to one half. Use a melon baller or small spoon to neatly remove the core from each pear half. Cut the halves into thin slices, cutting almost but not quite to the stem, and place them, skin-side down, in the mixture in the skillet. Bring to a boil once again, reduce the heat, and simmer, covered, for about 6 minutes or until pears are barely tender. Do not overcook. Remove each pear half with a slotted spoon and arrange in a fan shape on individual serving plates. Reduce the liquid in the pan to half (about ¼ cup) and spoon over pears. Decorate with rose petals.

A Southwestern Supper

MENU

*Fresh Black-Eyed Peas, Tomato,
Onion, and Jalapeño Pepper
Stewed in Beer and Served on a
Slab of Corn and Pepper Bread*

French-Fried Sweet Potatoes

SUGGESTIONS

*This vegetable stew served on Corn and Pepper Bread is healthful food indeed.
The cornbread is excellent prepared with sweet peppers only.*

Fresh Black-Eyed Peas, Tomato, Onion, and Jalapeño Pepper Stewed in Beer and Served on a Slab of Corn and Pepper Bread

Fresh (or frozen) black-eyed peas have been blessed with a delicacy not to be found in dried beans. A light, rather than an overbearingly, heavy beer is the best choice for the final simmering. For the same reason I sprinkle in what many would consider a miserly amount of jalapeño—it's just enough to add excitement, not to overwhelm. But if fiery is your preference, by all means fire away. The bacon is here for a touch of smoky flavor and may be omitted. The dish is still delicious without it.

Serves 6

2 cloves garlic, peeled
½ teaspoon dried thyme leaves
1 large bay leaf
4 cups fresh or frozen shelled black-eyed peas
2 slices lean bacon
3 tablespoons olive oil
½ sweet white onion, peeled and cut into ¼-inch-wide vertical slices (about 1½ cups)
1 small whole jalapeño pepper
2 large ripe red tomatoes, peeled, seeded, and coarsely chopped
1 teaspoon freshly ground pink peppercorns
1 can light beer
Corn and Pepper Bread (recipe follows)

Bring 2½ quarts water, the garlic, thyme, and bay leaf to a rapid boil in a large, heavy saucepan. Drop in the peas, immediately lower the heat, and simmer, covered, for 40 minutes or until the beans are not quite tender.

Meanwhile, in a large skillet, fry the bacon in the oil until crisp, then remove it and drain on paper towels. Make sure the onion slices are dry, then toss them, along with the whole jalapeño pepper, in the combined fats for 2 to 3 minutes over medium heat. Add the tomatoes, peppercorns, and 1 cup of the beer.

Add the well-drained beans and enough additional beer to nearly cover the ingredients in the pan. Simmer, uncovered, for 10 to 15 minutes. Taste a bean and a little broth occasionally if the liquid is drying up, and when spicy enough, remove the jalapeño. Most of the broth should be absorbed.

Serve the peas hot, spooned over a slab of Corn and Pepper Bread. If it pleases you, carefully cut the jalapeño open, discard the seeds and stem, mince the flesh, and use as an additional garnish.

Corn and Pepper Bread

Peppers, scallions, creamed corn, and cornmeal all lend their goodness to this satisfying and simple-to-prepare loaf. A great backup for soups or stews and equally pleasing on its own.

½ cup vegetable oil
¼ cup mixed minced sweet and hot peppers (according to taste)
1 whole egg plus ½ cup (4 ounces) egg substitute equivalent to 2 eggs
½ cup plain yogurt
3 medium-size scallions with 3-inch green tops, thinly sliced
2 cups creamed corn
1½ cups yellow cornmeal
2 teaspoons baking powder
Salt to taste

Preheat the oven to 350° F.

Heat the oil in a medium-size skillet and sauté the peppers for 2 minutes, then remove from the heat and cool to room temperature. Stir in the egg, egg substitute, yogurt, scallions, and creamed corn. In a medium-size bowl, mix the cornmeal, baking powder, and salt, and lightly stir in the vegetable-egg mixture, leaving the batter a bit lumpy. Generously oil a 9-inch earthenware, cast-iron (or other heavy) pan or dish, pour in the batter, and bake 45 minutes or until the bread springs back when the center is lightly pressed. Remove from the oven and let stand for 15 minutes, then unmold or serve from the pan or dish.

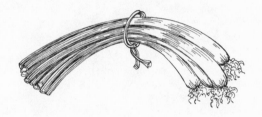

French-Fried Sweet Potatoes

Fried sweet potatoes are a treat with almost any meal. Try them either shaped like traditional french fries or sliced in thin rounds. I prefer the former with their crusty outsides and custardy insides, but the crispness of the latter is also appealing.

Serves 6

5 medium-size sweet potatoes, peeled and dropped immediately into cold water, to which 2 tablespoons of lemon juice have been added
3 heaping tablespoons all-purpose flour
Vegetable oil for frying
Vinegar-Soy Sauce (page 61)

If the sweet potatoes have pointed ends, cut these away and discard them so that you end up with a round or oblong oval potato. Cut these into ¼-inch-thick rounds or into french fries roughly ¾ inch by ½ inch by 3 inches long, or slightly broader and thicker than traditional french fries. Place the potato pieces back in the acidulated water and bring to a boil over medium heat. The potatoes must remain pliable, so do not overcook them. Drain well and pat dry with paper towels or a clean kitchen towel. Toss the fries with just enough flour to lightly dust them, shaking off any excess. Fry in deep hot oil until golden brown. Blot to remove excess oil and serve immediately. Pass the Vinegar-Soy Sauce.

A Winter Dinner Party with a Middle-Eastern Accent

MENU

Pumpkin Soup with Crabmeat and Pernod

Eggplant and Zucchini Timbale with a Middle-Eastern Accent

Fried Potato-Carrot Pancakes

Apricots in Rosewater

SUGGESTIONS

Prepare the soup 1 day early, following recipe directions.

The timbale is served at room temperature and refrigerates nicely. Get the major work accomplished a day early. Don't forget to remove the timbale from the refrigerator early enough for it to reach room temperature.

The potato-carrot pancakes, while very tasty, may be omitted if time is a factor, or they may replace the soup as a first course.

The flavor of the apricots improves as the days pass. I've kept them for as long as a week and enjoyed the last bite more than the first.

Pumpkin Soup with Crabmeat and Pernod

Wonderfully warming is this cold weather soup. The pumpkin provides the vitamin C so necessary when chill winds are blowing, and the oats not only add vital fiber and nutrition, but also thicken the soup. Don't hesitate to serve this soup chilled; it's delicious either way, even if the crabmeat is omitted.

Serves 6–8

½ cup rolled oats (*not* instant)
2 tablespoons vegetable oil
2 medium-size onions, peeled and coarsely chopped
5 medium-size ribs celery, trimmed and coarsely chopped
2 cloves garlic, peeled and minced
6 cups fresh pumpkin, peeled, seeded, and coarsely chopped or shredded
3 tablespoons Pernod
1 tablespoon minced fresh thyme or 1 teaspoon leaf thyme, dried
  Salt and freshly ground black pepper to taste
  Dash of nutmeg
½ cup low-fat milk
5 cups Fish Stock or Vegetable Stock (pages 185 and 184)
1 cup plain low-fat yogurt
½ pound crabmeat, picked over and any bits of shell discarded (optional)
  Garlic Croutons (page 188)

Heat the oats in a large, heavy non-stick skillet, stirring frequently until they are golden brown. Do not let them burn. Transfer the oats to a bowl and set them aside.

Heat the oil in the skillet and sauté the onions, celery, and garlic for 1 minute. Add the pumpkin and sauté until tender and golden in color, stirring frequently. Sprinkle 2 tablespoons of Pernod over the vegetables, and toss over low heat until the liquid evaporates. Stir in the seasonings.

Finely chop the mixture in a food processor or blender. Add the milk and turn the machine off and on just enough to mix. The puree should retain a nice texture. The soup may be refrigerated at this point until just prior to serving.

To serve the soup hot, stir the pumpkin mixture and the oats into the hot stock and simmer for 5 minutes or until the oats are tender, stirring occasionally. Add the yogurt, crabmeat, if using, and the remaining tablespoon Pernod and simmer for 2 minutes more. Serve hot sprinkled with Garlic Croutons.

Substitute bottled clam juice for homemade stock when time is short. Or, better yet, buy fresh clam juice at your friendly fish store.

For a hurry-up version of the soup, unsweetened canned pumpkin or frozen winter squash puree could pinch-hit for the fresh pumpkin. The texture won't be as toothsome but the flavor will still be extremely pleasing.

Replace the crabmeat with flaked cooked fish for a more reasonably priced potage.

When preparing the dessert, substitute vanilla extract if rosewater isn't available.

Eggplant and Zucchini Timbale with a Middle-Eastern Accent

Here's an excellent opportunity to rid yourself of those zucchini that seem to grow into monsters overnight. Medium-size specimens are excellent here, *not* the arm-length variety. Pick eggplant and squash of similar size, or, if squash are not available in this size, use eggplant only. But don't prepare this with zucchini alone; the unique texture and flavor of eggplant are essential.

Fried vegetable slices are a little more flavorful, but broiled slices use less oil. And about that oil—flavor is most important here, so do go for quality and a nice, fruity taste. Since these oils can be pricey, you could substitute vegetable oil for up to half the total amount.

The seasonings are traditionally Middle Eastern and unusually flavorful . . . unusually rich.

Serves 6

- 3 medium-size (about 8 inches long) zucchini
- 3 medium-size (about 8 inches long) eggplant
  Salt
- 1 cup all-purpose flour
- 1 cup flavorful olive oil, or half olive oil and half vegetable oil
- 1 large onion, peeled and chopped
- 1 large clove garlic, peeled and minced (optional)
- 8 medium-size mushrooms, chopped
- 1 tablespoon each minced fresh mint and thyme leaves
- ½ cup currants
- ½ cup pine nuts
- 1 recipe Fresh Tomato Puree (page 181), or use 1½ cups canned tomatoes in thick puree
  Freshly ground black pepper to taste
- 6 tablespoons soft bean curd (if you substitute firm bean curd, it should be pressed through a sieve)
- 2 slices low-fat muenster cheese, slivered
- ¾ cup egg substitute
- 1 cup plain low-fat yogurt
- 2 tablespoons each finely chopped fresh mint and dill

Cut away and discard 1 inch from the stem ends of the squash and eggplants, then cut into lengthwise slices, ⅓ inch thick. Discard the side pieces that are mostly skin. Arrange the remaining slices on paper towels, sprinkle lightly with salt, and let stand 15 minutes, or until beads of moisture form. Pat dry with paper towels, turn, sprinkle with salt, and let stand 15 minutes more (most of the salt is exuded with the moisture). Pat dry with paper towels.

To fry: Dust the slices lightly with flour and brown in hot oil a few at a time, turning once to prevent sticking. Drain immediately on paper towels. Reserve 2 tablespoons oil. *To broil:* * Do not dust slices with flour but brush them thoroughly on each side with oil. Arrange them on a baking sheet without overlapping, place on the top shelf, and broil for a few minutes, or until golden brown on both sides, turning once. The slices will be soft, so handle with care.

Heat the reserved 2 tablespoons oil in a non-stick skillet and sauté the onion and garlic for 1 minute. Add the mushrooms and sauté until lightly browned. Stir in the mint and thyme leaves, currants, pine nuts, and tomato puree, and cook over low heat until mixture is fairly thick. Season with salt and pepper.

To assemble, preheat the oven to 350° F. Arrange alternate slices of eggplant and zucchini in an overlapping pattern in an oiled 2-quart soufflé dish (with the widest ends of the slices at the bottom of the dish

---

* This method requires much less oil.

and the narrower ends hanging over the sides of the dish). Cover this bottom layer with about one half of the onion-mushroom mixture. Sprinkle with the bean curd and half the slivered cheese. Arrange eggplant and zucchini slices over the cheese layer, again with the widest ends down and the narrower ends hanging over the edge of the dish. Cover with the remaining onion-mushroom mixture and the remaining slivered cheese.

Carefully poke holes through the layers without disturbing the pattern and pour the egg substitute over the layers. Turn the dish from side to side to make sure the egg substitute seeps down through the timbale. Fold the overhanging vegetable slices in an attractive spiral pattern over the timbale and press down gently. Bake for 45 minutes or until the egg substitute has set. Remove from the oven and let cool in the dish for 15–20 minutes. Use a sharp, thin-bladed knife to carefully loosen around the edges without tearing or disturbing the outer layer. Let stand 15 minutes more (or until cool enough to handle). Place a large serving plate over the dish and unmold it by turning the soufflé dish and plate over quickly. If necessary, gently raise one side of the dish a little and lightly shake it along with the plate to induce the timbale to free itself. If the vegetable slices have been disturbed, return them to their perfect order. Cool to room temperature. Serve, cut in wedges, with a mixture of cold yogurt and mint. An electric knife cuts this carefully layered dish without tearing it.

VARIATIONS

In a pinch, when currants and pine nuts are nowhere to be found, I have substituted golden raisins and finely chopped almonds.

Let peeled, seeded, and finely chopped cucumber pinch-hit for the mint.

Fried Potato-Carrot Pancakes

If you combine the mellow sweetness of Pommes de Terre Crecy with the crispness of old-fashioned potato pancakes you have these especially tasty cakes.

Makes 12 pancakes

4 medium-to-large potatoes, peeled
1 medium-size onion, peeled and cut in quarters vertically and then thinly sliced
2 large carrots, scraped
⅓ cup egg substitute
⅔ cup matzo meal
1½ teaspoons salt
½ teaspoon freshly ground black pepper
Vegetable oil for frying

Finely grate the potatoes, dropping them immediately in cold water as you go to prevent discoloration. If you are using the food processor grating disk, the strands of potato, as well as the onion, may be too long to produce the desired consistency. If this is the case, finish them up by using the steel cutting blade to cut the strands, a handful at a time, with a quick chop or two. Finely grate the carrots. Drain the potatoes, squeeze them out to extract as much moisture as possible, then press them between several thicknesses of paper towel to remove any remaining moisture. Mix with the carrots. Stir in the egg substitute, matzo meal, and seasonings.

Drop the potato-carrot batter by tablespoons into hot oil and fry until golden brown on both sides, turning once. Drain briefly on paper towels before serving hot.

Apricots in Rosewater

Prepare the apricots at least 2 days in advance of serving.

Serves 6

2 11-ounce boxes fancy dried apricots
1 quart canned apricot nectar
¼ cup granulated sugar
2 teaspoons rosewater or vanilla extract
½ cup slivered or whole blanched (untoasted) almonds

Rinse the apricots several times in cold water, drain them and place them in a large bowl. Mix the apricot nectar, sugar, and rosewater, or vanilla extract and pour over the apricots. Stir in the almonds and refrigerate, covered with plastic wrap for at least 2 days or up to 5 days, stirring once a day. To serve, place in a large glass bowl or spoon into individual dessert dishes.

Basic Recipes and Techniques

Sashimi Dipping Sauce

Makes about 1 cup

1 teaspoon Wasabi (horseradish powder), or more if a hotter sauce is desired
¾ cup soy sauce
1 cup grated white daikon radish
1 teaspoon peeled and grated fresh ginger

Mix the Wasabi with enough water to form a thick paste. Mix with the soy sauce, daikon, and ginger.

Sweet and Salty Dipping Sauce

Partner this with sushi or strips of fresh sweet pepper, blanched cauliflower and broccoli florets, and cooked sweet potato slices.

Makes about 1½ cups

½ cup each soy sauce, saki, and mirin (a sweet Japanese cooking wine)
1 teaspoon granulated sugar
1 tablespoon sesame oil
Drop or 2 of Tabasco or hot oil (to taste)

Boil together the soy sauce, saki, mirin, and sugar until syrupy. Stir in the sesame oil and Tabasco or hot oil.

Your Own Fresh Tomato Juice

Makes about 1 quart

10 medium-to-large fully ripe tomatoes, peeled, cored, and cut in quarters plus 2 large fully ripe tomatoes, peeled, cored, and coarsely chopped
½ teaspoon granulated sugar (optional)
Fresh lemon juice
Salt and freshly ground pepper to taste

Put the 10 tomatoes in a large saucepan with the sugar and simmer over low heat until soft, stirring frequently. Add the chopped fresh tomatoes. Cool slightly, then puree in food processor or blender. Strain and season to taste with lemon juice, salt, and pepper before serving cold.

Fresh Tomato Sauce with Orange

The freshness of this sauce is enhanced by three very important ingredients: freshly squeezed orange juice, orange zest, and a last-minute addition of chopped golden tomatoes.

Makes about 5 cups

1 large leek, trimmed of roots, tough outer leaves, and all but 3 inches of green top
3 tablespoons good-quality olive oil
1 large onion, peeled and finely chopped
3 cloves garlic, peeled and minced
10 large, ripe red tomatoes, peeled, seeded, and coarsely chopped
1 tablespoon each finely chopped fresh basil, oregano, and thyme leaves (or 1 teaspoon of each dried)
3 cups Homemade Chicken Broth (page 186) or canned
2 cups freshly squeezed orange juice
2 1-inch strips orange zest (thin outer skin of the fruit, with none of the bitter white under-skin included), minced, or 1 teaspoon grated
Tabasco to taste
1 tablespoon fennel seeds
2 teaspoons minced hot red pepper (or more or less to taste)
Generous pinch of saffron
Salt and freshly ground black pepper to taste
4 low-acid golden tomatoes, peeled, seeded, and coarsely chopped

Split the leek, wash it thoroughly, and finely chop it. Heat the oil in a large saucepan, and sauté the leek, onion, and garlic until the vegetables are soft but not brown. Add the tomatoes and herbs, cover, and cook over low heat for 5 minutes. Uncover, add the broth and orange juice and bring to a boil. Skim off and discard any froth that rises to the top. Stir in the orange zest, Tabasco, fennel seeds, red pepper, saffron, and salt and pepper. Simmer the sauce, uncovered, for 45 minutes. Add the golden tomatoes and boil 10 minutes or until the sauce is nicely thickened. Skim off and discard any froth. The sauce will be chunky. If you prefer a smoother sauce, puree half and stir it into the remainder of the sauce. Serve hot.

VARIATION

To prepare this sauce out of season, substitute canned tomatoes packed in puree for the fresh red tomatoes simmered in the sauce, and instead of the golden tomatoes added at the end, use chopped fresh red ones. Not quite as zesty as the original recipe, but still excellent.

Salsa Cruda

This is one of those all-purpose wonders, a simple but remarkably versatile sauce for enhancing greens, pasta, polenta, beans, eggs, fish, or meat. There is only one constant . . . the tomatoes must be red and ripe. If only the pink, golf-ball-like variety is available, choose another sauce.

Makes 3–4 cups

3 pounds ripe red tomatoes
3 garlic cloves, peeled and minced
⅓ cup chopped fresh basil (or other herbs; Italian parsley, perhaps)
¼ cup extra-virgin olive oil
  Salt and freshly ground black pepper to taste

Spear each tomato with a fork and hold it over a gas burner (or plunge it into boiling water) until the skin cracks. Pull off and discard the skin. Quarter the tomatoes; seed, core, and cut them into ½-inch cubes; then place them in a bowl along with the garlic, herbs, oil, and seasonings and any additional ingredients you might choose to include. Let stand at room temperature for at least 1 hour, but preferably 2. Mash lightly with a fork. Serve warm, chilled, or at room temperature.

VARIATION

Any number of ingredients may be added to vary the impact of this terrific sauce—minced fresh sweet or hot peppers, minced scallion, anchovies, chopped black or stuffed olives, and whatever fresh herbs you might like to try.

Fresh and Easy Tomato Sauce

Makes about 3 cups

3 tablespoons olive oil
1 medium-size onion, peeled and finely chopped
1 medium-size carrot, scraped and finely chopped
1 rib celery, trimmed and finely minced
1 clove garlic, peeled and finely minced (or more to taste)
1 tablespoon minced fresh basil (or 1 teaspoon dried)
4 pounds red or golden plum tomatoes, peeled, seeded, and coarsely chopped
½ teaspoon granulated sugar (optional)
  Salt and freshly ground black pepper to taste

In a large, heavy kettle, heat the oil and add the onion, carrot, celery, garlic, and basil. Cook over low heat until the vegetables are soft, then add the tomatoes and bring to a boil. Add the sugar and salt and pepper, turn the heat *very* low and simmer, covered, 2–3 hours, stirring occasionally to keep the sauce from sticking. The sauce should be fairly thick.

Fresh Tomato Puree

Makes about 2 cups

- 1 tablespoon olive oil
- 16–20 fully ripe tomatoes, cut in eighths
- ½ teaspoon granulated sugar (optional)

In a heavy stainless steel pan, heat the oil and add the tomatoes and sugar. Cook over medium heat, uncovered, until the juices evaporate and the mixture has a nice thick consistency.

Puree the tomatoes in a blender or food processor or rub them through a food mill or sieve. If the mixture seems too watery, return to the pan and cook until thick enough to cling to the spoon, stirring occasionally.

Green Tomato Puree

Makes about 2 cups

- 16–20 medium-size green tomatoes (use only those that have begun to turn white on the bottom; the dark green ones will be bitter)
- 1 tablespoon olive oil
- 1 teaspoon granulated sugar (optional)

Wash the tomatoes, cut them in quarters, scrape out the seeds, and coarsely chop them by hand or in a food processor. In a heavy stainless steel saucepan, heat the oil and add the tomatoes, sugar, if desired, and ¼ cup water. Cook over medium-low heat for about 1 hour, or until fairly thick, stirring occasionally. Lower the heat and allow the mixture to reduce to the consistency you desire, stirring continuously. Strain.

White Turnip Puree

Makes about 1½ cups

- 8 small white turnips
- 2 tablespoons soft margarine or vegetable oil
- Salt and freshly ground black pepper

Peel the turnips and cut into cubes. Cook in boiling salted water until tender, about 20 minutes. Drain thoroughly and puree, then simmer over low heat, stirring continuously, until all excess moisture has evaporated. Add the margarine or oil and simmer just enough to firm the consistency. Season to taste with salt and pepper.

Salsify Puree

Salsify is also known as oyster plant, apparently because someone, somewhere thought it tasted like oysters. It doesn't. But it can be extremely tasty when properly prepared.

Serves 6

2½ pounds salsify
  2 tablespoons lemon juice
    Homemade Chicken Broth
    (page 186)
  2 tablespoons soft margarine
    Pinch of nutmeg
    Salt and freshly ground black
    pepper to taste
    Low-fat milk

Scrape the salsify roots and cut them into 1-inch pieces. Be sure to drop them immediately into cold water with the lemon juice added to prevent discoloration. Cook in broth to cover 30–40 minutes, or until tender. Drain and puree.

Press through a sieve to remove any tough fibers. Mix the resulting puree with the margarine and seasonings and just enough milk to produce a smooth, thick mixture. Serve hot.

Squash Puree

Makes 3–4 cups

1 ripe medium-to-large butternut,
  acorn, or other winter squash (or
  about 2–3 pounds)
  Vegetable oil or soft margarine
  Pinch of ground nutmeg
  Salt and freshly ground pepper to
  taste

Preheat oven to 350° F. Cut the squash in half, then spoon out and discard all seeds and stringy fibers. Set the vegetables in an ovenproof pan, add hot water to the depth of 1 inch, and bake 1½–2 hours, or until the pulp is tender. Scrape the hot pulp into a food mill or food processor, add oil or margarine, nutmeg, salt and black pepper, and puree.

VARIATION

Add 1–2 tablespoons maple syrup to the puree.

To heighten the flavor, replace the hot water in the squash halves with chicken broth, orange juice, or pear nectar.

Fresh Green Pea Puree

Makes about 2 cups

4 cups shelled green peas (about 4
  pounds unshelled)
2 teaspoons soft margarine
2 teaspoons vegetable oil
  Salt
  Pinch granulated sugar (optional)

Cook the peas in 1 cup water, covered, stirring every few minutes. This will take about 10 minutes. Do not overcook. Drain the peas well and puree, then place in a saucepan with the margarine and oil, and simmer over low heat, stirring continuously, until thick. Season to taste with salt and sugar, if desired.

Basic Duxelles

Makes about 1½ cups

2 teaspoons light olive oil
2 teaspoons soft margarine
8 ounces very fresh, perfect mushrooms, wiped, trimmed, and
 very finely chopped
1 shallot, peeled and minced
2 teaspoons minced fresh parsley
 Salt to taste

In a heavy saucepan, heat the oil and margarine and cook the mush-rooms and shallot until all the cooking liquid evaporates. Remove from the heat, stir in the parsley, and season to taste with salt.

Basic Brown Rice

Brown rice is far more nutritious than white rice, cooks only a few minutes longer, and is less likely to overcook and become mushy. You owe it to yourself and your family to include it.

Serves 6

1½ cups brown rice
 Salt to taste
1 teaspoon vegetable oil
 (optional)

Bring 3½ cups water to a boil, stir in all the ingredients and cook tightly covered until water is absorbed (about 50 minutes, or follow package instructions).

Basic Bulgur

Makes about 3 cups

1 tablespoon soft margarine or
 vegetable oil
1 cup bulgur
1 small onion, peeled and finely
 chopped
⅛ teaspoon salt
 Pinch each rosemary, thyme,
 and grated fresh nutmeg
2½ cups chicken, fish, or vegetable
 broth

In a large skillet, heat the margarine or oil and add the bulgur, onion, and seasonings. Cook over medium heat until the bulgur and onion are golden. Add the broth and bring to a boil, then lower the heat and simmer gently for 15 minutes, or until the bulgur is tender. Serve hot or refrigerate and use in other recipes.

VARIATION

Prepare Basic Bulgur. Toss with 3 tablespoons light soy sauce, 2 tea-spoons dark sesame oil, and ¼ cup minced chives. Serve warm or hot.

Basic Polenta

Better known for years in this country as plain old cornmeal mush, served in a variety of forms and found primarily in Southern and farm-house dishes, delicious Italian polenta has finally come into its own to become the darling of food lovers everywhere. It's about time.

 Although it's an unusually straightforward pursuit, preparing polenta has the reputation for being somewhat difficult to master, and it can be

(continued)

unless you know a few tricks. First, begin cooking it in cold water, rather than the boiling water most recipes recommend. This method assures that you'll have no sticky lumps to strain or press out with the back of your cooking spoon. Next, although polenta in its moist form should be used within minutes of cooking, you can keep it warm and hold off serving it for a few minutes by stirring in tablespoons of boiling water as needed to keep it from stiffening. Better yet, if serving must be postponed, try chilling the dish in loaf form, then slicing and frying, baking, or grilling it. Fine cornmeal cooks up smooth and silky. Coarser cornmeal has more texture and is superb served with heartier dishes.

Serves 6

5 cups **Homemade Chicken Broth (page 186), Vegetable Stock (page 184), or water**
1½ cups **yellow cornmeal**
2 tablespoons **extra-virgin olive oil, vegetable oil, or margarine (optional)**
Salt and freshly ground black pepper to taste

The stock or water should be at room temperature or cold, not boiling, when you stir in the cornmeal.

Stir over low heat as the polenta comes to a boil. Once the polenta is smooth and fairly thick, you can stir less frequently until it is very thick, about 30 minutes all together.

To serve, stir in the oil, if desired, and the salt and pepper.

You can also bake, fry, or grill polenta.

To bake: Preheat the oven to 350° F. Spread the polenta in an oiled loaf or cake pan, sprinkle with 2 tablespoons grated Parmesan, and bake 15 minutes. Turn out on a hot plate, slice, and serve immediately.

To fry: Place the polenta in an oiled loaf pan and chill until ready to use. Cut into ¾-inch-thick slices and fry in vegetable oil until lightly browned. If you prefer, the slices may be dusted very lightly with flour before frying for extra crispy texture.

To grill: Proceed as for frying but brush slices lightly with oil before lightly browning on a well-oiled grill.

Vegetable Stock

Vegetable stock can be made in many ways. In this rich, nutrition-packed version, excellent use is made of those fresh vegetable trimmings you might ordinarily discard. A few days before you decide to make this stock, save up parsley, watercress, spinach, or mushroom stems, the outer leaves of lettuce, leek greens, pea pods, slightly soft overripe but not spoiled tomatoes, in other words, any wholesome albeit slightly unattractive vegetable pieces except those from members of the cabbage family, whose strong flavor may overwhelm the others.

Makes about 10 cups

- 3 medium-size onions, peeled and quartered
- 3 large carrots, cut into ½-inch pieces
- 2 ribs celery, with yellow inner leaves only, coarsely chopped
- 2 leeks, well washed and thinly sliced
- 3 tomatoes, cored and cut in eighths
- 10 medium-size mushrooms, chopped
- 5 scallions, cut into ½-inch pieces
- 5 parsley sprigs
- 1 small white turnip, peeled and sliced
- 2–3 cups leftover vegetable trimmings (or more)
- 12 cups water and/or any combination of leftover liquids from cooked vegetables (other than cabbage family members)

In a large stockpot, bring the vegetables and water slowly to a boil, skimming off the grayish foam that rises to the surface. Adjust the heat and simmer, partially covered, for 1½–2 hours, or until the flavors are well blended. Line a fine strainer with several layers of dampened cheesecloth and strain the stock through, pressing down with the back of a spoon to release all the juices. Divide into containers and refrigerate or freeze. Season as desired when reheating.

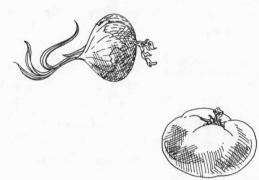

Fish Stock

Makes about 2 quarts

- 2 tablespoons vegetable oil
- 1 medium-size onion, peeled and coarsely chopped
- 2 medium-size carrots, scraped and thinly sliced
- 2 ribs celery with pale yellow leaves only, trimmed and thinly sliced
- 2 pounds fish heads (with gills removed), bones and trimmings from any white-fleshed, non-oily fish
  Cooked lobster, shrimp, and/or mussel shells* (optional)
  Dry white wine
- 2 tablespoons chopped fresh parsley, including some stems

In a heavy stockpot, heat the oil, add the onion, carrots, and celery and cook, stirring occasionally, until the vegetables are barely tender but have not taken on any color. Add the fish parts and shellfish shells. Pour in water and wine to suit your taste (5 cups water to 4 cups wine makes an excellent stock but less wine may be used). Bring the mixture to a very low boil and skim off any gray scum that rises to the surface. Reduce the heat, add the parsley, and allow to simmer, uncovered, for 20 minutes. Strain through several layers of dampened cheesecloth arranged over a fine sieve. Cool and refrigerate or freeze. Season when reheating.

---

* Your fish store might contribute fish heads or seafood shells if you ask nicely.

Homemade Chicken Broth

When preparing this or any broth that will be frozen, it's better to omit the seasonings and then add them at reheating time.

Makes about 3 quarts

1 3- to 4-pound stewing chicken with skin discarded
Carcass from a cooked roast chicken, with bits of meat (but not skin) attached, or 8 skinless chicken necks

1 veal knuckle (optional)
Chicken gizzards

3 medium-size carrots, scraped, trimmed, and cut into 1-inch slices

2 leeks, white part only, trimmed and cut into 1-inch lengths

1 large onion, peeled and cut into eighths

12 cups water or any combination of leftover liquid from freshly cooked vegetables (cabbage family members impart a strong taste that drowns out other more subtle flavors and are therefore usually omitted)

1 small bay leaf

¼ teaspoon black peppercorns

2 teaspoons minced fresh thyme and marjoram (or ½ teaspoon dried)

In a large stockpot, slowly bring the chicken, chicken carcass, veal knuckle, if using, gizzards, vegetables, and water or other liquid to a boil. Reduce the heat, partially cover, and allow to simmer very slowly for 1 hour, skimming off and discarding the grayish foam as it rises to the surface. When no more foam appears simmer, partially covered, for 2 hours longer, or until the chicken is very tender. Remove the chicken and reserve for another use. Remove and discard any large bones in the broth.

Line a large strainer with several layers of dampened cheesecloth and set it over a clean stockpot. Pour in the broth and solids, pressing the vegetables with the back of a wooden spoon to release as much flavor as possible. Discard the solids, pour the broth into containers, and chill quickly, skimming off and discarding any fat that forms on top, then refrigerate or freeze. Season when reheating.

Rich Beef Broth

Makes 10–12 cups

3–4 pounds beef and veal bones, cut into small pieces by your butcher

2 large carrots, scraped and sliced into 1-inch pieces

2 large onions, peeled and quartered

1½ pounds lean beef

Leftover scraps of good lean meat

2 pounds skinless chicken necks and backs

3 large ribs celery, with tender yellow leaves only, cut into ½-inch pieces

1 large white turnip, peeled and sliced

5 sprigs parsley

1 small bay leaf

Preheat the oven to 450° F. Put the beef and veal bones and half the carrots and onions in a large roasting pan and roast for 30 minutes, then transfer the bones and vegetables to a large soup kettle. Discard the surface grease from the roasting pan, add 3 cups of the water, and bring to a boil, deglazing the pan by scraping any brown bits that cling to the sides and bottom. Add this liquid to the soup kettle along with 11 cups water, the lean beef, meat scraps, and chicken parts. Partially cover and bring to a boil, skimming off and discarding the grayish foam that rises to the surface.

When no more foam appears, add the remaining ingredients. Continue to cook the broth over low heat, partially covered, for 4 to 5 hours. Remove and discard the meat bones and use a soup spoon to scoop off as much fat as possible. Line a large sieve with several layers of dampened cheesecloth and strain the broth into a clean bowl, pressing down with the back of a spoon to release the flavors. Discard the solids, divide the broth into pint or quart containers, and chill quickly, removing any fat that rises to the surface. Refrigerate or freeze. Season broth when reheating.

Chicken Consommé

Consommé is broth that has been clarified until it is crystal clear, then reduced to enhance and intensify its flavor. To clarify, use 1 egg white and 1 crushed eggshell for each 4 cups of liquid. Be sure to chill and completely degrease your homemade stock or broth first; the presence of fat particles will hinder the clarification process.

Makes about 8 cups

3 egg whites

Shells from 3 eggs, crushed

12 cups well-skimmed Homemade Chicken Broth (page 186)

Beat the egg whites to a froth and add them, along with the eggshells, to the broth. Bring the mixture to a boil, stirring continuously, and continue to boil and stir until the egg whites thicken into a mass and rise to the surface. Immediately remove the pan from the heat and let stand for 5 minutes while the egg whites settle. Line a fine sieve with several layers of dampened cheesecloth, and taking care not to agitate the broth too much, pour the soup through into a clean saucepan.

To prepare consommé, simmer the clarified broth over low heat until it is reduced to two thirds of its original volume.

VARIATION: PEPPERY CONSOMMÉ

Simmer a small whole serrano or jalapeño pepper in 8 cups chicken consommé or beef broth until the liquid is peppery enough to suit your taste. Use the pepper for another purpose.

Garlic Crusts

Serves 6

6 slices day-old bread
2–3 tablespoons fruity, extra-virgin olive oil
2–3 large garlic cloves, peeled and split

Trim the crusts and cut each bread slice in half to form 2 triangles. Put the oil and garlic halves in a skillet, and heat until the oil begins to smoke, then remove and discard the garlic. Add the bread triangles and fry until golden brown on both sides, turning once. Keep warm.

VARIATION: GARLIC CROUTONS

Follow directions for Garlic Crusts but cut the trimmed bread slices into ½-inch squares.

Cornbread Crumbs

Makes 3–4 cups

1 recipe Corn and Pepper Bread (page 171), prepared with or without peppers, or any other cornbread
3 tablespoons vegetable oil

Coarsely crumble the cornbread. Heat the oil in a medium-size, non-stick skillet, add the crumbs, and quickly toss to distribute the oil evenly. Continue to toss the crumbs over medium-low heat until they are lightly browned. Serve hot or at room temperature. Store leftover crumbs in a tightly closed container in your refrigerator or freezer.

Alternatively, you may prepare the crumbs in your oven. Preheat oven to 350° F. Crumble the cornbread, toss with the oil, spread on a cookie sheet, and bake until lightly browned, stirring every few minutes. Serve hot or at room temperature. Store leftover crumbs as above.

Frybread Rolls

These make excellent sandwich rolls or breakfast treats.

Makes about 12–15 rolls

1 recipe Indian Fry Bread (page 68)
Vegetable oil for frying

Prepare dough as directed for Indian Fry Bread but roll out in one large sheet. Tear off circular pieces about 2½ inches across, poke a hole in the middle, and drop, one by one, into ¼-inch-deep hot oil. Brown each piece on both sides. Serve hot.

Toast Points

Serves 6

Olive oil
Soft margarine
12 slices white bread

Preheat the oven to 350° F. Mix enough olive oil into the margarine so that it barely holds its shape. Toast the bread, trim the crusts, and cut each slice diagonally into 4 triangles. Just before serving, spread the oil-softened margarine on one side of each triangle, then bake in the oven 10–15 minutes, or until crisp.

VARIATION

Add ½ to 1 teaspoon anchovy paste to taste. Serve with vegetable or fish dishes.

Vinaigrette Dressing

It's fun to mix and match flavored and plain oils with subtle and not-so subtle vinegars available at gourmet markets. Dress up salad fixings with strawberry vinegar and hazelnut oil or a touch of orange juice and balsamic vinegar mixed with Garlic Enhanced Olive Oil. Experiment until you discover your own house specials.

Makes 1 cup

¼ cup red or white wine vinegar
Salt to taste
Generous pinch of freshly ground black pepper
¾ cup olive oil (plain or flavored)

Beat together the vinegar and seasonings until well blended. Slowly add the oil and continue beating until the dressing is well mixed.

Capered French Dressing

Makes about 1 cup

⅛ teaspoon anchovy paste
1 large clove garlic, peeled and minced
Tabasco to taste
1 cup Vinaigrette Dressing (recipe above)
2 teaspoons drained capers

Use a fork to beat the anchovy paste, garlic, and Tabasco into the dressing, then add the capers. Or whirl the dressing, anchovy paste, garlic, and Tabasco for a few seconds in the bowl of a food processor. Add the capers and whirl a second longer.

Rosemary Vinaigrette

Prepare Vinaigrette Dressing as directed, but substitute rosemary olive oil for the olive oil. Proceed as directed.

Herb-Enhanced Oils

Makes 1 bottle

6 sprigs fresh herb (thyme, rosemary, oregano, or marjoram)
1 bottle olive oil

Do not wet the herbs. To clean them, simply wipe them with a damp (not wet) cloth and pat dry with paper towels. Pick the leaves from half the herb sprigs, discard the bare stems, and mince the leaves with a stainless steel knife. Pour off a few tablespoons of oil from the bottle and use for another purpose. Add the minced herbs and the remaining herb sprigs to the bottle, replace the cork (or otherwise cover), and let stand in a cool, dark place for 1 to 2 months.

Garlic-Enhanced Olive Oil

Makes 1 bottle

  1 bottle olive oil
10–20 garlic cloves, peeled and cut in quarters lengthwise, with a stainless steel knife

Pour off ¼ cup olive oil from the bottle and add the garlic. Pour back enough oil to fill the bottle and replace the cork (or otherwise seal). Let stand several weeks in a cool, dark place. When all the oil has been used, mince the cloves and toss with pasta or salad greens.

Olive Oil with Peppercorns

Makes 1 bottle

3 tablespoons dried whole peppercorns (black, white, pink, etc.)
1 bottle olive oil

Crack the peppercorns with a mortar and pestle. Pour off a few tablespoons of the oil from the bottle, reserving for another purpose, then add the peppercorns, seal, and store for 2 weeks in a cool place.

Oil-Cured Garlic Cloves

I very often arrange the peeled and halved cloves from several heads of garlic in a pint jar, cover them with olive oil, and set them aside for several weeks in a cool, dark place. By the time I use them, the garlic itself is somewhat oil-cured and milder on the tongue. The oil, on the other hand, is wonderfully robust and assertive.

I sliver the garlic cloves and use some on plain-tasting fish, fowl, or vegetables. The oil is saved to be used alone, as a dip for crusty bits of breads, or to puddle on saucers of olives or other hors d'oeuvres. Superb.

Rosemary Olive Oil

Makes 1 cup

1 sprig fresh rosemary
1 cup olive oil

Rub the rosemary between your hands to slightly bruise it. Place the sprig in the olive oil and allow to stand for 36 hours. Discard the herb and use the oil as directed in individual recipes.

Basic Crêpes

Your food processor whirls these up in seconds.

Serves 6

1 cup (8 ounces) egg substitute equivalent to 4 eggs
1½ cups low-fat milk
A pinch of salt (optional)
3 tablespoons vegetable oil
1 cup all-purpose flour
2 tablespoons oat bran or wheat germ
Additional oil or margarine as needed

Whirl all ingredients except additional oil or margarine in food processor using the steel blade. When well mixed, refrigerate batter for 2 hours.

Rub inside of a 6-inch, non-stick skillet (or crêpe pan) generously with oil, heat for 1 minute, and wipe away most of the oil with a paper towel. Stir the crêpe batter. Heat ¼ teaspoon oil or margarine, tilting the pan from side to side to coat the bottom and sides evenly. Quickly pour 2–3 tablespoons batter into the pan and rotate it rapidly around and from side to side to spread the batter evenly all over the bottom. As soon as bubbles appear over the surface, loosen one edge of the crêpe with a spatula. When the bottom is lightly browned, turn the crêpe over to lightly brown the other side. Slide the crêpe from the pan onto a plate.

Prepare subsequent crêpes in the same manner rubbing the bottom of the pan with a well-oiled paper towel between crêpes. Stack one crêpe atop another as they come from the pan.

Freeze the crêpes in a Ziploc plastic bag until needed. Reheat in a microwave oven or remove the pancakes from the plastic bag, wrap in foil and reheat on the middle rack of a warm oven.

Onion and Orange Marmalade

Tart and sweet. Crunchy with onion. Fruity with orange syrup. Tangy with citrus peel. Perfect with just about anything.

Makes 5–6 cups

1 teaspoon salt
3 cups granulated sugar
16 small yellow onions, peeled, cut in half vertically, and thinly sliced
1 cup freshly squeezed orange juice
1 cup seedless raisins
Zest (the thin outer skin of the fruit with none of the bitter white underskin included) from 4 oranges or enough to make 1 cup thin strips

Mix the salt and sugar. In a large stainless steel pot, arrange alternate layers of sliced onions and the sugar and salt mixture. Allow to stand overnight. Add the orange juice and bring to a boil over medium heat, reduce the heat to lowest possible setting and simmer, uncovered, for 1½ hours, stirring occasionally to keep the mixture from sticking. Stir in the raisins and orange zest and cook for 1½ hours longer, stirring more frequently to avoid burning as mixture cooks down. Pour into clean jars and refrigerate until needed.

Toasted Pumpkin Seeds

Makes about 1 cup

1 cup pumpkin seeds
2 teaspoons vegetable oil
Salt to taste

Wash the seeds, taking care to remove and discard any bits of pumpkin flesh that cling to them, and pat dry. Spread on paper towels and let stand overnight. Heat the oil in a large heavy skillet, add the pumpkin seeds, and cook, stirring frequently, until the seeds take on a golden brown color. Remove from the heat and toss with salt to taste.

Toasted Sesame Seeds

Makes ¼ cup

¼ cup sesame seeds

Put the sesame seeds in a large, heavy non-stick skillet over medium heat and cook, stirring continuously, just long enough for the seeds to take on a rich brown color. Take care not to let them burn.

Garam-Masala

This lively combination of spices is frequently available in Indian or gourmet food stores, but just in case you can't find it, here's the recipe. It will help you get used to using out-of-the-ordinary seasonings when they're called for—and even when they're not.

Add this to meatballs, or rub it on chicken before it's roasted. You'll be surprised at how quickly humdrum dishes turn into something special. This particular seasoning mix dates back to biblical times. The authentic article is made from the whole spices, finely ground but not powdered. If you can find the whole ingredients and grind them yourself, by all means, do so. If not, mix the powdered variety, but make sure they're fresh.

3 tablespoons each coriander, cardamom, black peppercorns, and caraway seeds
1 tablespoon each cloves and cinnamon

Whirl all ingredients in a tightly covered blender or small food processor until the caraway seeds are fine. Wait for the spices to settle, then store in an airtight container.

Carrot Flowers

Use as a garnish or prepare a plateful to see how an unusual shape can make an ordinary vegetable very special.

Makes about 3 cups

4 medium-size carrots, scraped and trimmed

Use a sharp knife to make 4 shallow V-shaped cuts, at equal distances, along the entire length of each carrot. Slice the carrots vertically at ¼-inch intervals to form 4-petaled "flowers."

VARIATION

Cook in chicken broth flavored with a pinch each ground cardamom, cloves, cinnamon, and black pepper. No need to add salt.

Scallion Tassels

12 very slender scallions trimmed of roots

Line the scallions up with their roots in a line side by side and cut off the green tops evenly (including about 1 inch of green). Discard the cut off tops. Use a small sharp knife to make narrow, 1 inch slits in the tops of the scallions to feather the edges. Chill in ice water to cover until the scallion tops curl slightly. Use as a garnish.

Radish Roses

Cut off and discard root end from any small radish. Trim away all but 2 small leaves. Holding the radish by the leaf end, make parallel cuts ¼ inch apart in the root end. Do not cut through to the leaf end. Give the radish a half-turn and make similar cuts perpendicular to the first ones. Refrigerate in ice water until the bottom half of the radish "rose" spreads out attractively. Serve icy cold.

Charred Carrot Shreds

A pile of these naturally sweet carrot shreds can add interesting texture and flavor to any number of dishes. Try them on baked potatoes, fish, or chicken.

1¼–1½ pounds medium-size carrots, scraped
3 tablespoons fruity olive oil
Salt and freshly ground white pepper to taste

Shred the carrots and fill a heavy 8-inch pan (cast iron is best) with them. Cook over high heat, turning regularly with a spatula until the shreds become dehydrated and lightly browned. When they are dry and just beginning to blacken around the edges, lower the heat, add the oil, salt, and pepper, and toss carefully until the oil is distributed. Serve immediately.

Orange-Glazed Carrots

Serves 6

24 very small carrots, scraped and trimmed
2 cups orange juice
2 tablespoons honey
Salt, freshly grated pepper, and nutmeg to taste

Place the carrots in a large skillet, add the remaining ingredients, and cook over low heat until the carrots are just tender, but still have a bit of "crunch." Serve hot.

VARIATION: ORANGE-GLAZED SWEET POTATOES

Follow directions for Orange-Glazed Carrots but substitute slightly undercooked boiled and peeled sweet potato cut into 1-inch cubes.

How to Prepare Chestnuts

To roast 1 pound of chestnuts, preheat oven to 350° F. Use a sharp knife to cut a small cross on the flat side of each chestnut shell to allow steam to escape. Arrange nuts on a cookie sheet, cut side-up, and bake for 15 minutes. Remove shells and inner skins while nuts are still hot. Coarsely chop.

To boil 1 pound of chestnuts use a sharp knife to cut a cross on the flat side of each chestnut shell. Place the nuts in a saucepan, add water to cover, and bring to a boil over medium heat. Cook for 15 minutes, then drain. The outer shell and inner brown skin will come off much more easily if removed while the chestnuts are still hot.

Mixing, Kneading, Forming, and Baking Yeast Breads

Of all the culinary arts, perhaps the most creative and satisfying is breadbaking. Although many cooks approach this art with caution, it can also be one of the easiest, once you acquaint yourself with the basic procedures.

Mixing the Ingredients

Different types of breads may call for different ingredients and methods of preparation, but the aim in most is to produce a dough that is well mixed, firm, smooth, and not too sticky to handle.

Begin with lukewarm water or milk, broth, or juice that feels pleasantly warm (105° F. to 115° F.) when a few drops are touched to the inside of the wrist. (Compressed yeast requires liquid that is neither warm nor cool, but a neutral 95° F.) Add oil or soft shortening, sugar, and salt, and sprinkle the dry active yeast over it. Never shock the yeast with ingredients that are too warm or too cold.

Measure the flour called for and set aside ½ cup to sprinkle over your kneading surface. Stir in the remaining flour, 1 cup at a time, mixing well after each addition. Each cup added will firm up the dough and make it less sticky. As soon as the dough pulls away in a mass from the sides of the bowl, turn it out onto the floured surface and begin kneading. You may end up using more than the amount of flour called for if the day is humid and/or if the other ingredients were inaccurately measured.

How to Knead Dough

Kneading is the process whereby you vigorously push, pull, fold, and refold the dough once it has become too stiff to work any other way. Kneading is a one-on-one contact with the dough that smooths it and makes it flexible, eliminates air bubbles, and imparts a fine texture to the finished loaf. If time is short you may let your dough hook or let your food processor do your kneading for you, although hand kneading does add a deeply satisfying sense of participation that rewards the baker long before the first slice of bread is enjoyed.

Begin by sprinkling your kneading surface lightly with flour. Flour your hands lightly, too. Turn the dough out onto the work surface and press it firmly into a ball. If the dough seems sticky, add some of the reserved flour.

With the heels of your hands on the part nearest you, push the dough ball down and away from you to stretch and flatten it. Pull up the far side with your fingertips and fold the dough back toward you, then place the heels of your hands on the dough again and repeat the stretching and flattening motion. Give the dough a quarter-turn clockwise, pull the far side toward you, and push away again with the heels of your hands.

Continue to turn, pull, and push the dough for the length of time specified in the recipe (usually 10 minutes by hand, 2–3 minutes by machine). Knead vigorously; the dough should have firm but loving handling. After about 5 minutes, turn the dough over and continue as before. As kneading continues, the dough should become progressively firmer, smoother, and more elastic, with little blisters on its surface.

How to Test for "Double in Bulk"

Yeast dough must be allowed to rise until it is roughly twice its original size. Place the kneaded dough in a large, deep, oiled bowl, smooth side down, and turn the dough over to grease the top. Cover with a clean dish towel or other light cloth. Choose a warm, draft-free spot (an unlit oven will do nicely) where the dough can rise undisturbed in its bowl for the time specified in your recipe (usually about 1 hour).

To determine whether the dough has risen sufficiently, press two fingers firmly into its center. If the indentations remain after you withdraw your fingers, the dough is ready to be punched down. If the indentations disappear in a minute or so, re-cover the dough, allow it to stand another 15–20 minutes, and repeat the test.

Once the dough doubles in bulk, it is ready to be punched down. This is accomplished by pushing your fist firmly into the center of the dough, folding the edges in toward the center, and pressing out the air bubbles.

If your recipe indicates, you may shape the dough at this point. However, if a second rising is called for, turn the dough over in the bowl, re-cover lightly, and return it to its warm, draft-free place for the specified time. Punch down the dough again before shaping your loaves.

How to Shape Loaves

Turn the punched-down dough out of the bowl onto a lightly floured board or other work surface. Lightly dust a rolling pin with flour and shape the dough according to individual recipe directions. Bread may be shaped in many ways, none difficult to do. The conventional loaf is formed by flattening the dough (or half the dough at a time if your recipe produces two loaves) into a rectangle ¾ inch thick and roughly the length of your loaf pan. Roll this dough up tightly and pinch the seams together, then place it, seam side down, in a lightly oiled pan.

For a round loaf, pat dough into one large or two smaller rounded mounds, and place on a lightly oiled baking sheet. The dough should be firm enough to hold its shape. Dough may also be braided or formed into a large pretzel shape. Most doughs must be allowed to double in bulk in the pans (for approximately 1 hour).

How to Test Loaves

Your bread is perfectly baked when the loaf is smooth, shiny, and golden brown. A too-pale loaf means further baking is necessary. An additional test for doneness is to tap the bottom of the loaf pan lightly with your fingernail. If a hollow sound results, the bread is ready to serve.

Star Vegetables!

In-depth information on 132 new, unusual, and traditional vegetables including:

When and how much to buy

How to choose and store

Basic preparation

Introduction to Vegetables

At peak season your home garden, farm stand, or greengrocer's stalls overflow with a bounty of perfect vegetables. Yours for the picking or choosing are gorgeous green, gold, red, orange, purple, brown—even black—sweet peppers. Cherry and plum and Big Boy and beefsteak tomatoes. Bouquets of red oakleaf lettuce, bronze-leaved mignonette, radicchio, arugula, spinach, and watercress. Mint and coriander, lemon balm and borage, hyssop and sweet cicely, nasturtium and squash blossoms. Baby okra with its tiny pearl-like seeds. Vermillion beets. Fat tangle-rooted leeks. And best of all, in addition to being beautiful and delicious, these vegetables also supply energy-giving carbohydrates and health-promoting fiber (page 19 to 20) and are excellent sources for vitamins and minerals needed to promote good health.

Leafy green vegetables are rich sources of both vitamin C, necessary for maintaining connective tissue, and vitamin A, essential for eyes and skin. Root vegetables and tubers are high in vitamins B and C. Yellow, orange, and red vegetables provide both vitamins A and C. Both peas and beans supply important sources of protein. Some vegetables in combination (succotash for example) can provide the complete range of amino acids that make them complete proteins.

The following guide to vegetables outlines peak season, quantity to buy, selection, storage, and basic preparation for certain vegetables, both commonplace and exotic. While the simplest cooking techniques—blanching, steaming, sautéing, or broiling—are all that are needed to bring out natural goodness when vegetables are stereotypically relegated to tedious side dishes, something more imaginative is called for when these are given star treatment as an entrée. What this section aims to do is to introduce you to the new and unusual, to explore the myriad possibilities of vegetables when they are presented with the respect they deserve.

Artichoke

• Good all year long, or whenever available, but best in March, April, or May. One large artichoke serves one per person.

• Select plump, firm, fleshy leaved specimens of even green coloration. Beware of softness, darkening, or spreading leaves.

• Wash thoroughly in cold water and cut off the stem and enough of the bottom so that the artichoke stands upright.

• Use a stainless steel knife and acidulate all cuts with lemon juice or vinegar to avoid discoloration. Cut about an inch off the top and trim all sharp, exposed points with scissors. Keep in cold, acidulated water until ready to cook.

Place in a deep enamel or stainless pot, base down (aluminum discolors artichokes), cover with boiling water or stock, and maintain at boiling for 30 minutes. Test for doneness with a small, sharp knife inserted into the soft stem end. When done, the knife will penetrate easily. If this is still tough, cook 10–15 minutes more, or until soft. Serve hot or cold.

Arugula

• Available off-season in better markets but at its peak from May to October. Usually one bunch serves 2. Mixed with other greens, one bunch will serve 6–8.

• Select fresh-looking, smaller leaved bunches. Beware of tired, wilting, discolored, dry, or bruised leaves.

• Arugula is quite delicate, wilts easily, and thus cannot be stored for long. If you must store, place unwashed leaves in a tightly closed plastic bag or container and store in a cold part of the refrigerator.

• If sandy, rinse thoroughly but gently in cold water. Remove roots, pat dry, and serve broken or whole.

Asparagus

• Available April–June. Prepare ½ pound per person with the meal or, if used as a separate course, 5 or 6 thick stalks or the equivalent in thin ones.

• Choose straight, fresh, bright green stalks. Believe it or not, in most cases the thicker the stalk, the more tender. Beware of white streaks and flat stalks.

• To store, cut about an inch off the bottoms, wrap the asparagus in wet paper towels, and refrigerate in a plastic bag for a day or 2.

• Break or cut off woody ends and discard them. Wash asparagus thoroughly in cold water and place upright in an asparagus cooker, coffee pot, or bottom of a double boiler, add several inches of water, and, if necessary, cover the tops with aluminum foil. Boil the bottoms 4–6 minutes while the tops steam.

Or, peel the stalks to within 2 inches of the tips and place flat in about 3 inches of salted boiling water for 5–8 minutes. Test for doneness with a sharp paring knife, which should pierce the ends without resistance.

Wrap the stalks in foil and bake them to desired doneness (page 61).

Dried Beans

WASHING

Packaged dried beans have been pre-sorted and usually require no more than a rinsing to remove broken bean fragments or bits of dust. Beans bought loose or in bulk generally contain bits of debris—often pebbles—which should be removed before soaking and cooking.

SOAKING

This important procedure softens the beans and, by returning lost moisture, greatly reduces the cooking time. Reduced cooking time, in turn, saves vitamins and other nutritional elements, which break down under prolonged cooking. Use water liberally—at least 3 or 4 times as much water as beans.

Note: Another bonus of soaking is its role in reducing flatulence. The sugars—oligosaccharides—that create flatulence break down during soaking and are discarded with the water. Changing the soaking water 2 or 3 times will produce even better results.

SALTING

Don't add salt to the soaking or cooking water. Salt prevents the beans from absorbing water and hence slows down the soaking and virtually stops the softening process. If you do use salt, add it only after the beans have achieved their desired degree of softness.

COOKING

The slower the beans are cooked, the more easily they are digested. Be sure to add water as needed during the cooking process. Very hard water can keep your beans from cooking. If you have this problem, ⅛ teaspoon of baking soda per cup of beans will help, but any more will darken the beans, make them too soft, and will reduce their nutritional content as well. Beans cook best in soft water.

Note: Don't transfer the beans from the cooking water to any acidic sauce (chili, etc.) until they are as soft as you want them. They won't get softer in such a sauce no matter how long they are cooked.

QUANTITIES

Dried beans swell up to at least twice and sometimes 3 times their former size during cooking.

1 cup dried beans =
- 2–3 cups cooked
- 1–1¼ pounds cooked
- 4 servings
- 1 pound dry weight

Beans, Green (or Yellow)

- Always available but best from June through August. One pound serves 3–4.
- Select young, bright green (or yellow) beans. They should snap crisply and easily. Beware of old, leathery, bulging pods.
- Wash in cold water and place in the crisper in an air-tight plastic bag. Flavor and quality will start to deteriorate in 2–3 days, so use as soon as possible.
- Beans may be washed in cold water and prepared in a variety of ways. Slender, young beans

may be served whole. To prepare larger ones, cut or break them into 1- to 1½-inch lengths; slice into thin strips for frenched beans, or on the diagonal for Oriental dishes.

Beans may be blanched by dipping them briefly in boiling water, then immediately into cold; steamed for 15 minutes, covered, over boiling water; or boiled. Bring a large amount of water to a boil and add the beans a few at a time so that the water continues to boil. Boil 10–15 minutes, testing frequently to avoid overcooking.

Beans, Lima

- Best in spring and summer. About ¾ of a pound of fresh limas weighed in the pod will serve one person.
- Pick green, crisp, well-filled pods. Beware of blemishes and soft or flaccid pods. Baby limas are generally the most tender.
- Store in the refrigerator, unshelled and tightly covered. Use within 3 to 5 days.
- Pop the beans from their shells, discarding any that are blemished. Cook in a tightly covered pan in ½ inch of boiling, salted water 15–20 minutes, testing frequently to prevent overcooking.

Beets

- Available year-round but best from June through October. A bunch of medium-size beets, usually 5–7, will serve 3–4 people.
- Pick globular, regularly shaped specimens. Color should be a crimson-maroon (unless they are the golden variety), and the flesh should be firm and smooth. Small or medium beets are sweeter and more tender then the larger ones. Beware those with soft, moist spots and a rough surface.
- Remove all but 2 inches of the large top leaves (reserve the nourishing small bright-green leaves

Dried Beans

NAME	SHAPE	SIZE	COLOR	SOAKING TIME	COOKING TIME (approx.)
Adzuki azuki	oval	¼ inch	red-brown thin white heel	4 hrs.	60 min.
Black beans turtle beans, Mexican blacks, etc.	kidney	⅝ inch	shiny black, white heel	4 hrs.	90 min.
Black-eyed peas black-eyed bean, cowpeas, etc.	kidney	½ inch	creamy white	4 hrs.	70 min.
Canellini fasolia	oval	½ inch	white	4 hrs.	70 min.
Chick-peas garbanzos	round	⅜ inch	tan	4 hrs.	2 hrs. 15 min.
Fava broad bean, horse bean	flattish	¾ inch	creamy brown	12 hrs.	3 hrs.
Haricot great Northern bean, navy bean	oval	⅜ inch	white	1 hr.	20 min.
Lentils, brown	round	¼ inch	light brown	do not soak	35 min.
Lentils, green	round	¼ inch	olive green	do not soak	40 min.
Lentils, red	round	¼ inch	pink orange	do not soak	35 min.
Lima bean	flattish	1¼ inch	creamy white to pale green	4 hrs.	60 min. +
Baby limas	flattish	½ inch	pale green	3 hrs.	25 min.
Mung	round	¼ inch	olive green	4 hrs.	50–60 min.
Peas, pigeon	round	¼ inch	yellow-gray	do not soak	30 min.
Peas, split	half-round	¼ inch	green	do not soak	30 min.
Peas, whole	round	¼ inch	green	do not soak	30 min.
Pinto	oval	⅜ inch	tan	1–1½ hrs.	20 min.

for use in salads, soups, etc.). Place the beets in a plastic bag and refrigerate for up to 2 weeks.

• Wash the beets gently and simmer in boiling water in a covered pot 30–45 minutes for young beets and up to an hour for older specimens. Don't puncture to test for doneness or the beets will "bleed." Test by pressing the outside to see if they are soft.

Bok Choy (Chinese Chard)

• Available most of the year at Chinese markets and some supermarkets. Amounts depend on the dish you're preparing. One pound will generally suffice.

• Choose shiny green, unblemished leaves. Avoid wilted or limp specimens.

• Wrap in plastic and store in crisper 2–3 days. Use as soon as possible.

• Wash leaves, cut as directed in your recipe, and cook until tender, usually 8–10 minutes.

Broccoli

• Always available but best from October to May. A 2-pound bunch, the usual amount sold, will serve 4.

• Pick fresh, green, tender, and firm plants. Beware of large, loose buds and yellow flowers. These last, however, are lovely in salads.

• Wash thoroughly, place in a large plastic bag, and store in the refrigerator 2–3 days.

• Cut the broccoli into florets and peel the stems. Cook rapidly in a small amount of boiling, salted water 8–10 minutes, or until tender. Or steam 10–12 minutes, depending on the size of the florets.

If you are restricting fat and/or calories the vegetable is best boiled or steamed. To sauté the stems must be sliced to ¼-inch thickness and the florets must not be too large. To prepare broccoli for stir-frying, drop into boiling water, remove from the heat, let stand a minute, drain, rinse with cold water to stop the cooking, and then dry well to prevent oil splatters during stir-frying.

Brussels Sprouts

• Available most of the year but best from October though December. One pound will serve 4 people.

• Select sprouts that look fresh, have a nice green color, and are firm and compact. Beware of yellowing, soft, puffy-looking specimens.

• Although it is best to use these as soon as possible after purchase, you can refrigerate them in the crisper in an air-tight plastic bag for 2 or 3 days. If you grow your own and live in an area where winters stay below freezing (without intermittent thaws), wrap each plant in plastic bubblewrap, then unwrap and harvest throughout the winter.

• Slice off the stems (not too closely), discard loose or discolored leaves, and cut a shallow cross in the stem end to permit quicker cooking. Place in boiling salted water and continue to boil briskly in an uncovered pot until tender, from 5 to 15 minutes depending on their size and your taste. Or steam 10–18 minutes.

Cabbage

One of our oldest and best-known vegetables, and the major member of a large family that includes kale, collars, turnips, Brussels sprouts, and broccoli, among others, cabbage is astonishingly versatile. Possibilities include use in mixed salads, coleslaw, sauerkraut, or soups, or being stuffed (whole heads or leaves), boiled, or braised.

The three main varieties are the smooth leaf-green cabbage, the crinkly Savoy, and the red.

• Available all year long. A 2- or 3-pound head will serve 4.

• Pick neat, solid heads. Beware of wormholes, soft spots, flabbiness, or wilt.

• Store unwashed in a plastic bag in the refrigerator for up to 10 days. Savoy cabbages don't store as well, so use these as soon as possible.

• Remove outer wilted leaves from smooth-leaf green or Savoy cabbage. Use a stainless steel knife to avoid discoloration (of both knife and cabbage), and cut into eighths. Steam, covered, over boiling water 10 minutes; or cook in ½ inch water for 10 minutes in a large, covered pot. If you prefer, cut into ½-inch shreds and steam for 5 minutes as directed above or sauté in a lightly oiled pan until tender but not limp. The strong cooking odor is primarily the result of overcooking.

Prepare red cabbage as directed for green, but toss with a little lemon juice, wine, or vinegar to retain the color.

Cardoon (Cardoons, Cardoni, Cardi)

Up to 2 feet long with notched, fleshy, silver-gray stalks that are similar to celery in appearance, cardoon is actually a member of the artichoke family (which it resembles in flavor). It is low in calories, rich in potassium, calcium, and iron, but unfortunately high in sodium. Found occasionally late winter and early spring in Italian or gourmet markets. Two pounds (less considerable waste) serves 4.

Choose smallest specimens available (these are hard to find). Leaves should be fresh and dark green but there will be some browning and wilting.

Wrap the base in a damp towel and then in plastic and refrigerate up to 2 weeks.

Discard outer stalks and tops, halve and trim off base and cut stalks crosswise. Tender, sweet young stalks may be eaten raw, dipped in olive oil, or finely chopped and fried in egg batter in the Italian manner. Otherwise, boil until tender in water, to which has been added a splash of vinegar or lemon juice to help prevent discoloration. Dice and add to salads; broil with a sprinkle of cheese, or puree and add to mashed potatoes.

Carrots

• Available—and good—all year long. An average bunch, usually from 1–1½ pounds, will serve 3–4.

• Select well-shaped, crisp, smooth carrots of a deep hue. Beware of greenish specimens or those with yellowed tops.

• Remove tops and refrigerate in a plastic bag for 2 to 3 weeks.

• Wash, trim, and scrub with a stiff vegetable brush or scrape with a vegetable peeler. Slice, dice, shred, or cut as desired and cook in water to cover in a tightly covered saucepan. Whole carrots take up 30 minutes to cook; sliced, 10–12; and shredded, 4–5. Steamed take 2–3 minutes longer in each case.

Cauliflower

This creamy white, relatively new member of the cabbage family is now also more widely available in purple or green. It is excellent prepared whole or broken into pieces and served in a number of interesting ways—deep fried, pickled, curried, pureed, raw in salads, or as crudités. Like its cousin the cabbage, offensive odors may be minimized or eliminated by not overcooking.

• Usually available all year but most plentiful from September through November. A medium-size head will serve 4.

• Select white, firm heads with bright green leaves. Beware yellow or speckled heads or yellowed, wilted leaves.

• Plastic-wrap and store in refrigerator crisper for up to 5 days.

• Remove all but the smallest leaves, wash well, and cook whole or break into florets. Cook in 1 inch of water in a covered pot. Florets will be ready in 10–15 minutes, the whole head in about 20–30 minutes. A teaspoon of fresh lemon juice will keep the vegetable white as it cooks.

Cauliflower may also be steamed 12–18 minutes for florets, 25–35 for whole heads.

Celeriac (Celery Root)

This round, brown, rough-skinned root is very popular in Europe, and is becoming more well known in this country. Serve it cooked or raw.

• Available during the winter in specialty markets; 1½–2 pounds serves 4.

• Choose small or medium solid roots. The smoothest roots are easiest to peel. Beware of soft spots near the stalk end or overly large, woody roots.

• Discard any straggly root ends. Scrub with a brush, remove tops, and refrigerate for up to a week.

• Peel, cube or slice, and cook at a low boil until tender (5–10 minutes) in water to which has been added a splash of vinegar or lemon juice. Add to soup or stews several minutes prior to serving. Lovely cooked and mashed with potatoes. Or peel, grate, julienne, or shred and marinate in Vinaigrette Dressing for up to 24 hours. Serve as is or stir a little low-fat mayonnaise into the sauce.

Celery

• Available year-round. A whole, cooked celery will serve 4.

• Select fresh, crisp stalks. Light, glossy green celery is tastiest. Avoid soft areas, brown tinge, rot, and wilt.

• Trim, wash, and shake off excess water and store in a plastic bag in the refrigerator for 2 weeks or, if it is still firm, even a little longer.

• Wash well, cut into desired lengths, and chill in ice water prior to serving. To cook, remove leaves and prominent strings and boil in 1 inch salted water in a covered saucepan for about 8–10 minutes. Steam 10–12 minutes, covered, over boiling water.

Chard

• Available from July through September. Two pounds serves 4.

• Choose crisp, fresh, unblemished leaves.

• Store in a plastic bag in the refrigerator for several days.

• Wash well in cold water, remove thick stems, and reserve for cooking as you would asparagus or celery. Cook leaves as for spinach.

Chicory and Chicory Relatives

CHICORY

Chicory, in some areas mistakenly called endive, has narrow, curly-edged leaves and grows in a loose head. The pale imported French chicory is mildest in flavor and most tender to the tooth. Outer leaves are darkish green, inner leaves are yellow or white. Rinse and dry, wrap in damp paper towels, and refrigerate up to a week. Toss in salads.

ESCAROLE

Often confused with its cousins, escarole is frequently called chicory or endive. It has wide leaves, uncurled at the edges, and forms a somewhat bushier head than chicory.

RADICCHIO

Radicchio (the Italian name for chicory) is a star vegetable if ever there was one. With it's gorgeous, satiny, swirling leaves that frequently begin life as bright green, mellowing into a rich darker green and finally into the flashy white-streaked red-purple treasure we know and love, radicchio can grace a salad, highlight a pasta dish, or go it alone.

Don't let the price, once outrageous now only expensive, put you off. A little of this treasure goes a long way.

Available all year in many markets, these have turned out to be surprisingly untemperamental for all their beauty. Just so long as you choose a head that is firm at the base, with no holes showing, you can be fairly sure it will produce leaf after perfect leaf right down to the center. Radicchio stores well, too. Unrinsed, loosely wrapped, and refrigerated it will await your pleasure up to 2 weeks.

When ready to use, carefully loosen, rinse and dry, and toss in salads. Or cut in quarters, drizzle with olive oil, and sauté, grill, or bake. The cup-shaped leaves make perfect "bowls" for garnishes.

Collards

• Most abundant from February through April but available all year long.

• Choose crisp, clean, nicely colored, unblemished leaves. Avoid shriveled, limp, insect-damaged, or discolored leaves.

• These do not store well so use them as soon as possible. In the meantime, store in a bag in the refrigerator along with a few ice cubes.

• Wash well in cold water, shred, and simmer until tender in water to which has been added a little vinegar.

Corn

Corn on the cob at its peak is generally available for only 8–10 weeks, or even less. It's something to wait for, something to savour. The early, or green, corn, extremely fragile and lacking in sweetness, is sought after, nevertheless, more as a reminder of meals to come than for its own sake. Though admittedly nothing quite compares to corn cooked just minutes after being cut from the stalk, corn that is cut from the cob and immediately frozen does extend the pleasure of the season somewhat.

• Let's stretch it and say corn is available from May to September in some fortunate locales. More often, peak season is much shorter. Figure on from one ear to a dozen per person, depending on degree of mania.

• Select ears with fresh, green husks. If you can get away with it, puncture a kernel or two with your thumbnail—the freshest, ripe kernels will have delicate skin and exude a milky fluid; unripe corn will produce a thin, watery fluid; old corn will have a tough, hard-to-puncture skin and exude a thick white paste. The sugar in corn turns to starch as it ages.

• Cook just as soon as you can husk it and pop in into boiling water.

• Husk, place in boiling water, and when water boils again, turn off the heat and allow corn to remain in the water for up to 10 minutes, depending on taste. Serve immediately. Corn may also be roasted in its husk or the kernels cut from the cob, simmered a few minutes and served or frozen.

Cucumbers

• These are found in markets year-round but are more plentiful in summer. One medium-size cucumber will serve 2 when cooked, or 5–6 when eaten raw in a salad. Purchase one per person of the small, crisp pickling cukes.

• Select firm cucumbers of a rich green color. Avoid dull green, yellowing, or shriveling specimens.

• Store cucumbers wrapped in plastic in the refrigerator crisper for up to 1 week.

• These are generally eaten raw, peeled, unpeeled, or partially peeled, but are excellent peeled, seeded, and sautéed, steamed, or fried. In any case they require only a few minutes' cooking.

Dandelion Greens

This lovely bitter herb grows wild in country fields and may be gathered on spring days for turning into salads or wine. Be sure you collect plants far from any pollutants or car exhausts.

• Gather in spring or purchase in fancy food markets. One pound will serve 4.

• Choose tender, clean, fresh-looking leaves. Avoid wilted yellow or damaged plants. (Cultivated varieties are less bitter and of better size then wild ones.)

• Store, if you must, in a plastic bag in the refrigerator, but use as soon as possible.

• Serve raw as a salad green tossed with hot or cold dressing, prepare as spinach, or use in soups and stews. Roots, too, may be eaten in salads or fried.

Eggplant (Also Japanese, Oriental, Chinese, White, or Italian)

As a prime ingredient in countless satisfying entrées, the eggplant has proven itself as versatile as any leg of lamb. It's low in calories, rich in fiber, potassium, and folic acid. It's delicately flavored and eloquently formed. In short, a treasure.

• Traditionally, eggplant is lightly salted and set aside prior to cooking to reduce moisture and acridness. Most of this salt washes away as the vegetables ooze juice; however, very nearly the same effect may be achieved by simply placing the cut vegetables between towels and weighting them down lightly with a cutting board or plates for about 10 minutes. Try both ways. If you don't notice any difference, forgo the salt to gain a healthful benefit, not to mention saving a little time and trouble.

• Japanese or Oriental eggplant are thin-skinned, straight, narrow, striated, and rich purple with sweet meat and few seeds. These produce neat, attractive, and uniform slices.

Chinese eggplants are pale violet in color, smooth and slim with thin silky skin, a dearth of seeds, and exceptionally flavorful flesh.

White eggplants of all kinds, from the small egg-shaped ones up to the large round ones, have the advantage of having firmer, fine-grained, more delicately flavorful flesh along with the disadvantage of possessing thick skins which must be peeled off before cooking. Use in any recipe where firm white flesh is an advantage, in white or pastel sauces, for example.

• Available all year, but best and most plentiful in August and September. A large eggplant or two medium-size ones (approximately 1¾ pounds) will serve 4.

• Select firm medium-size eggplants, smooth, dark, shiny, and uniform in color. Beware of overly large eggplants or ones that feel light for their size. The flesh tends toward softness and they contain an abundance of large seeds. Stems and caps should be fuzzy and bright green. You are seeking specimens that have sweet, dense, moist meat.

• Keep in a cool, not cold, place. Store in a plastic bag and, if this is impossible, use within 24 hours.

• Eggplants are very versatile. Peel only the very large or the tough-skinned white fruits unless your recipe directs you to do so. Cut off the top and the stem, then slice, partially slice, dice and sauté, steam, of bake.

Endive (Belgian Endive)

• Look for endive from October through May. Generally buy a single endive per person. When serving raw, 1 will usually serve 2.

• Choose firm, clean stalks approximately 5 inches long, well bleached and creamy in color. Beware of discoloration, blemishes, wilt, or rot.

• Remove several of the outer leaves, dampen the stalk, wrap in plastic, and refrigerate. Store up to 3 days, but, ideally, use at once.

• Serve leaves whole, cut lengthwise into halves or quarters or broken into small pieces in a mixed salad. For cooked endive, cut in half lengthwise and braise in consommé (10–15 minutes) or steam whole for 15 minutes over low heat in a pan with a tight lid.

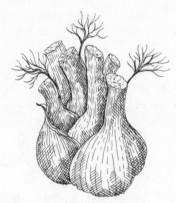

Fennel (Fenucchi, Fenocchio)

What other vegetable is so crunchy, so refreshing, so fragrant, so versatile? What other sports feathery green tops, celerylike stems, a bulbous base, all with a light licorice flavor that becomes even more subtle as it cooks? Versatile fennel.

• Available from October through March. In most cases, 4 or 5 small or 3 large bulbs serve 4 persons.

• Select crisp, round white bulbs with bright green leaves and celerylike stems.

• Refrigerate wrapped in plastic wrap.

• Trim off the feathery fronds and use as you would dill as a garnish or to flavor various dishes. Cut the bulb into thin shreds or slivers and cook or stir-fry as you would celery. Peel the stems and use

in soups and stews. Cook by removing the stalks from the bulbs and cutting out the hard core in the center. Cut the bulbs in quarters or ½-inch-vertical slices and braise them in broth until tender (20–25 minutes).

Fiddlehead Ferns

Increasingly popular, these tender scrolled shoots of the Ostrich fern have a distinctive flavor that falls somewhere between that of asparagus and artichoke. They are lovely in salads and are good fried or steamed.

• Fiddleheads may be found in gourmet food markets in early spring, but are quite expensive. To serve as a vegetable, buy about ¾ cup per person. When added to a recipe with other ingredients, purchase ½ cup per person.

• Choose the smallest, freshest-looking specimens, the smoother (less fuzzy) the better. Avoid rotted ends and any ferns over 1½ inches.

• Refrigerate in a plastic bag and use as soon as possible.

• Wash well in cold water and serve very small ferns raw in salads. Braise in consommé for 2 minutes. Or dry well and stir-fry, or dip in batter and deep-fry.

Garlic

• Readily available all year.

• Choose firm, heavy, full bulbs with creamy white peels. Squeeze an individual clove to make sure it has not dried inside. Avoid any soft, sprouting bulbs.

• Keep several bulbs on hand stored in a ceramic jar (they are sold this way) or refrigerated in a jar with a screw-top lid.

• Flatten a garlic clove by pounding it beneath the side of a heavy-bladed knife. The peel will pull right off. Mince or thinly slice the clove, or crush with a mortar and pestle following the directions in your recipe. Avoid burning garlic or its glorious flavor will turn bitter. Follow recipe directions.

- To flavor olive oil, see page 190.

Ginger

- Available all year long. A good-size root should last for weeks.
- Select firm, smooth-skinned, fresh-looking tubers with a large central piece and very few small surrounding knobs. Most recipes call for large, thin slices, either whole or evenly slivered or minced. Avoid bruises, rot, or shriveling skin.
- Wrap loosely and refrigerate for up to 2 weeks. Or scrape or peel, cut in slices, cover with dry sherry, place in a screw-top jar, cap tightly, and store in refrigerator indefinitely.
- Peel or scrape and grate, slice, or shred as directed in your recipe.

Horseradish

This zesty fresh root (member of the mustard family) hides its excellent qualities beneath a dark, gnarled, particularly Grimm exterior. Its clean, sharp, potent taste adds zip to meat, poultry, seafood, soups, stews, salads, and other vegetables.

- Available all year. If covered with leaves to keep the ground soft, horseradish can be harvested 11 months a year from a winter garden.
- Choose firm, crisp roots. Beware of soft spots, shriveled ends, sprouts, or greenish tinge. Hard-to-find Wasabi, a Japanese root, has similar qualities and uses and is especially good with Japanese dishes.
- Wrap first in a damp towel and then in a dry one and store in the refrigerator for up to 3 months. Do not store longer, or an unpleasant taste might develop.
- Wash, peel, grate raw, and use in seafood cock-

tails or with other shellfish, and in fish and chicken dishes. Add vinegar or lemon juice if desired. Best served raw. Heat destroys the flavor.

Jerusalem Artichoke

Although this relative of our native wild sunflower grows abundantly in home gardens even under the most adverse conditions, it is usually found only in gourmet markets. Its texture is similar to that of the other popular tuber, the potato, but it is less starchy and has a nuttier flavor. Use raw as a substitute for raw water chestnuts, adding it at the last minute so that the crisp texture does not soften. Jerusalem artichokes are high in nutrition, low in calories, and extremely versatile.

- Available year-round but best in autumn and winter. One pound serves 4.
- Select firm, crisp specimens. Shun any that are rotted or shriveled. The larger, smoother ones are easiest to handle. Avoid green or sprouting, 'chokes, but tan or reddish ones are fine.
- Place in a tightly sealed plastic bag in the refrigerator for a week. In home gardens, mulch heavily and harvest as needed over the winter.
- Brush or scrub well and skin before or after cooking if desired. Prepare as you would potato or peel, slice thinly, and serve in salads or use as a garnish. (After peeling, immerse in cold water to which has been added vinegar, salt, or lemon juice to avoid discoloration.) When cooking, test frequently so as not to overcook (5–15 minutes depending on size).

Kale

This hearty cabbage-plant member with finely curled bluish-green leaves has been a food favorite at least 2000 years. Popular in chilly climes— Scotland, Scandinavia, Germany, and the like—in the United States it has found favor in the South and among new-food aficionados. Small wonder; it's high in nutrition and fiber and low in calories, with first-rate texture and distinctive flavor.

• Available all year long but best after it has been touched by frost, from September through the winter. This hearty crop may be picked by home gardeners throughout the winter if heavily mulched. One pound serves 2.

• Select clean, crisp, dark-green kale. Beware of crushed, bruised, limp leaves with worm damage or brown edges.

• Wash well, drain, and store in a plastic bag in the crisper for several days—it tends to become bitter as it ages.

• Rinse in cold water, discard tough stems and damaged leaves, and cook in boiling water for about 5–10 minutes, barely wilted for the new American cuisine or well wilted for the traditional Southern style. Or blanch in boiling water 3–4 minutes, drain well, and sauté or stir-fry. Add a few of the smallest leaves to a tossed salad.

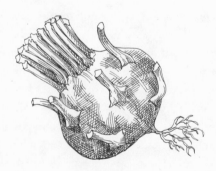

Kohlrabi

Kohlrabi comes in white or purple varieties, each with smooth texture and sweet, firm white flesh and delicate cucumber-cabbagelike flavor.

• Available May through late fall but more abundant in summer. Four small to medium-size bulbs serve 2 persons.

• Choose small (2 inches) to medium (3 inches) bulbs. Tops should be fresh, clear green, and free of blemishes. Those larger than an apple are generally less tender. Buy them with their tasty collardlike tops, if possible.

• Store in the refrigerator and use within 1 week.

• Cook before or after peeling away skin. Trim off leaves at bulb. Steam, boil, or braise whole bulbs about 20 minutes. Or cut into pieces or strips and cook in boiling water until tender (10–25 minutes depending on the size of the slices) then use in a variety of recipes. Pickled, sliced kohlrabi is excellent raw—a fine addition to salads or a plate of crudités. Raw kohlrabi is excellent sautéed or stir-fried.

Leeks

An ancient and highly considered vegetable to which was attributed many health-inducing properties, from relieving coughing to eliminating gray hair, this sweetest member of the onion family is much more popular in Europe than in the United States—an oversight we would be wise to correct.

• Available all year long but most abundant from October to June. Four small leeks serve 2 persons.

• Select small or medium-size leeks with fresh green tops and long white stems. They are best when they give slightly to the touch. Leek tops, usually discarded, make a fine soup or sauce (page 119).

- Refrigerate, unwashed, for up to 4 or 5 days.
- Cut the green stems off to within 3 inches of the white section and split lengthwise. Then stick a sharp knife through the white section and cut a slit from ½ inch of the roots up to within an inch of the green. Revolve shaft ¼ turn and repeat.

Wash thoroughly in cold, running water, spreading the cut parts to remove all dirt. Fill bowl with cold water, add a tablespoon of lemon juice or vinegar, and soak leeks for 30 minutes. Steam leeks in a small quantity of salted, boiling water for 20 minutes, or until tender. Served hot or cold. Leeks may also be braised in consommé or chicken broth for 40 minutes or so.

Mâche (Corn Salad, Lamb's Lettuce, Lamb's Tongue, Field Salad)

This most delicate of greens is a sophisticated European harbinger of spring. A most temperamental leaf that as yet has not responded enthusiastically to cultivation in this country, mâche or corn salad has been grown since Neolithic times in France, Belgium, Holland, Italy, Britain, Austria, and Germany. Its sweet, nutty flavor and downy texture cannot be surpassed. You'll find it in the finest gourmet markets.

- Available in the spring by the bunch at outrageous prices.
- It's best served alone so it can be fully appreciated; however, it may be tossed in salads with mild-tasting Boston or Bibb lettuce. Walnut, olive, or hazelnut oils set this jewel off to advantage as does a sprinkling of sieved, hard-cooked egg, grated cooked beets, lemon juice, or mild vinegar.
- Wash gently but thoroughly, trim off roots, and dry on a towel. Chill. Use as soon as possible.

Mushrooms

- Available all year long and most plentiful November through April.
- One pound of sliced mushrooms cooks down to approximately 2 cups. One pound of mushrooms includes 40 or so small buttons, 25–30 medium mushrooms, or 12–15 large ones.
- Choose fresh mushrooms that are white, firm, round, and short stemmed. Beware of open caps. Gills should not show.
- Store unwashed in the refrigerator in a tightly lidded container for 2 or 3 days, but, ideally, use at once.
- Don't peel! Wipe clean with a damp towel, and slice off and discard hard end of stem. Mince, slice, or use whole and serve raw, baked, fried, or sautéed.
- The current surge of interest in new and alluring foods has resulted in the availability of a variety of fresh and dried wild mushrooms, some cultivated, others gathered wild from woodland dells by expert mushroom hunters. Now, once-little-known mushrooms, such as shiitakes, chanterelles, enokis, oyster mushrooms, and porcini, nestle snugly alongside their cultivated white mushroom counterparts on the produce shelves in supermarkets and specialty shops.

Mushrooms perform beautifully in many dishes, but the distinctive woodsy flavor of wild mushrooms shines forth best in uncomplicated ones.

DRIED MUSHROOMS

Store these in an airtight container in a cool (not cold) place and they will keep indefinitely. Soak

30–60 minutes in hot water or stock or in cold water overnight. Squeeze out excess moisture and cut off the stems (save these for flavoring stocks).

MORELS

These rare, expensive wild mushrooms are highly sought after for their earthy-rich, smoky flavor. They are not cultivated and are mostly available in dried form.

CHINESE OR JAPANESE BLACK MUSHROOMS ("winter" mushrooms)

These are large and meaty with flat caps. (Those with specked rounded caps are the northern variety.) Bigger is better here, with the larger more tender and flavorful. A flower-shaped variety is most expensive and is used primarily for banquets.

TREE OR CLOUD EARS (silver ears are the albino variety)

When soaked in hot water for 30 minutes or so, these small, ruffled chips swell to 4 or 5 times their original size. Rinse well. Cut away stems and the woody centers or eyes and use these to flavor stocks. Tree ears have very little flavor but they lend a pleasant gelatinous texture and absorb the flavors of their accompanying ingredients.

SHIITAKE

Perhaps these are the most popular of all dried mushrooms. Their rich flavor and meaty texture add character to any braised, simmered, or stir-fried dish. Rinse briefly and soak large specimens up to 60 minutes (15 minutes for smaller ones) as directed above. Cut away stems and use with broth for flavoring.

EXOTIC FRESH MUSHROOMS

Store these vulnerable treasures loosely wrapped in paper towels in the refrigerator and use them as soon as possible.

ENOKI (enoki-dake)

With their slender stalks and delicate, creamy button tops, these delightful mushrooms lend enchantment to a variety of soups, salads, stir-fries, and tempura. Rinse gently and trim away base of stems. Cook very little, if at all.

OYSTER MUSHROOMS (tree-oyster mushrooms)

Clusters of these pale gray, oyster-flavored mushrooms are harvested from trees that grow in Asian forests. Rinse them briefly and dry them well just prior to stir-frying or adding sparingly to salads.

FRESH SHIITAKE

These dark, velvety caps are harvested in the spring and fall in Japan—in this country we snap them up whenever we find them. Cut away the stems and save them for flavoring stocks. Use the caps interchangeably with dried shiitake or braise, stir-fry, or grill.

Mustard Greens

• Available 12 months a year. Two pounds serves 4.

• Choose small leaves that are tender, crisp, and fresh-looking. Beware of wilted, dirty, discolored, or spotted leaves.

• Wash well, shake off excess water, and dry with paper towels. Refrigerate in a plastic bag for up to 7 days.

• Discard brown or faded leaves. Use the young, tender leaves in salads. Place more mature leaves in a tightly covered saucepan, sprinkle lightly with salt, and cook until leaves wilt (about 15 minutes) in water that clings to the leaves after washing. Drain well and chop if desired.

Onions

The story goes that a child who was asked in school to define *onion* answered, "that without which the stew would be ruined." The tale might not be true, but the sentiment certainly is. What is the first vegetable you reach for when you begin to prepare a soup? a stew? a sauce? a salad? The onion, of course (either sweet or hot), or one of its close relations—the scallion, the chive, the shallot, the leek, or that other star, garlic.

• Happily, onions are available all year. Most households keep a few pounds on hand at all times.

• Select firm, well-formed specimens with dry, brittle skin. Beware of onions with soft necks or those that are beginning to sprout.

• Store onions in a dry, cool area for weeks, but use before they begin to sprout or turn soft. Store away from potatoes, because onions tend to absorb excess moisture from the former and therefore soften or decay more quickly.

• As we all know, onions are extremely versatile and may be boiled, baked, fried, roasted, sautéed, steamed, pickled, creamed, or certainly served raw. Onions sweet enough to eat like an apple seem to be the newest stars, with Vidalia, Texas, Giant Walla Walla, Red Mac, White Bermuda, White Sweet Spanish, and Yellow Sweet Spanish all vying for attention.

SCALLIONS

May be served raw and trimmed of roots and all but 3 inches of stems, either whole or sliced or minced; or steamed, simmered, or sautéed whole.

CHIVES

Rinse, dry, and snip into foods raw, for flavor and garnish.

SHALLOTS

This mild-mannered member of the onion family that grows in clusters of cloves, like garlic, is more similar in flavor to the leek than to its cousin, the scallion. Use whenever a subtle touch is required.

• Available all year long. Always keep a few on hand.

• Choose firm bulbs, gray to red-brown, with dry, paperlike skins. Avoid soft, moist, or sprouting bulbs.

• Store in a well-ventilated spot, cool and dry, from 4 to 6 weeks.

• Serve raw in salads and/or use to flavor sauces or to accompany vegetables, fowl, fish, or seafood.

Okra

As delicious as this can be in gumbo or deep fried, if you're repelled by slippery texture, avoid okra. For those who fancy it, it's well loved for that very trait.

• Available year round but most abundant June through November. One pound serves 4.

• Choose only young, fresh pods 2–4 inches long. Avoid large, shriveled, soft, moldy, or discolored pods. If perfect specimens are not available, don't purchase any.

• Use immediately or, if you must, store in a paper bag in the refrigerator.

• Cut off stems and tips of caps without exposing the seeds. Rinse. Steam the smallest pods over a small quantity of boiling water until tender (around 2–5 minutes). Add at the last minute to stews or gumbos. For a crisp texture, cook whole and quickly to keep juice from escaping.

Parsley

Both curly parsley and the flat-leaved Italian parsley are herbs extraordinarily rich in vitamins and minerals. Once most frequently used as a garnish and ignored by diners, it is now coming into its own in salads, pasta sauces, even fried. And, incidentally, it is true that it freshens breath and negates the odor of onions and garlic.

• Available all year but most plentiful and of best quality from October through December. It keeps well so it's wise to always have a bunch on hand.

• Choose crisp, firm, dark green parsley. Avoid old (yellowing) or bruised (black) bunches.

• Rinse, shake out excess water, and store in a plastic container in the refrigerator crisper, or place stems in a glass of water, cover with plastic wrap, and refrigerate for a week or more.

• Although parsley is extremely nutritious—with several times as much vitamin C as in oranges, more A than carrots, and more iron than spinach—it is still mainly relegated to use as a garnish. To be a little more adventurous with parsley yourself, double up on the quantities you usually use and add it to soups, stews, sauces, spreads, and dips.

Parsnips

This delicious, underappreciated member of the carrot family is best during the winter, particularly if harvested after the first frost.

• Available all year long but best during the winter months. Two pounds will serve 4–5 persons.

• For tender, fine-grained flesh with delicate flavor, choose clean, medium, or smaller parsnips with smooth, slender roots and well-shaped shoulders. Beware of soft, discolored, or large specimens.

• Store in the refrigerator or root cellar for months.

• Scrub well and steam or boil in boiling water until tender (around 30 minutes). Best in boiled dishes and hearty soups and stews, mashed with potatoes, or even deep fried.

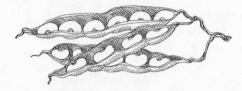

Peas

From the conventional varieties through the more refined sugarsnap peas and Chinese snow peas, one of the favorite vegetables of millions is what was once thought of as the common garden pea. There are early peas, more prolific peas, peas that grow best in cold weather, and peas that love the sun, but unless you grow them yourself it's difficult to find a really fresh old-fashioned green pea these days. And since peas are similar to corn and artichokes in that their sugars rapidly turn to starch once they are picked, most peas in markets are not sweet enough to bother with. This is one case when the frozen product may be superior to the so-called fresh one. The exceptions are the sugarsnap pea and the Chinese snow pea. Their extra sweetness seems to help them taste fresh longer. These do not freeze well.

• Available from March through June. One pound garden peas equals about 1 cup after shelling. Four pounds serve 4.

• Choose young, plump, evenly green pods purchased as soon as possible after picking.

• Use as soon as possible after picking. If necessary, store in the pods, uncovered, in the refrigerator.

• Serve immediately after shelling, add a bit of sugar (if needed) to enhance sweetness but don't salt until after cooking. Use a minimum amount of water or a dampened lettuce leaf or two for moisture, and cook over low heat just until tender. Do not overcook.

PEAS WITH EDIBLE PODS

These are favorites among food lovers in general and Chinese cooks in particular. Both the pods and the peas are edible, adding crisp texture, bright color, and sweet flavor to seafood, stir-fries, soups, salads, and crudités arrangements.

Chinese Snow Peas

• Available in some form and in some supermarkets or gourmet markets year-round but best from March through June. Quantity will depend on how they are to be used.

• Choose tender young fresh green pods no longer than 2–3 inches. Select those with clean, dry stems and no yellowing.

• Use as soon as possible.

• (Dwarf varieties are best for using whole in stir-fry dishes.) Remove strings from larger specimens. Boil snow peas for 1½ minutes, sauté 2 minutes, and steam for 3 minutes, or until barely tender. Blanch and chill (if desired) for salads and snacks. Serve whole or sliced.

Sugarsnap Peas

• The information in the first two paragraphs for Chinese snow peas applies here too.

• Choose the stringless "Sugar Daddy" variety, if available.

• Remove strings on larger specimens. Boil for 2 minutes; steam or sauté 3 minutes, or until barely tender. Blanch and chill (if desired) for salads and snacks.

Peppers

For sheer brilliance of color and clarity of flavor, I pick the pepper. Once confined to red or green, peppers now blaze forth in orange, yellow, purple, brown—even pure black. And peppers have gained not only in eye-appeal. What once were small, rather puny, metallic-tasting, dull green bells have been transformed into hybrids of big, voluptuous-looking globes—thick-walled, sweet, and meaty. Whether sweet or fiery, even the array of shapes dazzle—round, button shaped, with just a tempting touch of heat; bland and waxy 6-inch banana peppers; juicy, heart-shaped pimientos; wedge-shaped gypsy peppers; monstrous blocky 4-lobed big bells—and all add their unique flavor and sizzle to many otherwise plain dishes.

Actually, what we call sweet peppers and chili peppers are not properly "peppers" (members of the piper nigrum family) at all, but members of the capsicum family that originated in Mexico and were discovered by Columbus when he was searching for spices and happened upon the New World. Since we are in the New World and most of our chilies are grown here, we will go along with this less complex appellation.

SWEET PEPPERS

• Available all year but are most plentiful, with more varieties, from May through October. When serving stuffed peppers, figure on 1 large pepper per person.

• Select firm, well-shaped, crisp-looking peppers with a healthy-looking sheen. Avoid soft spots or bruised, shriveled skin.

• Use as soon as possible or store in a plastic bag or airtight container in the crisper for up to 5 days.

• Wash and remove the stem, core, seeds, and pith, leaving only the shell. Cut to suit your taste or recipe. Serve raw in salads, as a garnish, or with a dip. Add to soups, stews, sauces, etc. Or stuff and bake.

To sauté, heat 1–2 tablespoons oil in a nonstick skillet and stir over medium heat for several minutes or until pepper pieces are tender-crisp and just beginning to brown on the edges.

Charbroil peppers by turning them over hot coals (or under the broiler) until their skins are evenly browned. Place the peppers in a double brown-paper bag to steam for a few minutes. Rinse under cold running water until the skins separate from the flesh. Use a dull knife to scrape away any skin that still adheres. Make a small slit in the side of the pepper and remove any pith and seeds. Dry well. Place in olive oil, garlic oil, or oil and vinegar, and store in the refrigerator 4–5 days.

Most Popular Sweet Peppers

Bell Boy: Medium-size, thick-walled, bright, 4-lobed green fruits. Crisp and delicious with no bitter aftertaste.

Golden Summer: Pale lime-green fruits that gradually turn to golden color. Big, blocky, thick-walled, sweet and mild.

Purple Beauty: Most of the qualities of Golden Summer, but gorgeous color that makes an enticing addition to salads and stir-fries.

Big Bertha: Thick, meaty red-orange fruits with sweet yet spicy flavor.

Hungarian Wax: A sweet banana pepper with golden-yellow 6-inch fruits. No bite or bitterness.

CHILI PEPPERS

• Available 12 months of the year. Amounts will be determined by your recipe.

• Choose fresh-looking, smooth-skinned specimens. These will most likely be found in summer at vegetable stands or, out of season, in Mexican markets or supermarkets in the Southwest.

• Rinse if dirty, dry well, wrap in paper towels, and store in refrigerator for up to 3 weeks.

• Use rubber gloves and handle chilies with care. The capsaicin they contain can cause a painful reaction in those who are sensitive to it. Follow directions for charbroiling sweet peppers on pages 214 to 215, but take extra care when removing the seeds. Always wash your hands thoroughly after handling chilies. Touch your finger to your lips to determine if any capsaicin remains on them. Never touch your eyes or any sensitive areas until you are sure your hands are clean. If chilies are too hot for your taste, soak them in salted water for 15 to 30 minutes to make them milder. Discard the soaking water.

Most Popular Chili Peppers

Relleno Mild: More spice than heat, more flavor than fire. Six-inch peppers, good for stuffing or canning.

Jalapeño: Long, blunt peppers turn red when ripe. Nice and spicy.

Cayenne Long Slim: Liquid fire! Makes powdered cayenne pepper seem mild.

Ancho 101: Black-green, nicely spicy but not terribly hot.

Pepperoncini: Flat, greenish yellow and 4 inches long. Not hot, just warm. Great for pickling. Makes soups and sauces sizzle.

Numex Big Jim: Big, mildly hot, 10-inch peppers. Great for Mexican food.

Potatoes, White

• Available all year. Serve one medium-to-large potato per person (approximately ½ pound).

• Choose firm, well-formed, unblemished potatoes. Avoid potatoes that have sprouted, and especially beware of "greening," which can actually cause illness. Peel green away and, if excessive, discard the potato.

• Store in a dry, cool, dark place (not next to onions) for 2 to 3 months. Use before potatoes begin to sprout. (New potatoes last 3–4 weeks.) Use slightly blemished potatoes first.

• If possible, cook potatoes with the skins on to best preserve nutrients. Boil in a minimum amount of water in a covered pot 25–40 minutes, depending on size. To bake, scrub well and dry, rub with cooking oil, cut a thin slice from each end of the potato, and bake in the oven at 400° F. from 45 minutes to an hour. Serve immediately.

SWEET POTATOES AND YAMS

If you're confused about which vegetables are sweet potatoes and which are yams, and where they both come from, and whether they are one and the same, you're in good company. Actually, the answer is not only confusing but basically unimportant since the two are so similar that any recipe that is good for one is also good for the other. And the same holds true for the taro root. If you are really interested enough to play detective, you might begin with this—true yams are actually a different species, not native to the United States.

- Available all year but most plentiful from October through December. Three medium-size sweet potatoes average 1 pound, or almost 2 cups (mashed). The two primary varieties are the dry (yellow flesh) and the moist (soft, orange flesh).
- Choose firm, unblemished, medium-size sweet potatoes with tapering ends. Avoid bruised, shriveled, or excessively dried-out specimens.
- Store in a cool, dark, dry, and well-ventilated place for a week or a little longer. They don't store nearly as well as white potatoes.
- Scrub and bake in a 400° F. oven until soft (40–60 minutes). Or boil, unpeeled, in lightly salted water to cover. At this point they may be fried, mashed, glazed, or used in stuffing or for baked goods, in pies, cakes, biscuits, muffins, etc.

Radishes

This plentiful member of the mustard family is enjoying increasing popularity with knowledgeable cooks who serve them not only cooked but also with cheeses and French bread. There are so many varieties of radishes, and each adds a nice touch of crunch, color, and peppery goodness to a meal. I guess most should be mentioned, if only briefly.

- One or more varieties are available all year, but there are more varieties, which are more plen-

tiful, from May through July. One bunch should be ample for 4 persons.
- Choose solid, smooth, unblemished radishes with fresh green leaves. Avoid dull, soft, pithy ones with rotting leaves.
- Remove tops (unless you prefer to retain a few on each radish to make a more attractive assortment of crudités) and store in the refrigerator for up to 2 weeks.
- Wash, scrub, and serve raw, sliced, or whole in salads or separately. Summer radishes may be steamed or braised and used as a turnip substitute.

SPECIAL RADISHES

Daikon: This huge, increasingly popular white radish grows to a length of 12 inches (or much more), up to 1½–2½ inches in diameter, and 40–50 pounds. Of a somewhat more delicate texture, and generally hotter than our common round red variety, daikon is excellent peeled and thinly sliced, served cold in salads, pickled, grated and used as a garnish, or stuffing for Indian parathas or Chinese pastries, or served with other vegetables in stir-fried dishes or soups. Or slice ¼ inch thick and use as a low-calorie, no-cholesterol cracker for soft cheese.

Long White Radish: Pure white, torpedo-shaped, and 5–6 inches long; mild, sweet, and extra crisp.

Long Scarlet: Basically the same as the Long White, but with gorgeous scarlet skin and snowy flesh.

French Breakfast: Crisp, mild, and sweet with a vivid red skin except for the white tip.

Pink Beauty: Soft rose-pink skin and extra white meat. Extra sweet and beautiful in salads.

White Glove: Large, sweet, snowy flesh, and white skin.

Black Spanish Radish: Interesting coal-black skin and pure white extra-sharp flesh. Should be used sparingly.

Red Meat Radish: White globes with bright red centers; tender and sweet.

Japanese Giant Sukurajima Radish: Grows to a large size (up to 15 pounds) and has snow-white tangy flesh. One will feed a whole family.

Rutabaga

These belong to a different family, but they are much like turnips, though a deeper and richer yellow-orange in color, somewhat sweeter and stronger-flavored, and far superior nutritionally.

• Available most of the year but best from October through February. One pound cooked makes about 2 cups. One large rutabaga serves 4.

• Choose heavy, solid, smooth-skinned specimens.

• Store in a cool (not cold) place for several months. A root cellar is ideal.

• Peel, slice, or cut into pieces and boil in ample water until tender. Serve mashed or pureed and combined with carrots, mashed potatoes, or Jerusalem artichokes. May also be eaten raw.

Salsify (Vegetable Oyster)

Similar to carrots in size but black-skinned (a white-skinned variety is usually available as well), this bland, pleasant root, like parsnip, was once used primarily as one of a group of soup greens but is now more often used in fritters, purees, and other dishes. Some think it has a slight oysterlike flavor.

• Available most of the year but best from October to November. Eight roots serve 4.

• Choose firm, small- to medium-size roots, with no blemishes or soft spots.

• Store in the refrigerator crisper for up to several weeks.

• Cook after scrubbing well, unpeeled or well scraped, but submerge immediately in cold water to which has been added a splash of lemon juice to avoid discoloration. Cook whole or in pieces in salted, boiling water until tender (10–15 minutes).

Sorrel (Oseille)

More popular in Europe than here, sorrel has a piquant flavor that provides zest to soups, salads, egg dishes, and sauces.

• At its peak from May through September. Two pounds serves 4 persons as a vegetable, 1 bunch for salads.

• Choose fresh, clean, young leaves. Avoid bruised, wilted, yellowing, or woody stems.

• Use as soon as possible. If you must store sorrel, rinse and dry it well and store in a plastic bag in your refrigerator crisper for 1 to 2 days.

• Discard stalks, shred leaves, and use in salads. Cook until wilted for 8 to 10 minutes in the water that remains on the leaves after rinsing and use in soups, sauces, etc.

Spinach

More versatile than most cooks realize, this most popular and nutritious green is superb in salads (or as one) and in soups, sauces, and soufflés.

• Available all year long. One pound yields 1½ cups of cooked spinach, enough to serve 2 persons.

• Select good green, fresh-looking leaves. Beware of crushed, yellowed, or wilted leaves.

• Ideally, use as soon as possible, or wash, drain well, and store in a plastic bag in the refrigerator for up to 4 days.

• Remove roots and heavy stems and wash carefully in lukewarm water to remove all traces of sand. Steam 5–8 minutes in a covered pot—the water that remains on the leaves will be sufficient. Also excellent stir-fried in hot oil. Tender young leaves may be served raw in salads.

Sprouts

Sprout-growing is easy to do and fascinating to observe. Even if sprouts weren't extremely nutritious and a tasty addition to very nearly any meal, I'd advise that you grow some just for the fun of it. Most seeds can be sprouted, providing that they are whole (rather than split) and raw. Most delicious are probably sweet winter wheat, delicate alfalfa, spicy mustard or radish seed, sesame seed, and lentil, mung, or soy bean sprouts.

My interest began some twenty years ago, before commercial sprouters were readily available. I experimented until I discovered the following foolproof methods. I still prefer these even though commercial sprouters are probably more efficient.

Dampen several thin, sponge dishcloths, wring them out, and place them on a cookie sheet. Arrange seeds or beans in the wafflelike depressions. These may be close together but should not be on top of one another. Cover the pan loosely with waxed paper (don't use plastic wrap, as it droops down rather than stands up). Place the pan in an unlit oven. Every day, unwrap the pan, sprinkle the seeds or beans with a few drops of water, re-cover with waxed paper, and replace in the oven until your sprouts are ready to harvest (usually a few days).

A second, equally simple method involves rinsing seeds or beans and soaking them overnight in 1 cup of tepid water. Drain and rinse until the water is clear and place in a 1-quart jar topped with cheesecloth held in place with a rubber band.

Place in a warm, dark spot (never in sunlight) and rinse with cool water and drain well (to prevent mold) 4 times daily. When the sprouts are 1 inch long or a little longer, rinse, drain well, and use immediately or refrigerate in a tightly lidded jar.

Mung Bean: Sprouts in about 3 days and has creamy white stems and pale yellow, barely developed leaves.

Soybean: Sprouts in about 6 days and looks very much like mung sprouts, but has longer stems and fairly large cotyledons not yet developed into leaves.

Alfalfa: Have thin, threadlike white roots with 2 tiny green leaves.

Radish: Relatively large, with dark green leaves and long, thin, peppery sprouts.

• Available all year long. Follow recipe directions. Raw sprouts diminish to half their bulk when cooked, so purchase or grow accordingly.

• Choose sprouts that are fresh and crisp. Generally, the shorter ones are more tender.

• Place in the refrigerator crisper in an air-tight container or bag.

• Rinse and wash thoroughly in cold water to remove some of the remaining seeds or beans. Prior to serving, place in ice water for ½ hour, drain well, pat dry, and serve cold. To sauté or stir-fry, add at the last minute and cook for only a few seconds so that sprouts retain their crunch.

• Sprouts will keep 3–5 days.

Squash

The ancestors of our present-day squash varieties were domesticated in Mexico and cooked up over primitive fires both as a seed and flesh food as long ago ago as 5000 B.C. By the time Columbus sampled his first bite in the West Indies on his premiere voyage, squash was undoubtedly flourishing in Central and North America from coast to coast. And before you could say Queen Isabella, squash was on its way to becoming a worldwide favorite.

Little wonder! How could anyone resist those

glossy, succulent zucchini, bumpy golden crooknecks, scallop-edged patty pans, and meaty, goldenfleshed winter acorns, Hubbards, and butternuts? There are dozens of varieties to choose from—all slightly different, all delicious, all nutritious. Quickgrowing and marvelously productive, squash performs with equal facility in either gourmet recipes or farm favorites, whether prepared alone or in concert with other foods.

Squash belongs to the warm-weather-loving gourd family, a group of tender, vine-bearing annuals that includes purely ornamental as well as edible fruits (cucumbers, melons, pumpkins). Horticulturally speaking, these are known as *Cucurbita,* a gourd-family genus whose chief characteristics are hairy vines, oversized leaves, lovely yellow flowers, and large fruits with smooth or furrowed skins. Whatever you call them, they are delicious.

SUMMER SQUASH

This is one instance in which "smaller is better." When harvested early, before they reach the huge size they are capable of, immature squash—lightly steamed, sautéed, or eaten raw—are tender, tasty, and delicately flavored. (Squash are cousins to cucumbers and these generally may be used interchangeably.)

• Some variety is always available, but all are most plentiful during the summer. Two pounds will serve 4 people.

• Choose squash that looks fresh and has good color and few blemishes. These are easily bruised and very perishable. Generally speaking, the smaller ones are more tender and tasty.

• Place in plastic wrap and store in the refrigerator up to 2 or 3 days.

• Tender young squash does not have to be peeled. Small squash may be cooked whole or sliced, eaten cooked or raw. Steam until barely tender or cook in a minimum of water. May be sautéed, fried, or pureed.

Traditionally, summer squash is lightly salted and set aside prior to cooking to reduce moisture. Most of this salt washes away as the vegetables ooze juice; however, very nearly the same effect may be achieved by simply placing the cut vegetables between towels and weighting them down lightly with a cutting board or plates for about 10 minutes. Try it both ways. If you don't notice any difference, forgo the salt and save a little time and trouble in the bargain.

Most Popular Summer Squash

Black Zucchini: Slender, glossy, cylindrical, uniform glossy, dark-green skin and creamy flesh.

Gray Zucchini: Light green fruits with gray markings. Delicate flavor and fine quality.

Early Straightneck Squash: Golden fruits with fine texture and flavor.

White or Green Patty Pans: A lovely scalloped fruit with a mild nutty flavor.

Yellow Crookneck Squash: Long, cylindrical, light yellow with creamy yellow flesh. Darker when mature.

Hairy Squash: A Chinese variety pronounced dzeet-gwa. Dark green and hairy. Best when stirfried or used in soups.

WINTER SQUASH

Many winter squash are the same varieties as summer squash, but grown to maturity. Their tough rinds protect them and keep them fresh and capable of being stored for long periods of time.

• Available all year but most plentiful during the fall and winter months. About 2½ pounds will serve 4.

• Choose hard, unblemished specimens. Avoid a soft rind, breaks in the skin, soft spots, and mold.

• Store in a cool, dry place for months.

• Cut in half (or wedges), remove seeds and fibers (but leave the rind), and bake until tender. Or peel, cut into pieces, and boil or steam and serve mashed. May also be peeled and grated and cooked, covered, with a little margarine or oil, over low heat until tender.

Most Popular Winter Squash

Golden Acorn: Deeply ridged, with dark green skin. Serve raw when young, baked when fully mature.

Buttercup: Turban-shaped fruits with thick orange flesh and deep green skin with gray flecks. Tastes like sweet potato.

Butternut: Popular and delicious, with tan skin, pear shape with a thick, long neck, and deep orange flesh.

Hubbard: Huge (up to 15 pounds), sometimes lightly ridged, bluish or orange or green rinds. There is also a baby variety that weighs in at only 5 or 6 pounds. Thick, sweet, yellow-orange flesh.

Pink Banana: Can grow to 40 pounds but is usually about 30 inches with an average weight of 12 pounds. Banana shaped with a pinkish shell and rich orange flesh.

Pumpkin: These members of the squash family are bright orange, ridged, and vary in size from 200-pounders to tiny one-pounders. Flesh is bright orange and unusually sweet.

SPAGHETTI SQUASH (VEGETABLE SPAGHETTI, SUZZA MELON, CUCUZZI)

Available year-round in some markets but generally just through the summer. Three pounds will serve 4.

Choose unblemished specimens with hard, firm, smooth rinds.

Store in a cool, dry, dark place for many weeks.

Wash, puncture in 5 or 6 places, and bake in a 325° F. oven for 1 hour, or follow recipe directions. Cut, remove seeds, and serve in the shell, or better yet, use 2 forks to toss and gently lift out the vegetable threads and serve as spaghetti.

To cook in a microwave oven: Puncture in two dozen places with the point of a thin, sharp knife. Put in the microwave for 15–20 minutes, turning occasionally. Cut in half, remove seeds, and test for doneness. The strands should be al dente. If underdone, put the halves in the microwave until they test done.

CHAYOTE

With colors ranging from cream through celery green to dark green and skin textures from smooth to hairy, these pear-shaped squash are a surprise inside and out.

• These small, popular Latin American squash are available year-round in Hispanic or Mexican markets but are usually most plentiful in winter. Two chayote (about 2 pounds) serves 4, although younger specimens may weigh much less.

• Small is better and the darker the green, the better the applelike flavor and patty pan texture.

• Store unwrapped in the refrigerator for up to 3 weeks.

• Scrape or peel and dice or cut into small pieces and simmer in salted water until tender (approximately 10 minutes), or cook and serve as you would any other squash. When you cook chayote in the skin you might be surprised to discover an irritating slippery membrane as you pull off the peel. If this makes your fingers numb its best to lightly oil your hands first or work under running water. Cook the crunchy seed with the squash. It's delicious.

Swiss Chard

This is a beet that has been encouraged by breeders to produce leaves and stalks rather than a rounded root. As a matter of fact, it is really two vegetables rather than one—the leafy tops, similar to spinach, and the slightly bittersweet pale-green celerylike stalks.

• Most frequently available from early spring through to autumn. Choose bunches with crisp stalks and perfect leaves.

• Rinse thoroughly, cut off the stems from the leaves with a knife or scissors, cut away and discard the midribs. Pull off the strings from the stalks as you would from celery. Cut the stalks into ½-inch slices and boil until tender in acidulated water. Drain well, pressing out as much liquid as possible.

• Small and medium chard can be quickly sautéed.

Taro Root (Dasheen)

A brown, shaggy tuber with encircling rings and creamy or gray flesh with a nutty artichoke flavor. Known as poi in Hawaii, taro root is now raised in the Orient, the Caribbean, North Africa, and South and Central America as well as several of our most southern states.

• Taro root is available year-round in those areas where it is cultivated.

• Choose solid, smooth, unblemished roots about the size of turnips. Avoid those that are soft.

• Store in the refrigerator for a few days. If it softens, use it at once.

• Taro must never be eaten raw and should be peeled using rubber gloves.

• Wash well, and then bake, boil, or steam until tender. Remove the skin after cooking. Alternately, it may be sliced, chopped, and cooked in soups and stews.

Tomato

The tomato is the superstar of the vegetable world. Granted the humble onion is necessary and hard-working, and the bean feeds nearly as many hungry people as does rice, and a squash is satisfying (not to mention versatile), but this gorgeously designed, delicious, and nourishing fruit makes thousands of dishes worth sampling. For instant eating pleasure there is nothing more delectable, and in a dazzling variety of cooked dishes the brilliant tomato goes forth from soup to dessert with consummate good taste.

First cultivated as a food crop by the Indians of South America, it was brought to Europe by way of Mexico, probably by the conquistadores, and found its way to Italy, where the early yellow variety was named *pomi d'oro,* or "apple of gold." It was regarded by the rest of Europe as an ornamental plant, dubbed *pomme d'amour,* or "love apple," and as an aphrodisiac until the eighteenth century. Today we see the tomato as something more than just another plant with a pretty fruit. Though tomato pie may not be quite as American as apple pie, the tomato is surely as all-American a favorite as the adored apple.

• Good, vine-ripened tomatoes are available from June through August or September in northern America, longer in southern parts. During the rest of the year what could be called commercial tomatoes are mealy, tasteless, bred primarily for their ability to withstand shipping—and thus should be avoided. One large tomato should serve 1 (or follow your recipe).

• Select firm, plump, unblemished tomatoes with a characteristically good tomato smell. Beware of odorless specimens which are usually gas-ripened, as well as fruits with soft areas, bruises, or cracks. If necessary, ripen in a warm, shaded place and when ripe use immediately. Their flavor is best when fruits have never been chilled but they may be refrigerated for a few days if necessary to delay spoilage. Avoid bruising.

• To prepare, wash well in tepid water, and if skins are tough, scald in boiling water and peel. Serve raw, straight from the garden, or barely chilled, or use in soups, stews, sauces, etc.

GREEN TOMATOES

Green tomatoes are not merely red tomatoes that are underachieving, they are every bit as perfect in their own right as their more colorful cousins. They are more firm and less acidy when cooked than a ripe tomato; and in flavor, they are not too dissimilar to a tart apple. Green tomatoes perform brilliantly in specialized recipes—I remember them fondly from my Pennsylvania Dutch childhood. The tomatillo used in Mexican cooking is a real "taste-alike."

• Available from July to October in the northern United States; slightly longer in the southern states. One pound of cooked makes 1½ cups.

• These are most often available from farm stands or country gardens. Choose tomatoes that are light green or almost white on the bottom. Dark green tomatoes are bitter (and never ripen).

• Store in a cool, dark place. If kept too long they will ripen.

• May be used with or without peeling. Cut into quarters or slice and remove seeds. Follow recipe directions.

TOMATILLO

This is similar to a small green tomato with a papery husk although the flavor is somewhat sweeter. They may be used interchangeably.

• Available fresh in Latin American markets or in markets in the Southwest. One pound equals 1 cup cooked. Widely available canned.

• Choose firm, green specimens that have not ripened and turned yellow.

• Store in a paper bag, refrigerated, for up to 3 weeks.

• Tiny specimens, some no bigger than a large pearl, are glorious when allowed to ripen to full golden color in their husks. Place on a napkin in a small basket and serve as an hors d'oeuvre with guests husking their own and enjoying the very sweet, fresh taste.

Remove the husks from larger specimens, rinse, and simmer in water to cover until barely tender. Do not overcook. Drain (reserve ⅓ cup cooking liquid for pureeing). Puree with the reserved liquid and a pinch of sugar. Or grill the fresh tomatillo in the husk until soft, remove the skins, and mince or puree for use in Mexican dishes.

To peel and seed ripe tomatoes: Spear the stem end of a tomato with a fork and plunge it into scalding water for 10 seconds. Loosen skin at blossom end with a small knife—and pull. The tomato will obligingly slip out of its skin.

MOST POPULAR TOMATOES

Cherry tomatoes: These come in red and yellow, are sweet and bite-size. Terrific in salads, on platters of crudités, and as a garnish.

Pear tomatoes: Sweet red or yellow pear-shaped varieties are excellent for sauces, canning, or eating raw.

Beefsteak: Fruits up to 2 pounds each, mild, sweet meaty, and nearly seedless. Wonderful for sandwiches and salads.

Big Boy: Smaller than beefsteak, with up to 1-pound fruits; extra juicy and unbeatable for slicing.

Pink Girl: Rosy-pink slices from large, smooth, juicy fruits.

Golden Low Acid: Golden colored fruit, extra sweet with less acid. Beautiful in sauces, salads, and on sandwiches.

Lemon Boy: Large, lemon-yellow rather than golden fruits. Striking in salads and vegetable mixtures.

Snowball: Very nearly white with few seeds and a mild, sweet flavor. Beautiful when sliced.

Truffles

• Found only in Italy (white) and France, truffles, which are becoming increasingly rare and expensive, are always available canned or fresh during October and November.

• Beware of white, less-expensive truffles that have been dyed black!

• To store, place in a bowl of dry rice, cover, and refrigerate for up to 10 days.

• Black truffles may be cooked but are usually sliced thin and served raw. They are widely used in fine pâtés. White are generally sliced thinly and served over meat or poultry dishes.

Watercress

• Always available, but the best selection is May through July. Keep a bunch on hand.

• Choose fresh, crisp cress with deep green leaves. Beware of yellowing, limp, bruised, or obviously mishandled bunches with leaves turning black around the edges.

• Wash several times in cold water, keeping an eye open for lingering snails. Drain thoroughly and wrap in paper towels to dry somewhat. Place in tightly covered rigid container and store in the coldest part of refrigerator for 7 to 10 days.

• Discard thickest stems and use cress on sandwiches, in salads and soups (both hot and cold), as a garnish, and pureed.

Turnips

• Available all year. Two pounds serves 4.

• Choose small, smooth young turnips. Leaves, if still on, should be fresh and green. Beware of large turnips with tough, fibrous roots.

• Store in the refrigerator for months.

• Remove the tops, reserve tender leaves for use as cooked, leafy vegetables, or serve raw in salad. Cut off the root top, peel, and cook whole or sliced or diced in salted, boiling water until tender (about 15 minutes for sliced, 25–30 minutes for whole). Or bake and/or use in stews and soups.

Liquid and Dry Measure Equivalencies

CUSTOMARY	METRIC
¼ teaspoon	1.25 milliliters
½ teaspoon	2.5 milliliters
1 teaspoon	5 milliliters
1 tablespoon	15 milliliters
1 fluid ounce	30 milliliters
¼ cup	60 milliliters
⅓ cup	80 milliliters
½ cup	120 milliliters
1 cup	240 milliliters
1 pint (2 cups)	480 milliliters
1 quart (4 cups, 32 ounces)	960 milliliters (.96 liters)
1 gallon (4 quarts)	3.84 liters
1 ounce (by weight)	28 grams
¼ pound (4 ounces)	114 grams
1 pound (16 ounces)	454 grams
2.2 pounds	1000 grams (1 kilogram)

Oven Temperature Equivalencies

DESCRIPTION	°FAHRENHEIT	°CELSIUS
Cool	200	90
Very slow	250	120
Slow	300–325	150–160
Moderately slow	325–350	160–180
Moderate	350–375	180–190
Moderately hot	375–400	190–200
Hot	400–450	200–230
Very hot	450–500	230–260

Additional Reading List

Cheraskin, Emanuel, M.D., D.M.D., and Orenstein, Neil S., Ph.D. *Lower Your Cholesterol in 30 Days,* Perigee Books, 1989.

Connor, Sonja, M.S., R.D., and Connor, William, M.D. *The New American Diet,* Fireside, 1986.

Cooper, Kenneth H., *Controlling Cholesterol,* Bantam Books, 1989.

Fisher, Hans, and Boe, Eugene. *The Rutgers Guide to Lowering Your Cholesterol,* Warners Books, 1986.

Fletcher, Anne M., M.S., R.D. *Eat Fish, Live Better,* Perennial Library, 1989.

Goor, Nancy and Goor, Ron. *Eater's Choice,* Houghton Mifflin, 1989.

Kowalski, Robert E. *The 8-Week Cholesterol Cure,* Harper and Row, 1989.

Kowalski, Robert E. *The 8-Week Cholesterol Cure—Personal Diary,* Perennial Library, 1989.

Kwiterovich, Peter. *Beyond Cholesterol,* Johns Hopkins University Press, 1989.

Mintz, Penny. *The Complete Cholesterol Counter,* Ballantine Books, 1990.

Netzer, Corinne T. *The Complete Book of Food Counts,* Dell Publishing, 1988.

Piscatella, Joseph C. (recipes by Bernie Piscatella). *Choices for a Healthy Heart,* Workman Publishing, 1987.

Pritikin, Robert. *The New Pritikin Program,* Simon and Schuster, 1990.

Robbins, John. *Diet for a New America,* Stillpoint Publishing, 1987.

Roth, Eli M., and Streicher, Sandra. *Good Cholesterol, Bad Cholesterol,* Prima Publishing, 1988.

INDEX

A Tastemaker award winner for *The Great East Coast Seafood Book*, Yvonne Young Tarr has written 22 popular cookbooks, including the best-selling *The New York Times Natural Foods Dieting Book*, *The New York Times Bread and Soup Cookbook*, *The Great Food Processor Cookbook*, and *The 10-Minute Gourmet Diet Cookbook*.

Wife of the sculptor, William Tarr, and mother of two sons, Jonathon and Nicolas, she lives, works, and cooks in East Hampton, New York.